PSYCHOKINESIS
A Study of Paranormal Forces Through the Ages

JOHN L. RANDALL

SOUVENIR PRESS

First published 1982 by Souvenir Press Ltd,
43 Great Russell Street, London WCıB 3PA
and simultaneously in Canada

ISBN 0 285 62540 3

Photoset, printed and bound in Great Britain by
Redwood Burn Limited
Trowbridge, Wiltshire

Dedicated to the memory of my good friend
Dr Joseph Banks Rhine

Acknowledgements

Many people have helped me, directly or indirectly, in the production of this book. I am especially grateful to the following: Miss Renée Haynes and the Society for Psychical Research for permission to reproduce material from the Society's publications; Dr John Beloff and Mr Julian Isaacs for their helpful advice and encouragement; the librarians of the Royal Leamington Spa Public Library; Mr Kenneth Cooper, Head of the Art Department at King Henry VIII School, Coventry, for re-drawing Figures 1, 3, 4, and 5 from the originals; Mrs Doreen Leach for photocopying; and Mr Peter Davis and Mr Robert Sadler for their work on the photographs. Last but not least, I wish to thank my publishers, Souvenir Press, for their patience and forbearance during the preparation of the manuscript.

John L. Randall
Royal Leamington Spa,
1982.

Contents

	Acknowledgements	vi
	Introduction	11
1	Shamans, Sorcerers and Witch-Doctors	15
2	Wise Men from the East	24
3	Jews and Gentiles	38
4	Saints and Sinners	46
5	The Age of Enlightenment	59
6	The Phenomena called Spiritual	67
7	Science Lends a Hand	79
8	The Man who was called Mad	95
9	Mediumship and the SPR	113
10	PK in the Twentieth Century	129
11	PK and the Laws of Chance	142
12	The Return of the Physical	155
13	PK in Everyday Life?	178
14	The Phenomena Surveyed	188
15	More than Meets the Eye?	199
16	Beyond the Quantum	217
	Epilogue	226
	Postscript	230
	Glossary of Technical Terms	234
	References	239
	Index	251

'MAGIC,' gasped the dull of mind,
  When the harnessed earth and skies
Drew the nomads of their kind
  To uncharted emperies –
Whispers round the globe were sped,
  Construed was the planets' song.

But the little boy playing in the orchard said,
Conning his tale in the orchard said,
  I knew it all along.

Power deduced from powerless dust,
  Nurture from the infertile grave;
Much the years may hold in trust,
  Space a thrall and Time a slave.
Hark the boasting of the wise:
  'First are we of those that know!'

But the little boy playing by the roadside cries,
Trundling his hoop by the roadside cries,
  I said it long ago.

John Buchan
The Magic Walking-Stick

Reprinted by permission of Lord Tweedsmuir

Introduction

In his *Life of Augustus,* which was probably written towards the end of the first century AD, the Roman writer Suetonius tells a fascinating story. It appears that near a place called Velitrae there was a country house which had once belonged to the Emperor Augustus's grandfather, and inside the house was a small room which was often shown to visitors as Augustus's nursery. Local people firmly believed that the Emperor was born there. Suetonius tells us that no one was allowed to enter this room without good reason, and even then only after performing religious rites of purification. It was generally believed that casual visitors would be overcome with a 'sudden awful terror'. This was shown to be true one night when a new owner of the mansion, either from ignorance or because he wanted to test the truth of the belief, went to bed in the room. A few hours after retiring he was hurled out of bed by a sudden occult force, and was found lying half-dead against the door, bedclothes and all.

Throughout the long history of the human race there have been innumerable recorded examples of phenomena similar to that described by Suetonius; examples, that is, of some kind of occult force (the word 'occult' simply means *hidden*) which can move objects and shatter or deform apparently solid pieces of matter. Ancient writers generally took such occurrences for granted, attributing them to the intervention of demons, spirits or gods, depending on the particular world-view of the writer. In most cases the activity of the force seems to have been merely mischievous, but occasionally it displayed itself in a malicious and even dangerous manner, throwing people out of bed and setting fire to furniture and houses. Only very rarely do we hear of the force acting in a helpful or constructive manner.

Around the year 593 AD Gregory the Great, one of the most famous of the early Popes, wrote his books of *Dialogues,* which recount the life story of St Benedict and some of the other saints. Gregory assures us that his information about Benedict is reliable, being based on the reports of four of Benedict's disciples: Valentinian, Simplicius, Honoratus, and Constantine. Whatever we may think of Gregory's reliability as a historian, there is no doubt that his writings contain some interesting tales. For example, he tells how on one occasion Benedict had gone to take over the government of a monastery which had recently lost its Abbot; when he arrived there, he found that the monks had fallen into a very slovenly and immoral style of living. Naturally, he set about trying to remedy this, much to the annoyance of the monks, who began to 'rage like men possessed'. They realised that under Benedict they would no longer be permitted to continue their luxurious lifestyle, so they began to consider what they could do to get rid of him. In the end, they decided to put poison in his wine:

'The glass vessel containing the deadly potion was set on the table before the abbott that he might give the wine his customary blessing. Benedict raising his hand made the sign of the cross, and at that sign the vessel, though distant from him, was broken, and broken exactly as though he had cast a stone at it instead of a blessing.'[66]

Despite this clear demonstration of supernatural support, Benedict seems to have decided that discretion was the better part of valour for, after delivering a hasty rebuke to the monks, he left them to their own devices and returned to his life as a hermit.

Of course, it is easy to make fun of these early accounts of occult forces, and dismiss them as merely old wives' tales (or old monks' tales as the case may be). It is a feature of the snobbery of our age to imagine that because we have a greater accumulated knowledge of natural phenomena than our forebears, we are therefore less gullible than they were. In fact, there is no reason to suppose that either the general intelligence of the human race or its ability to make accurate observations of spontaneous phenomena have increased very much over the past two thousand years or so. Actually, almost all the strange phenomena recorded in antiquity can be matched with accounts of similar phenomena from the nineteenth and twentieth centuries, and our present-day attempts to explain them are not much better than our ancestors'. A few years ago I was experimenting with a 'mini-Geller,' a schoolboy who apparently had the ability to deform pieces of metal by stroking them, in much the same way as the well-known Israeli performer. The boy was handed a metal bar which had been carefully sealed inside a thick-walled glass boiling-tube. The aim of the experiment was to see whether the boy could deform the metal bar by gently stroking the outside of the glass tube. To my surprise, within a few minutes the glass shattered into pieces. Now it is certainly not easy to break such tubes in one's hands; usually they will only break if thrown onto a hard surface or dropped on the floor. I was even more surprised when the glass-breaking occurred a second time, with another carefully prepared tube. Later, I met Professor John Taylor, who had been conducting similar experiments at King's College, London. He told me that he had also found that glass containers tend to shatter in this kind of experiment, and for that reason he enclosed his metal bars in tubes made of plastic or wire-gauze. I leave it to the reader to decide whether it is too fanciful to see a possible connection between this twentieth century effect and the shattering of the hapless Benedict's wine-flagon.

The late Dr C. G. Jung, the famous Swiss psychiatrist, gives two interesting examples of strange effects on matter. Both occurred when he was working on a doctoral thesis which was concerned with the psychology of mediumship. He was sitting working in his room one day when a loud noise came from the adjoining room, the door to which was ajar. On rushing in Jung found his mother staring in astonishment at the round dining table, the top of which had split from the rim to beyond the centre. There was no other person present in the room. Jung found it impossible to think of any normal explanation for the incident, since the table was of solid walnut, and at least seventy years old. Why should it suddenly split on a summer's day under conditions of relatively high humidity? This was not all. Two weeks later there was a further deafening report, and a steel-bladed bread knife shattered into five pieces. Jung took the knife to a local cutler who, after examining the fractures with a lens, stated that he could find no faults in the steel.[94]

This, then, is the kind of phenomenon we shall be mainly

concerned with in this book. The suggestion underlying all such accounts is that there exists some kind of force or energy whose *modus operandi* is unknown to present-day science. I shall refer to the effect of this unknown force as *psychokinesis* (or PK for short), a modern term which literally means 'movement by the mind'. However, the use of this term must not be taken to imply any particular theory about how the force operates, or even whether there is a force at all in the strictly scientific sense of the word. In this book the term 'PK' will be used merely as a convenient way of referring to a class of phenomena which seem to involve unexplained (or *paranormal*) effects upon matter. In the first part of the book we shall consider some of the reports of such phenomena which have come down to us through the ages from a variety of countries and cultures. Then we shall go on to examine the results of scientific investigations into the nature of the 'occult force', particularly those which have been conducted during the past fifty years. Finally, we shall attempt to arrive at some sort of classification of the various types of PK effect, and examine the implications of them for our understanding of space, time and matter.

1 Shamans, Sorcerers and Witch-Doctors

In the year 1920 there was an outbreak of trouble among the population of an Indian reservation in the north of Manitoba Province, Canada. The cause of the disturbance was the arrival in the area of a young self-styled medicine man who was challenging the authority of the established occupant of the post, an elderly shaman who had been resident in the area for many years. In an attempt to settle the dispute, the local corporal of the Royal Canadian Mounted Police decided to hold a competition in magic between the two wonder-workers. By this means, he hoped to discredit them both, and thus restore peace to the neighbourhood. On the appointed day of the contest the younger contestant built a 'tepee' or tent almost twenty feet high and made of four poles of poplar covered with canvas. There was no opening in the tent except for a small hole at the very top. Inside was a tin can filled with pebbles and suspended about ten feet from the apex. The rigidity of the tent was tested thoroughly by a number of people including the corporal, a clerk of the Hudson Bay Company, and several Indians. It was sufficiently narrow for two observers, standing on opposite sides, to keep the whole of it in view, and during the contest no one approached within three feet of it. The senior shaman was invited to make the pebbles rattle by exerting his occult powers, but after half an hour of singing and dancing without producing any effect whatever he retired from the contest, weary and dejected. Then came the turn of the younger contestant. He followed a similar, although more energetic, routine, and within ten minutes the tepee was vibrating and the pebbles rattling loudly. The corporal suspected that an accomplice had sneaked into the tent, so he slit the canvas with a knife, but there was no one inside. Not surprisingly, the prestige of the young shaman was greatly increased by this demonstration of paranormal ability, and within a few weeks his influence among the village folk was even greater than that of the chief and council[122].

The term 'shaman' is derived from a Siberian word, and first came into general use among ethnologists around the beginning of the twentieth century. It was used originally to describe the trance activities of certain primitive people in North and Central Asia, but nowadays it is also used to refer to similar phenomena occurring among the peoples of North and South America, Indonesia, and the Islands of the Pacific Ocean. Professor Mircea Eliade defines shamanism as 'a technique of ecstasy'. The shaman claims to be able to communicate with spirits by working himself up into a trance state, and it is this condition of trance or ecstasy which distinguishes the true shaman from the medicine man, sorcerer or magician. However, in practice the distinction is not clear cut, and a shaman may also be a magician and a medicine man, claiming to cure diseases and perform miracles of the fakir type; nevertheless, he is first and foremost an ecstatic.

Julien Tondriau points out that although the shaman goes into a trance and communicates with spirits, he does not usually allow himself to become *possessed* by them: 'If the shaman in his ecstasy communicates with the spirits of nature or with the dead, it is to impose on them his views and to utilise them, not to become, through possession, their docile instrument.'[180] Sometimes a shaman may indeed be found to be 'possessed', but this is an exceptional occurrence for which a special explanation is offered. In general his aim is to control the spirits, not to be controlled by them.

K. Rasmussen, in his book *Intellectual Culture of the Iglulik Eskimos*, describes how, after a young shaman has been initiated, he receives 'enlightenment'; he experiences 'a mysterious light which the shaman suddenly feels in his body, inside his head, within his brain, an inexplicable searchlight, a luminous fire, which enables him to see in the dark, both literally and metaphorically speaking, for he can now, even with closed eyes, see through darkness and perceive things and coming events which are hidden from others . . .' When he experiences this light for the first time 'it is as if the house in which he is suddenly rises; he sees far ahead of him, through mountains, exactly as if the earth were one great plain, and his eyes could reach to the end of the earth. Nothing is hidden from him any longer; not only can he see things far, far away, but he can also discover souls, stolen souls, which are either kept concealed in far, strange lands or have been taken up or down to the Land of the Dead'. We may notice, in passing, that this description of the internal experience of the initiated shaman is strikingly similar to some of the European descriptions of so-called 'out-of-the-body' experiences.[110,111]

Exceptional powers of ESP and PK are attributed to shamans. Some claim to interpret dreams and make prophecies; others are believed to be able to bring rain, halt the movements of clouds, or melt the ice on rivers, simply by singing or shaking a feather[46]. In North America some shamans are said to have the power to handle burning coals without being hurt, a feat which was also attributed to the nineteenth century medium Daniel Dunglas Home. Others are supposed to be able to undo instantly ropes and chains with which they are bound, or make a grain of wheat germinate and grow before the eyes of an audience. The phenomenon known to western spiritualists as *telekinesis* – the movement of objects without contact – is also reported, and so are instances of *apportation*, the disappearance of an object from one region of space and its reappearance in another. Eliade describes how, in the séances of the Tungus and other Siberian peoples:

'. . . voices of spirits are heard; the shaman becomes "light" and can spring into the air with a costume that may weigh as much as sixty-five pounds, yet the patient scarcely feels the shaman tread on his body; the shaman feels an intense heat during his trance, and hence can play with burning coals and red-hot iron, and becomes completely insensible (for example, he stabs himself deeply but no blood flows); and so on.'[46]

The mention of heat production during shamanistic séances is interesting, since this has been reported by some western investigators. During a séance in 1878, for example, a snail shell which had apparently passed through a solid wooden table was found to be so hot that the experimenter almost burnt his fingers on it.* In a computer analysis of pol-

*This case is described in more detail later. See page 104.

tergeist cases Gauld and Cornell found that 11% of the cases they examined involved incendiary effects, and 4% involved the transportation of objects which were subsequently found to be hot.[58] There may well be a connection here with the phenomenon known as *spontaneous human combustion*, which has been chronicled by Michael Harrison.[75] Eliade suggests that in some cases the generation of heat by an entranced shaman may be quite considerable:

'... shamans are not merely "masters over fire"; they can also incarnate the spirit of fire to the point where, during séances, they emit flames from their mouths, their noses, and their whole bodies.'[46]

One western scientist who has made a study of shamanism is Dr A. R. G. Owen; he was a research lecturer in mathematics at Trinity College, Cambridge, and from 1952 onwards lectured in genetics at that University. In 1963 Owen received an award from the Parapsychology Foundation of New York for a treatise on poltergeist phenomena, and the following year he was presented with the William McDougall Award for Distinguished Work in Parapsychology. Later he emigrated to Canada, where he took up the Directorship of the New Horizons Research Foundation in Toronto, and helped to establish the Toronto Society for Psychical Research. His book *Psychic Mysteries of the North* contains a chapter on shamanism among the North American Indians, whose presence in Canada antedates the coming of the white man by several thousand years. The story of the magical contest between the two shamans (p. 15) is taken from Owen's account, and he also describes many other examples of the phenomenon of the shaking tepee, which has baffled European observers for over three hundred years. Andrew Lang, the distinguished anthropologist and writer, also discussed shamanism in his book *Cock Lane and Common Sense*; he quoted the description of a séance attended by Pére Arnaud, a missionary who in 1853 visited the Naskapi Indians on the Labrador peninsula:

'The conjurers shut themselves up in a little lodge, and remain for a few minutes in a pensive attitude, cross-legged. Soon the lodge begins to move like a table turning, and replies by bounds and jumps to the questions which are put to the conjurer.'[99]

We have already noticed some striking resemblances between the phenomena of shamanism and those of nineteenth century spiritualism. Dr Owen draws an interesting parallel between the shaking tepee of the shaman and the curtained cabinet of the physical medium. He also sees a parallel, although a less close one, between 'the use of hymns and chants, the tambourine and the drum, as well as the trembling and shaking that sometimes preceded the medium's entry into trance.'[22] Indeed, he goes even further than this, suggesting that there may be a *direct* historical connection by means of the religious sect known as the Shakers, which flourished in parts of the North American continent around the middle of the last century. Some members of this sect believed that the spirits of deceased Indians visited their meetings and 'possessed' their members, and there is evidence indicating that the first recorded professional mediums, the Davenport brothers, were inspired by the Shakers. If this is so, it could explain the fashion for North American Indians as 'spirit guides' among the spiritualists of later generations.

Levitation, or the raising of the human body into the air without visible means of support, is yet another strange faculty often attributed to shamans. In this respect they are hardly exceptional among practitioners of the occult for, surprisingly enough, levitation is one of the most frequently reported of all the paranormal phenomena. References to alleged levitations or 'flights' are found not only among primitive shamans and witch-doctors, but also in the literature of Hinduism, Buddhism and Islam, among the alchemists and witches of the Middle Ages, in the biographies of many Christian saints, and in the records of the nineteenth century spiritualists. Levitation of the human body was also reported in 7% of the poltergeist cases analysed by Gauld and Cornell. There is even one report of a *post-mortem* levitation, that of the second century Rabbi Simeon Bar Yochai. It is said that when his dead body was being carried out of the house it was raised in the air, preceded by a column of fire![180] Eliade informs us that the ability to fly in the air is claimed by Siberian, Eskimo and North American shamans, as it is by sorcerers and medicine men all over the world:

'The power of flight can, as we have seen, be obtained in

many ways (shamanistic trance, mystical ecstasy, magical techniques), but also by a severe psychological discipline, such as the Yoga of Patanjali, by rigorous asceticism, as in Buddhism, or by alchemical practices.'[46]

Levitation, if it is a genuine occurrence, seems to imply some sort of neutralisation of the gravitational field which, under normal circumstances draws all physical objects towards the centre of the earth. Perhaps we can include in the same category an astounding performance which was witnessed by R. G. Trilles among African tribesmen, and described in a book by Ernest de Martino.[33] This performance took place during an initiation ceremony employed by the older medicine men for the admission of novices to their brotherhood. After various preliminaries, a see-saw structure similar to that shown in Figure 1a was erected in a suitable place. The older men then walked around the structure, clapping their hands and singing to the spirits while another medicine man beat upon a drum with a loud, regular beat. After this the novices were brought forward, and at a given signal they straddled the wooden beam MN as shown in diagram b. The medicine man took up his position as shown on the right of the diagram, with his arms raised and the palms of his hands in the form of cups directed towards the nearest end, N, of the beam. At this point the beam began to descend towards his outstretched hands, slowly at first and then more rapidly. When it came into the horizontal position it stopped, being at this point about 50 centimetres from the magician's hands (diagram c). The novices' feet were then about two metres from the ground. The bystanders now circled the structure three times, chanting all the while. The medicine man slowly knelt down, keeping his hands in the same position, and the beam followed the movement of his body (diagram d). Eventually, he lay flat upon the ground with his hands folded upon his chest while the beam, still untouched, remained in the position shown in diagram e. After a while the medicine man stood up, the beam returning to the horizontal position and remaining there while the participants circled it once again. Finally, the medicine man turned his palms downwards, and the beam returned to its original position, as in diagram b. The 'test' was considered highly successful, and the novices had gained their admis-

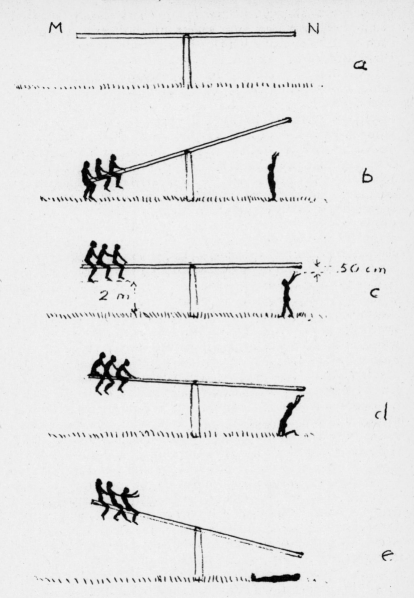

Fig. 1   An initiation ceremony among African tribesmen. (Redrawn from de Martino[33])

sion. At this point the medicine man, who appeared to be in a trance, collapsed upon the ground and was taken away to be revived.

Reflecting upon this report, the student of paranormal phenomena will undoubtedly recall similar examples in the literature of psychical research. A modern case with obvious parallels is that of the Russian housewife Nina Kulagina, who apparently sets small objects in motion by passing her hands above them, in a manner not dissimilar to that of the witch-doctor. After a successful session she is said to experience 'fatigue and sometimes extreme exhaustion', with dizziness, reduced coordination, thirst, and pains in the upper part of the spine and neck.[95] The resemblance to the medicine man's state of collapse following a successful initiation session is obvious.

All paranormal phenomena are capricious by nature, and therefore exceedingly difficult to record or bring under scientific control. This is particularly true of those physical phenomena which we describe as psychokinetic. In poltergeist cases, for example, objects usually move when the observer has turned his back for a moment, or when he is in the process of changing the film in his camera. For this reason, photographs of poltergeist missiles in motion are rare, although there are a few examples.[12] Attempts to gain objective records of PK phenomena with individual subjects have often been frustrated by the phenomena themselves. Scientists investigating the metal-bender Uri Geller have found that their electronic equipment malfunctions at the crucial moment, films become fogged in their cameras and magnetic recording tapes are mysteriously erased.

It is interesting to note that the inherent resistance of PK effects to scientific methods of observation is not confined to civilised countries. Robert Van de Castle describes an occurrence reported to him by a friend who became an apprentice to Rolling Thunder, a Shoshone medicine man living in Nevada. On one occasion a visitor wanted to take a Polaroid picture of Rolling Thunder, but the medicine man did not wish him to do so. Rolling Thunder told the visitor to take as many pictures as he wished, but warned him that none of them would come out properly because he would mentally cause the camera to malfunction. After three successive 'blackies' were obtained, the Indian began to feel sorry for his frustrated visitor. He asked a couple of young women to stand near him and smilingly told his visitor that a successful picture would now be obtained, since he was now in a better mood and would no longer jam the camera mentally. A perfectly normal picture was then obtained.[188]

A further instance of PK interference with sophisticated equipment is reported by St. Clair, who encountered a priest of the Brazilian Umbanda cult, a man called Edu. St. Clair took out a tape-recorder, hoping to get the exact words of the priest on tape, but Edu asked him to put it away:

'I told him that I wanted to get his exact words on tape. That it was important for a foreign journalist to capture exact phrases because so many Brazilian reporters just made up their own quotes. Still he said he wished that I would put the recorder away. I argued that in such an important project as I was writing, he would want to have his exact words on paper. Finally he shut his eyes, remained silent for a few seconds and then, looking at the machine, said, 'Turn it on'.

'Delighted, I pushed the button and the reels started to turn. But to my dismay the tape came gushing up out of the box like plastic spaghetti! I slammed at the stop button but it did no good. Soon his desk was a pile of forever-ruined tape. "This has never happened before," I spluttered.

'"You see?" he said with his soft voice and an even softer smile. "Yemanja didn't want you to use that machine either."'[156]

Sceptics will point out, with some justification, that many of the phenomena described in this chapter can be accounted for in terms of coincidence, fraud or malobservation. Later we shall examine the scientific evidence for PK, based on the results of hundreds of experiments. At this stage we are merely concerned with demonstrating that there is a widespread belief in such phenomena among primitive peoples, and that examples of apparent PK have been reported by educated travellers in most of the less civilised areas of the globe. The anecdotal evidence provided by ethnologists and anthropologists does not amount to absolute proof, but at least it provides a reasonable basis for pursuing the matter further.

2 Wise Men from the East

The origin of the human species is shrouded in obscurity, but it seems to be generally agreed by anthropologists that *Homo sapiens* evolved from his pre-human ancestors somewhere on the African continent, probably in the region of present-day Kenya. From there he spread northwards to the lands of the fertile crescent, developing the first civilisations along the valleys of the Nile, the Tigris, and the Euphrates, and expanding still further into India and China. There is evidence of widespread settlement in all these areas by about 4,000 BC. The first literate inhabitants of Mesopotamia, the Sumerians, appeared sometime between 4,000 and 3,000 BC, and the first Egyptian dynasty began in 3,200 BC, when King Menes united Upper and Lower Egypt to make a single nation. Bronze making had been established in the Middle East from about 3,800 BC, and there were flourishing cities along the valley of the Jordan river at least a thousand years before Abraham and his fellow tribesmen set foot in the area, probably around 2,090 BC.

Unfortunately we know much less about the early civilisations of India and China than we do about those of the Middle East. However, it is certain that there were cultured people living in these countries by about 3,000 BC. Sir James Jeans informs us that the Chinese were making accurate astronomical observations and keeping records of comets from the year 2,296 BC onwards, and adds that in the reign of the Emperor Yao two astronomers were put to death for failing to predict eclipses correctly.[92] The philosophy known as *Taoism* emerged in China during the second half of the first century before Christ, but it undoubtedly had its roots in a much earlier system. The earliest sacred writings of India, the *Vedas*, can be dated from around 1,000 BC, and reveal a very highly developed philosophy of life. It is probable that all these systems gradually evolved out of an earlier and more primitive form of practice and belief which was shamanistic in nature. As we have seen, shamanism involves communication with spirits through a form of trance mediumship, and it is often accompanied by apparently paranormal phenomena.

Levitations, flights or 'ascensions' are frequently mentioned in ancient Hindu and Buddhist texts. Joseph Needham quotes from a book called the *Pao Phu Tzu*, by the Chinese writer Ko Hung:

'The manuals of the immortals say that masters of the highest category (shang shih) are able to raise themselves high up into the aery void; these are called "celestial immortals". Those of the second category resort to the famous mountains and forests, and are called "terrestrial immortals". As for those of the third category they simply slough off the body after death, and they are called "corpse-free immortals"'.[114]

The prophet Elijah was reputed to have ascended into the heavens in a whirlwind of fire (2 Kings 2:11, 12); his Chinese rival the legendary Emperor Huang Ti performed an even more dramatic ascent:

'After Huang Ti had cast a bronze tripod cauldron once upon a time at Shou-shan (and doubtless brewed a chemical elixir in it), a celestial dragon vehicle came down from the heavens to fetch him, into the which he stepped – together with more than seventy other people, both ministers and palace ladies, and they all mounted up into the sky in full view of the populace'.[114]

A book called the *Shen Hsien Chuan* (probably written in the early 4th century AD) contains an interesting account of a holy man nicknamed 'Mr White-Stone', who deliberately chose to become a terrestrial rather than a celestial immortal. In the time of Phêng Tsu he was reputed to be already more than 2,000 years old, having achieved this remarkable longevity through the use of special drugs. One of these was a white mineral which he used to eat with his food, hence the nickname! The *Shen Hsien Chuan* continues:

'Phêng Tsu once asked him why he did not take the chemical which can make one rise into the heavens, to which he replied: "Can the joys of the heavens really compare with those that are found among men? If one can go on living here below without getting old and dying, one will be treated with the greatest respect; would one be treated any better in the heavens?!''

Joseph Needham, in quoting this passage, adds the following comment:

'On the other hand there was a widespread belief that certain immortals had been seen to ascend into the heavens in broad daylight. The *Hou Han Shu* itself contains a circumstantial account of a performance of this kind by an adept named Shangchhêng Kung, witnessed by two well-known scholars of the time . . .'[114]

Of course, it is extremely difficult to know what interpretation to place upon these very ancient descriptions. Some may be entirely fictitious, others may be descriptions of drug-induced hallucinations. Those who belong to the Erich von Däniken school of thought will no doubt find evidence for extraterrestrial visitations in some of the accounts. Needham mentions that the hallucinogenic mushroom known as the fly-agaric (*Amanita muscaria*) was used by the Gilyak, Koryak and Chukchi shamans of North East Asia to induce ritual ecstasies, imagined flights and visits to the gods. The same plant may have been the *Laoma-soma* of the Indian Vedas, for the Vedic hymns imply that those who participated in the ancient rites experienced ecstatic visions. However, it is also possible that some of these ancient descriptions refer to real levitations of the physical body, in which case they would come under our modern classification of PK phenomena. In any case, the writings prove that such phenomena were thought to be possible by the educated classes of that period.

For several hundred years now, the thought processes of western man have been mainly 'left hemispheric'; that is to say, they have been derived from that half of the brain which is mainly concerned with analytical, verbal, mathematical and logical thinking.[117] In contrast, eastern systems of thought have generally been of the holistic, intuitive kind which originate in the right hemisphere of the brain. Western man finds himself vaguely uncomfortable in the presence of these eastern systems, which do not fit neatly into any of his thought categories. Thus, western librarians have difficulty in classifying books on Yoga, which may be found on the shelves of public libraries under such varied headings as philosophy, religion, psychology, sport, medicine and physical education! In fact, Yoga is a remarkable technique designed to develop and integrate the *whole* person, not just one particular aspect of him as our western methods tend to do. The word 'Yoga' derives from a Sanscrit term meaning 'union', and it is defined by Ernest Wood as 'the method and practice leading to conscious union of the human being with the divine principle'.[189] Within this broad definition are many different kinds of Yoga, each with its own traditional techniques. Western devotees often confine their activities to the postures and breathing exercises of *Hatha yoga*, which can certainly lead to an improvement in health and a sense of physical well-being. However, Hatha yoga is only a small part of the total yogic system. The training of the body should lead naturally into the training of the mind and spirit through the practices of *Raja yoga*, the 'royal' yoga. Whereas many westerners have become proficient in performing the physical exercises of Hatha yoga, very few have acquired proficiency in the higher forms of yoga which seek to control the mind and bring the individual into union with the divine.

Exactly when yoga originated is not known, but some forms of it were certainly in existence before the birth of Christ. One of the earliest works on yoga, the *Yoga Sutras* of Patanjali, may be as old as the fourth century BC, although some scholars place it several hundred years later than this. Patanjali may be described as the great natural historian of yoga; in the *sutras* he set out to systematise the vast body of yogic philosophy and practice which had grown up over the centuries. Later yogic writers expanded and developed his teaching into the many different forms of yoga which exist today.

Many yogic books refer to the *siddhis*, or psychic powers, which may develop as a by-product of the practice of yoga. Usually, although not invariably, the ancient writers regard the appearance of such powers as something of a nuisance, since they may distract the mind from the practice of meditation, and thus retard the individual's progress towards the blissful state of *samadhi*. Ernest Wood distinguishes two kinds of psychic phenomenon in the yogic literature, and he refers to these as *faculties* and *powers*. The two divisions correspond roughly to the modern parapsychologist's distinction between ESP and PK. The faculties include the ability to become aware of events occurring in some other place or time (*clairvoyance, precognition, retrocognition*) and to receive other people's thoughts (*telepathy*). The powers are said to be eight in number, and are listed by Wood as follows:

1) Minuteness (*animā*). To be as small as an atom, at will.
2) Expansion (*mahimā*). To increase in size, at will.
3) Lightness (*laghimā*). Neutralisation of gravity, at will.
4) Reaching (*prāpti*). To obtain anything or to reach any place, at will.
5) Acquirement (*prākāmya*). To have the fulfilment of any wish, at will.
6) Lordship (*īshatwā*). Control of the energies of Nature, at will.
7) Self-control (*vashitwā*). Self-command and freedom from being influenced, at will.
8) Desire-control (*kāmavasāyita*). The stopping of all desires, at will.

At first glance, there does not seem to be much resemblance between the powers claimed here and the phenomena encountered in 19th and 20th century spiritualism and psychical research. However, it is only the terminology which is unfamiliar. If the descriptions are taken literally, they are seen to be virtually identical with those of later ages. For example, several of the nineteenth century physical mediums claimed the ability to elongate or shorten their bodies, and would thus be considered to be practioners of *animā* and *mahimā*.[85] *Laghimā* is just another name for levitation which, as we have seen, is one of the most frequently reported of all psychical phenomena. Apportation and translocation of objects, including the human body, is implied by *prāpti*, and *prākāmya* and *īshatwā* suggest rather extensive psychokinetic powers, though hardly more extensive than those attributed to D. D. Home or Uri Geller.

In discussing the flights or ascensions attributed to some of the sages of ancient China we considered the possibility that these might have been drug-induced hallucinations, perhaps akin to the modern parapsychologist's 'out-of-the-body experience', or OBE. Ernest Wood is careful to distinguish between what he calls 'travelling in the subtle body' (*sūkshma* *sharīra* in Sanscrit) and levitation of the physical body. True levitation is said to be achieved by the practice of the 1:4:2 breathing rhythm, carried to exceptional lengths. This breathing technique is one of the standard practices of Hatha yoga; it is performed by inhaling on a count of one, retaining the breath while counting four, and then exhaling on a count of two. After a great deal of practice the time intervals may be lengthened until the adept is breathing as slowly as 36:144:72, where the numbers are taken as seconds. According to Wood, it is at this point that physical levitation may occur.[189] It is interesting to note that in recent years some people claim to have levitated through the practice of Transcendental Meditation; however, from the few descriptions of this phenomenon which are available it would seem to be more like a kind of *leaping* into the air rather than a true sustained levitation.*

As far as I am aware, no yogi has ever levitated under test conditions in a laboratory, but there are many reports from travellers who claim to have witnessed the phenomenon in India or Tibet. Some of these reports include descriptions of levitations occurring in the open air, and these are particularly impressive since it is difficult to see how they could have been faked. Ernest Wood claimed to have observed one such example:

'I remember one occasion when an old yogi was levitated in a recumbent posture about six feet above the ground in an open field, for about half an hour, while the visitors were permitted to pass sticks to and fro in the space between.'[189]

He went on to quote an account by Princess Pena Choki, second daughter of the Maharaja of Sikkim, whose uncle '. . . did what you would call exercises in levitation. I used to take him a little rice. He would be motionless in mid-air. Every day he rose a little higher. In the end he rose so high that I found it difficult to hand the rice up to him. I was a little girl, and had to stand on tiptoe . . . There are certain things you don't forget.'

If we accept these reports as accounts of genuine paranormal phenomena, then we have here evidence of levitations apparently induced through the calm, deliberate practice of

*There is an interesting account of this by a practitioner of T. M., R. L. Franklin, in *Theoria to Theory*, 1980, *14*, pp. 43–63. Mr Franklin is a barrister by profession.

yoga techniques. However, there is also a certain amount of evidence that levitation may occur spontaneously, in circumstances which are by no means pleasant for the person concerned. E. A. Smythies, sometime Forest Adviser to the Government of Nepal, reported one such incident in 1951.[164] The phenomena centred around a young orderly called Krishna, who had been negligent in performing the sacrifices prescribed by his religion, and as a result was 'possessed' by his village spirit, or *Bhagwan*. On the evening when the principal phenomenon occurred Smythies had been holding a small dinner party; at about nine o'clock he was interrupted by Azmat, his Mohammedan bearer, who told him that Krishna was possessed by the Bhagwan:

'I did not want to disturb the party, so I slipped out quietly, and went to the back of the house where the servants' quarters were. These quarters were a building of brick and tiled roof divided into five rooms in a row, each room about ten feet by seven and eight feet high, with a small extension at the back for cooking food, and a door three and a half by six feet high in front, and well lit with an unshaded electric light bulb. In one of these little bare rooms – there was nothing in the room except a roll of bedding in one corner and a small box in another – my elder orderly, aged about twenty-two and also called Krishna, was squatting quite alone on the bare floor, dressed in a shirt and khaki shorts with bare legs. His attitude was approximately as shown in the accompanying illustration (Figure 2), cross-legged with his hands clasped between his legs. His head and body were shaking and quivering, his face appeared wet with sweat, and he was making the most extraordinary noises. He seemed to me obviously unconscious of what he was doing or that a circle of rather frightened servants – and myself – were looking at him through the open door at about eight or ten feet distance.

'This went on for about ten minutes or a quarter of an hour, when suddenly (with his legs still crossed and his hands clasped, see Figure 2b) he rose about two feet in the air, and after a second bumped down hard on the floor. This happened again twice, exactly the same except that his hands and legs became separated.

'One of the servants whispered that the *Bhagwan* was very angry with Krishna and was punishing him by bumping him

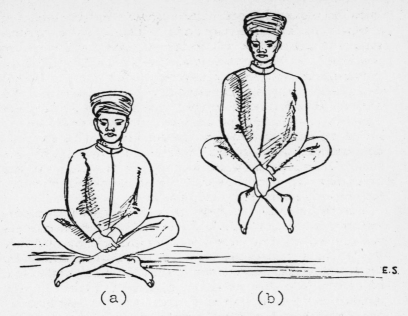

(a)   (b)

E.S.

Fig. 2 A case of levitation in Nepal. Drawn to Mr Smythies' specifica-
tions by Mrs Elizabeth Sulivan in December, 1950. (*Journal of the Society for
Psychical Research*, May 1951)

on the floor in this way, which, I must admit, was just what it
looked like. The servants were becoming very frightened and
worried, and I was feeling very creepy myself at this inexplicable sight. Then one of the Nepali servants produced a
splinter of resinous wood, which he lit and placed the burning
end in Krishna's mouth for a moment. The seizure continued
unaltered for a brief interval, and then suddenly it passed, and
Krishna opened his eyes and relaxed. He sat looking dazed
but otherwise normal. Shortly afterwards I left and returned
to our party, from which I had been absent for less than an
hour.'

Later, certain members of the Society for Psychical
Research set out to investigate this occurrence, and statements were obtained from Azmat and from other persons
present at the party. None of the information thus obtained
was in conflict with Mr Smythies' account, which seems to
have been very carefully and accurately compiled. It is diffi-

cult to see how such a happening, recorded by a reliable and intelligent observer and supported by independent testimony, can possibly be explained without invoking some sort of paranormal agency.

Another remarkable eye-witness account of a levitation occurring in the east is described by Olivier Leroy.[103] L. Jacolliot, a French magistrate who was *procureur impérial* at Pondicherry, India, in 1866, said that he saw a fakir named Covindassamy raised two feet above the earth. The fakir lived in a hut a short distance from Jacolliot's home. On one occasion the magistrate saw him suspended in the air on the terrace of his house, with only a stick for a prop. He remained there for twenty minutes. On another occasion the levitation took place without any support whatever: 'At the moment when he left me for lunch ... the fakir stopped in the doorway opening from the terrace into the backstairs, and folding his arms, he was lifted – or so it seemed to me – gradually, without visible support, about one foot above the ground. I could determine the exact height, thanks to a landing mark upon which I fixed my eyes during the short time the phenomenon lasted. Behind the fakir hung a silk curtain with red, golden and white stripes of equal breadth, and I noticed that the fakir's feet were as high as the sixth stripe. When I saw the rising begin, I took my watch out. From the time when the magician began to be lifted until he came down to earth again, about ten minutes elapsed. He remained about five minutes suspended without motion.'

One of the most popular books about yoga is *Autobiography of a Yogi* by Paramhansa Yogananda. Born at Gorakhpur, north-east India, in 1893, Yogananda spent his entire life in pursuit of the yogic ideal. For many years he studied under the watchful eye of his 'Christlike' master, Sri Yukteswar. Later he travelled to the west, giving lectures in both Britain and the USA, and establishing the organisation known as the Self-Realisation Fellowship. Yogananda's autobiography is a truly astonishing book, containing descriptions of a great variety of allegedly paranormal events. Thus, we are told of a silver amulet which 'materialised' between Yogananda's palms (p. 27), an electric lighting system which ceased to function at the mental command of a yogi (p. 77), a paranormal increase in body weight (p. 104), and the mental suppression of a photographic image (pp. 18–19). There is also a somewhat amusing account of a fakir, Afzal Khan, who used his powers of materialisation and dematerialisation to steal gold and jewellery; the story ends, as all such stories should, with the wonder-worker deprived of his paranormal gifts and compelled to repent in exile!

Confronted with such a profusion of apparently miraculous events, the scientifically-trained westerner is likely to shrug his shoulders or throw up his hands in despair. How can one ever arrive at any definite conclusions when presented with reports of phenomena occurring under such uncontrolled conditions? There is no doubt that most, if not all, of the events described by Yogananda could have perfectly natural explanations, such explanations ranging from simple malobservation or illusion to downright lying and fraud. Since no trained observers were present it is impossible to assess the veracity of the reports.

However, there is one modern yogi whose activities have been observed by experienced parapsychologists, although not under laboratory conditions. Sathya Sai Baba, born in 1925, has a considerable religious following and lives in the state of Andhra Pradesh in southern India. According to his close associates he has been a focus for paranormal occurrences ever since his childhood. His chief speciality is the materialisation and dematerialisation of physical objects such as amulets, gold rings, jewels, and statuettes, but he has also been said to produce paranormal healing, transformations of material objects, and direct mental effects upon photographic film.[25] Sai Baba's phenomena have been observed by a number of eminent Indian scientists, including several from the All India Institute of Science in Bangalore. The phenomena have also been studied by two experienced parapsychologists from the west, Dr Karlis Osis and Dr Erlendur Haraldsson, who published an account of their observations in 1977.[73] They witnessed some 21 appearances and disappearances of physical objects at close range, although none were under fully controlled conditions. Some of the objects 'materialised' by Sai Baba and given away to his visitors seem to have been quite expensive; for example, Dr Osis received a gold ring which was subsequently valued by a goldsmith at $100, while Dr Haraldsson was given a gold ornament valued at $80. Despite their very close and careful observation, Osis and Haraldsson were unable to detect any signs of fraudulent activity, and later examination of Sai Baba's robe showed that it contained no pockets, slings, suspicious seam corners or other places where objects might have been concealed. During the materialisations Sai Baba sat cross-legged on a concrete floor, well out of reach of any possible containers or hiding-places, and some of the objects produced by him seem to have been too large for concealment in the mouth.

Of all the phenomena produced by Sai Baba, the most difficult to explain in normal terms are the materialisations occurring at a distance. Thus, he is said to have caused fruit to appear directly in a visitor's hand, some prayer-beads to appear on the windscreen of a car being driven along an open country road (this observed by two senior research scientists), and some holy ash to appear on pictures of himself. Osis and Haraldsson observed only one of these distance effects, but it was an exceedingly puzzling one. As mentioned earlier, Osis had been given a materialised gold ring which had a large enamelled coloured picture of Sai Baba encased in it. The picture was set as firmly in the ring 'as if it and the ring were one solid article'; it could not have been removed without bending the frame and notches which held it. During an interview in which Osis and Haraldsson were trying to persuade Sai Baba to participate in some controlled experiments, the holy man seemed to become impatient and said to Osis 'Look at your ring'. On examination the picture was found to have vanished from the ring. The frame and notches which had held the picture were undamaged, but the picture was nowhere to be seen. At the time when Sai Baba made the investigators aware of the picture's absence they were sitting about five or six feet away from him. Both Osis and Haraldsson had seen the picture in the ring at the beginning of the session, and two other persons present certified that they had also observed it. When the picture could not be found, Sai Baba teasingly remarked, 'This was my experiment'!

If the claims made for Indian yoga are considered extravagant, those of Tibetan yoga are even more so. Tibetan yogis are supposed to be able to observe events hundreds of miles away, levitate, read people's thoughts, walk upon water, make themselves invisible, pass through rocks and transform stones into gold. 'The only difficulty', as Glen Barclay puts it, 'is to find a Tibetan yogi who has actually done some of these things, or who is prepared to say that he has seen any other Tibetan yogi do them'.[3] Nevertheless, there are a few instances where competent and educated observers have reported events which seem to be inexplicable on any natural-istic hypothesis. Madame Alexandra David-Neel was a French scholar of considerable distinction, having been awarded a gold medal by the Geographical Society of Paris and made a Knight of the Legion of Honour. She studied oriental languages at the Sorbonne, and spent many years of her life travelling in the east, covering vast tracts of Tibetan territory previously unexplored by Europeans. In her famous book *Magic and Mystery in Tibet* she describes the strange phenomenon of the *lung-gom-pa* lama, who travels across the mountains at an incredible speed, by what appear to be a series of leaps and bounds. Madame David-Neel was able to observe several of these adepts at close quarters, and on one occasion she calculated that the man must have maintained his rapid method of locomotion for at least two days non-stop. The *lung-gom-pa* runner – if such is the correct term – appears to be in some sort of trance state, and, according to the Tibetans, he must not be interrupted or he will die. Whether there is an element of levitation in this curious ability is not clear, but Madame David-Neel saw one of the adepts sitting upon a rock with iron chains rolled around his body; she was told that, through the practice of *lung-gom* his body had become so light that it was in danger of floating off into the air!

Although levitations of the human body are fairly fre-quently reported by travellers in the east, the paranormal movement of a physical object, such as a table, is much less common. In 1831, however, a M. Tschérépanoff described the following incident which he witnessed:

'The Lama, after being asked to trace an object . . . sits on the ground, reading a Tibetan book, in front of a small square table, on which he rests his hands. At the end of half an hour he rises and lifts his hands from the surface of the table: pres-ently the table also rises from the ground, and follows the direction of his hand. The Lama elevates his hand above his head, the table reaches the level of his eyes: the Lama walks, the table rushes before him in the air, so rapidly that he can scarcely keep up with its flight. The table then spins round, and falls on the earth, the direction in which it falls indicates that in which the stolen object is to be sought.' Tschérépanoff adds that he saw the table fly about forty feet before it fell. He searched in vain for hidden wires, or other evidence of trickery.[99] It is interesting to note that this account, so startlingly reminiscent of the 'table-turnings' of western spiritualism, took place some seventeen years *before* the date usually assigned to the birth of the spiritualist movement in America.

Some Tibetan lamas seem to possess another extraordinary ability which has been noted by Madame David-Neel and other western observers: the ability to withstand sub-zero temperatures:

'To spend the winter in a cave amidst the snows, at an altitude that varies between 11,000 and 18,000 feet, clad in a thin garment or even naked, and escape freezing, is a somewhat difficult achievement. Yet numbers of Tibetan hermits go safely each year through this ordeal. The endurance is ascribed to the power which they have acquired to generate *tumo*.'[30]

She goes on to explain that the term 'tumo' refers to a kind of mystical warmth which is generated by the practices of meditation, and which protects the adept from the normal consequences of exposure to extreme cold. The ability to generate *tumo* is only acquired after a lengthy training, and not everyone who attempts it is successful. Nevertheless, the fact that it can be achieved at all is remarkable. It suggests that there are reserves of power within the human body and mind which lie far beyond anything so far revealed by modern medical science.

There is no doubt whatever that a great deal of utter nonsense has been written and talked about the 'mysterious east', from the time of Madame Blavatsky onwards. It is quite understandable that many western scientists feel that they have neither the time nor the inclination to immerse themselves in the great morass of occultist literature which has developed over the centuries from the religious and philosophical systems of the orient, and which now threatens to become a mighty flood engulfing the hard-won gains of rational western thought. Even so, it would be a pity to throw out the baby with the bath-water. There is sufficient evidence to show that at least *some* of the claims of yoga are valid ones. Practitioners of yogic techniques have been tested under laboratory conditions and shown to have remarkable control over the autonomic processes of their own bodies.[53] Many medical men are convinced of the beneficial effects of both Hatha Yoga and Raja Yoga, and some have recommended courses in yoga for their patients, with very satisfactory results. Provided that we do not abandon our critical faculties, nothing but good can come from the attempts now being made to explore oriental techniques with the methods of western science. There is much we can learn from the wise men of the east.

3 Jews and Gentiles

Western civilisation as we know it is largely the result of the confluence of three ancient cultures: those of the Jews, the Greeks, and the Romans. Most of our present-day attitudes can be traced directly to one or other of the three. From the ancient Hebrews we have inherited the Bible with its powerful monotheistic imagery, its burning sense of justice and its concept of a patriarchal society. From Rome comes much of our legal system and our notions of military discipline and organisation. From the Greeks we derive our concepts of democracy, of logical thought, mathematics and science. It is of interest, therefore, to enquire whether these ancient peoples ever reported instances of paranormal phenomena, and if so, how they interpreted them.

Turning first to the Bible, one is struck by the fact that paranormal phenomena are only occasionally reported within its pages, and when they are reported they are usually attributed to the direct action of God. Compared with much eastern literature, the Bible is a sober book. With the exception of Elijah, there are no reports of people being taken into the skies on golden chariots such as we find in Chinese literature, nor of people having their severed heads restored, such as we find in some Arabic writings. Nevertheless, most of the paranormal phenomena investigated by modern researchers are mentioned occasionally in the Bible. Spiritualistic séances were certainly held in ancient Israel as they were in other Middle Eastern countries, although the Deuteronomic law forbade them (Deuteronomy 18:11). We are told that King Saul communicated with the spirit of the dead prophet Samuel through the mediumship of the witch of En-dor (1 Samuel 28:3–14), although we are not told exactly how the communication was effected. 'Direct voice' communication seems to have been known to the ancient Jews; certainly Moses heard the voice of God speaking directly to him from the burning bush (Exodus 3) and later from Mount Sinai (Exodus 19). Physical phenomena, apart from paranormal healings and voices, seem to have been rare. However, there is a curious account of what might be regarded as a partial levitation of a physical object in the Second Book of Kings, Chapter 6. Under the direction of Elisha, the prophetic brotherhood were cutting timber in order to build themselves a dwelling place when one of their members dropped his iron axe-head into the Jordan. '"*Alas*, my lord," he exclaimed, "and it was a borrowed one too!" "Where did it fall?" the man of God asked; and he showed him the spot. Then, cutting a stick, Elisha threw it at that point and made the iron axehead float. "Lift it out," he said; and the man stretched out his hand and took it.' (*Jerusalem Bible* translation).

The New Testament also contains relatively few miracles, apart from those concerned with the healing of the sick. No doubt fairly plausible naturalistic explanations can be suggested for many of the healing miracles. However, there are a few phenomena reported by the New Testament writers which cannot be easily explained in this way. If they occurred as described, these phenomena must have involved some interference with normal physical causation. Thus, we have the transformation of water into wine (John 2:1–12), the multiplication of food (Matthew 14:13–21), the walking on the water (Matthew 14:22–23), the raising of Lazarus (John 11) and, of course, the Resurrection of the Master himself. It is worth noticing that although Matthew, Mark and John all recount the story of Jesus walking on the water, only Matthew tells us that Peter tried to do it as well. At first the apostle was reasonably successful, but as soon as he felt the force of the wind he lost his confidence and began to sink. The story is interesting because it implies that the ability to perform physical miracles is not the prerogative of certain special persons, but is open to anyone who has sufficient faith in the possibility of the phenomenon and in his own ability to produce it. Twentieth century parapsychologists have demonstrated the importance of belief in influencing the production of phenomena in numerous laboratory experiments.

The Acts of the Apostles includes descriptions of several physical miracles. Thus, Peter twice escaped from prison as a

result of supernatural intervention (Acts 5:17 and 12:1–11).
On the first occasion we are told that an angel of the Lord
opened the prison gates; however, when the prison officials
arrived they found the gates still locked, although Peter and
his companions had disappeared from inside. This seems,
therefore, to be an instance of apportation or teleportation of
human beings. On the second occasion Peter imagined that
he was dreaming or seeing a vision when the angel struck the
fetters from his hands and the prison gates opened of their
own accord. It was only when he had walked the whole
length of a street that he 'came to himself' and realised that he
was physically free. There is a dream-like quality about the
whole episode which accords well with modern descriptions
given by people who have found themselves involved with
the paranormal.

Notwithstanding the precepts of their own Law, there
were a number of Jews who practised sorcery of one kind or
another. The Jewish historian Flavius Josephus, who was
born a few years after the death of Jesus, gives us an interesting account of the activities of a Jewish exorcist named
Eleazar. Under the eagle eye of the Emperor Vespasian and
several of his officers, Eleazar cured a man possessed by
demons, using the following procedure:

'. . . he put to the nose of the possessed man a ring which
had under its seal one of the roots prescribed by Solomon,
and then, as the man smelled it, drew out the demon through
his nostrils, and, when the man at once fell down, adjured the
demon never to come back into him, speaking Solomon's
name and reciting the incantations which he had composed.
Then, wishing to convince the bystanders and prove to them
that he had this power, Eleazar placed a cup or foot-basin full
of water a little way off and commanded the demon, as it
went out of the man, to overturn it and make known to the
spectators that he had left the man. And when this was done,
the understanding and wisdom of Solomon were clearly
revealed . . .'[93]

Although Josephus claims to have been an eye-witness of
this phenomenon, he does not tell us whether anyone
examined the basin containing the water for evidence of
trickery!

Turning now to the Graeco-Roman world, we find innumerable reports of paranormal phenomena of one kind or another. All the various forms of extrasensory perception – telepathy, clairvoyance, precognition – were known to the ancient Greeks and were incorporated under the general heading of 'divination'. Democritus, who flourished around 400 BC, actually developed a theory of telepathy based on the notion that persons and objects of all sorts emit impulses which can be transmitted across space. Aristotle also accepted the reality of ESP, and believed that it was particularly effective during sleep, a view which seems to be confirmed by modern experiments in dream laboratories. One of the most famous ESP stories of all time comes from the Greek historian Herodotus, who was born between 490 and 480 BC. He tells how Croesus, King of Lydia, set out to test the extrasensory abilities of seven of the leading oracles of the day. He sent messengers to each one, telling them to put a single question to each oracle: what is the King of Lydia doing at this moment? The question was to be asked at a specified time, and the answer carefully recorded in writing. When the time arrived, Croesus performed an act which he thought no one would be likely to guess; he cut up a tortoise and a lamb, and boiled them together in a bronze vessel. When the messengers returned he found that the only oracle to give the correct answer was the famous Priestess of Delphi.[83]

The late Professor E. R. Dodds was a great classical scholar who held the presidency of the Society for Psychical Research from 1961 to 1963. In 1971 he published a long and scholarly paper in which he reviewed many of the descriptions of paranormal phenomena in ancient Greece and Rome. He found that, with one exception, the phenomena reported in those far off days were much the same as the phenomena reported today. The one exception was the poltergeist; Dodds could find no evidence that the ancients were acquainted with these mischievous 'spirits' which move furniture, throw objects around, and tear bedclothes off their sleeping victims. Brian Inglis disagrees with Dodds on this point; he argues that although poltergeists are not identified as such, many of the manifestations associated with them are there in abundance in classical antiquity: 'lights, and fires, and objects moving – like the armour clashing around in the temple of Hercules, which warned the Spartans of their impending defeat by Epaminondas'.[91] There is also the story of the man hurled out of bed by a 'sudden, occult force', described in the introduction to the present book. It would be hard to think of a more typical poltergeist prank than this unpleasant event, reported from the first century AD.

Some modern spiritualist mediums hold what are called 'transfiguration' séances. In these, the features of the entranced medium become distorted into the likeness of a deceased person. The phenomenon is supposed to be produced by the exudation of a thin layer of ectoplasm which covers the natural face of the medium, and shapes itself to produce the required resemblance. A friend of mine described a visit to such a medium some years ago:

'. . . on each occasion her face underwent quite definite changes. First she showed us her four guides, among them an aged Chinaman and a young Japanese girl. No two faces could have been more dissimilar. As the face of the Chinaman built, she appeared to be quite toothless, and as far as we could see the teeth were not concealed by the lips, which were drawn tightly back. In the cases where men appeared, the change was most obvious, moustaches appearing, not hair, but shadow on the darkening of the skin, wrinkles appeared, a scar, hollow cheeks or full necks. Most startling instances of these phenomena were the lengthening of finger-nails perceptibly, even though the hands were never concealed from our eyes, an obvious thickening of the body, and a change in the luminosity of the eyes.'[102]

Whether or not such phenomena can be attributed to fraud or clever acting, it is instructive to compare them with such ancient examples as the transfiguration of Moses (Exodus 34:29–35), of Jesus (Matthew 17:1–8) and of the Sibyl described in Virgil's Aeneid:

'They had reached the threshold when the maid cried: "The time to ask your fate has come. Look, the God! The God is here!" As she spoke the words, there, before the double doors, suddenly her countenance and her colour changed and her hair fell in disarray. Her breast heaved and her bursting heart was wild and mad; she appeared taller and spoke in no mortal tones, for the God was nearer and the breath of his power was upon her.'

Elongation of the body was a common feat among the

nineteenth century mediums; an early example of what seems to be the same effect is described by Ovid (*Fasti*, vi, 540):

'A brief pause ensued, and then the prophetess assumed her heavenly powers, and all her bosom swelled with majesty divine. Of a sudden you could hardly know her again; so holier, so taller far was she than she had been but now.'

Apollonius of Tyana was a famous miracle-worker who was born during the lifetime of Christ and died during the reign of the emperor Nerva (96–98 AD). He seems to have been something of an ascetic, for his biographer Philostratus tells us that he took a vow of chastity, fasted, and for a time kept a vow of silence. Apollonius wandered all over the civilised world, including India, where he saw the Brahmans levitating themselves 'two cubits high from the ground, not for the sake of miraculous display, for they disdain any such ambition; but they regard any rites they perform, in thus quitting earth and walking with the Sun, as acts of homage acceptable to the God.'[127] It is interesting to have this very early testimony to the alleged paranormal faculties of the Indian sages. Also of interest are the many physical miracles attributed to Apollonius himself. Imprisoned on one occasion with his disciple Damis, Apollonius cheered up his friend by demonstrating that he could remove his leg from the fetters and replace it at will! On another occasion a demon expelled by Apollonius demonstrated its presence by a psychokinetic effect on a statue:

'"I will throw down yonder statue", said the devil, and pointed to one of the images which were in the king's portico, for there it was that the scene took place. But when the statue began by moving gently, and then fell down, it would defy anyone to describe the hubbub which arose thereat and the way they clapped their hands with wonder.'[127]

The young man from whom this demon had been expelled then appeared to be perfectly normal, 'as though he had been treated with drugs', an interesting phrase which suggests that the ancients were not unfamiliar with the use of tranquillisers.

Of all the ancient writings, there is no doubt that those emanating from the Neo-Platonist sect known as the *theurgists* contain the closest parallels to modern spiritualism. The founder of Neo-Platonism was reputed to be Ammonius Saccus (175–242 AD), although little is known about his life and work. It is from the writings of his successors, particularly Plotinus (c. 205–270 AD), Porphyry (c. 232–303 AD) and Iamblicus (c. 250–330 AD) that we learn most about the doctrines and practices of the sect. Whereas modern spiritualist mediums are usually middle-aged women, the occult practitioners of ancient times tended to use pre-pubescent boys as intermediaries between the visible and invisible worlds. Trances were induced by methods which were similar to those of the modern hypnotist; the young mediums were alleged to be totally unaware of the manifestations which occurred while they were in the trance state:

'Those . . . who draw down spirits invisibly are without vision, as if they were in the dark, and know nothing of what they do, except some small signs which become visible through the body of him who is divinely inspired . . .'[90]

Once possessed by the spirit or god, the body of the medium might undergo various startling changes, including elongation, levitation and translocation:

'For the inspiration is indicated by the motions of the whole body, and of certain parts of it, by the perfect rest of the body, by harmonious orders and dances, and by elegant sounds, or the contraries of these. Either the body, likewise, is seen to be elevated, or increased in bulk, or to be borne along sublimely in the air, or the contraries of these, are seen to take place about it. An equability, also, of voice, according to magnitude, or a great variety of voice after intervals of silence, may be observed . . .'[90]

The great classical scholar and historian Andrew Lang was one of the first writers to notice the many close resemblances between the phenomena described in ancient writings and the phenomena investigated by present-day psychical research. 'When the epidemic of "Spiritualism" broke out in the United States', he wrote in 1896, 'students of classical literature perceived that Spiritualism was no new thing, but a recrudescence of practices familiar to the ancient world.'[99] Lang constantly pleaded for a closer liason between anthropologists, classical scholars, historians, and psychical researchers. He drew attention to the similarities between the social conditions which led to the rise of theurgy in the early centuries of the Christian era, and the conditions which led to the rise of spiritualism in nineteenth century America. Both movements occurred at times when the old established creeds were falling into disrepute, and men were beginning to turn away from the practices of their forefathers. It is in such periods of philosophical confusion that the human mind seeks for tangible, or at least visible, evidence of a spiritual reality, and therefore turns toward those phenomena which seem to offer a glimpse into the unseen world. Whether the phenomena really do provide such an insight is a very different matter.

4 Saints and Sinners

On October 28th in the year 312 AD, the soldiers of the Emperor Constantine defeated those of his rival Maxentius at the battle of the Milvian Bridge. Tradition informs us that, in response to information received in a dream, Constantine had ordered the Christian *Chi-Rho* symbol to be embroidered on his standards. His military success was therefore interpreted as an indication of the efficacy of the Christian religion, which became an officially permitted religion after the proclamation of the edict of Milan in the following year. From that time onwards the power and influence of the Christian Church grew steadily until, under the mediaeval papacy, it came to dominate the whole of Europe.

Powerful religions seem to induce extremes of both holiness and wickedness, and Christianity is no exception. The Christian religion has spawned many great saints and many great sinners. An abundance of paranormal phenomena have been reported from both extremes of the spectrum of sanctity. We have already heard how St Benedict shattered a glass vessel with the sign of the cross; the following passage reports a partial neutralisation of the force of gravity:

'One day, when the monks were busy building that monastery, there lay by them a stone which they intended to raise and put into the structure. At first two or three of them attempted to move it, but not succeeding were joined by more. Yet the stone stuck fast as though it were rooted in the ground, and it became plain that if so many men could not move it, it must be because the devil was sitting on it. Faced with this difficulty the monks sent for the man of God, so that he might come and repel the enemy with his prayers and so release the stone. Benedict came at once, prayed and gave a blessing; and then the stone was moved so speedily that it seemed to have no weight at all.'[66]

As the Christian centuries progressed, hagiographers vied

with one another in their attempts to recount tales of extra-ordinary and miraculous feats. St Clare, foundress of the order of Poor Clares, was supposed to have been miraculously transported from her sick bed to the church and back again.[150] Her friend the great St Francis of Assisi had many miracles attributed to him, including the levitation of an astonished Franciscan brother:

'And Saint Francis went behind the altar and began to pray, and during his prayer he was filled by the visitation of divine grace with such overpowering fervour that his soul was set on fire with love for Holy Poverty; his face glowed and his lips parted strangely as though he were emitting flames of fire. And coming thus aflame to his companion, he said to him: "Ah, ah, ah, Brother Masseo; yield yourself to me." He repeated these words three times, and at the third time Saint Francis raised Brother Masseo into the air with his breath and cast him a long spear's length from him. This astonished Brother Masseo . . .'[150]

Levitation of the human body seems to have been regarded by the hagiographers as an important adjunct to sanctity; over two hundred of the Catholic saints are said to have levitated at some time or other. No doubt the vast majority of these stories from the Ages of Faith can be dismissed as mere pious exaggeration; certainly most of them were not written down until long after the events they purport to describe. However, there are a few accounts which cannot be so easily dismissed. The levitations of St Teresa of Avila (1515–1582), for example, were witnessed by a number of people, including bishops, and the saint herself left us an account of them in her *Life*. Far from wishing to make spiritual capital out of these strange occurrences, Teresa found them acutely embarrassing, and instructed her nuns never to speak of them. She also found them frightening, at any rate at first:

'It seemed to me when I tried to resist that a great force, for which I can find no comparison, was lifting me up from beneath my feet. It came with greater violence than any other spiritual experience, and left me quite shattered . . . I confess that in me it aroused a great fear, at first a very great fear. One sees one's body being lifted from the ground; and though the spirit draws it up after itself, and does so most gently if it does not resist, one does not lose consciousness. At least I myself was sufficiently aware to realise that I was being lifted. The majesty of One who can do this is so manifest that one's hair stands on end, and a great fear comes over one.'[151]

Like all the great mystics Teresa was very introspective, and has left us a very detailed and scientific account of her inner experiences in the various stages of prayer and meditation. Her writings could well repay careful study by anyone interested in medicine, depth psychology, or psychical research. There are, in fact, several features which seem to occur with exceptional frequency in the lives of people who produce dramatic PK effects. One of these is a tendency to psychosomatic disorders (Teresa suffered from a 'mysterious' illness in her early years). Another is the adoption of an ascetic lifestyle involving fasting, long hours of prayer or meditation, and sometimes mortifying practices such as flagellation. Whether these things have any connection with the release of the PK force we have no way of telling; but their occurrence in conjunction with paranormal physical phenomena is certainly suggestive. The apparent connection is not restricted to the phenomena of the Christian saints; similar mortifying practices occur in the lives of Hindu mystics and wonder-workers of the ancient world, such as Apollonius.

Perhaps the most famous of all the levitating saints is St Joseph of Copertino (1603–1663). He was the son of a poor carpenter, and was considered to be very backward as a child. Brought up under a system of strict religious discipline, he began to have ecstasies at the early age of eight. At school he would sometimes pass into a kind of trance, sitting motionless with his mouth open and his eyes turned upwards, a characteristic which earned him the nickname of 'openmouth'. He was refused admission by the Conventual Friars Minor on account of his lack of learning, but in 1620 he was taken on as a lay brother in the Capuchin order. Unfortunately, Joseph turned out to be virtually unemployable. Put to work in the refectory, his frequent fits and ecstasies caused so many breakages that he was transferred to the kitchen, where he was assigned the tasks of carrying firewood and doing various odd jobs. After eight months of this, the Capuchins were so fed up with him that he was dismissed.

Eventually, Joseph succeeded in gaining employment as a

stable-boy at the Franciscan convent of La Grotella, near Copertino. He was received into the order as a choir religious in 1625, and ordained priest in 1628. He had always lived an ascetic life, but now his asceticism began to exceed all bounds. Every day he scourged himself, using for this purpose a whip fitted with star-shaped pieces of metal. It is said that the walls of his cell were stained with the blood drawn from his self-inflicted wounds. He experienced frequent trances and ecstasies, the effects of which were so disturbing that he was not allowed to worship with the other friars, or even to eat with them in the refectory. His levitations began about 1630, and were observed by innumerable people including priests, monks, nuns, lay-folk, shepherds, bishops, cardinals, dukes, doctors, and even the Pope himself. Joseph did not merely rise into the air; he actually *flew*. It seems that the merest mention of anything joyful was enough to set him off. On one occasion a fellow monk happened to remark what a beautiful day it was; whereupon Joseph uttered a piercing shriek, rose in the air, and flew to the top of a tree, from which he had to be rescued by means of a ladder! On another occasion, the joyful sound of a group of shepherds playing their pipes in the church on Christmas Eve sent the entranced Joseph soaring onto the high altar, where he narrowly escaped being burnt by the candles.

It seems to be virtually impossible to explain Joseph's feats in naturalistic terms. If they had always occurred in church, it might perhaps be suggested that the Catholic authorities 'rigged' the phenomena – with invisible wires or whatever – in order to gain converts to the faith. However, Joseph's levitations occurred in many different places, both indoors and out, and were observed by a great variety of people, not all of whom were Catholics. He levitated not only at Copertino, his home town, but also at Naples, Assisi, and Rome. On several occasions he lifted other people into the air with him, including an unfortunate priest from a neighbouring village who was seized by Joseph and borne aloft in a fit of ecstasy. On another occasion a lunatic had been brought to Joseph for healing; seizing him by the hair and uttering his usual cry, the wonder-worker lifted him into the air and remained there with him for about a quarter of an hour. Apparently this form of shock treatment was effective, for the man became sane!

St Benedict's feat of reducing the weight of a stone (p. 46) was mirrored in a somewhat more dramatic form by Joseph of Copertino. On one occasion ten workmen had failed to lift a very heavy cross made of walnut wood. Joseph rushed forward, rising into the air like a bird, and after flying a distance of about twelve yards seized the heavy cross, carried it off, and placed it in the hole which had been prepared for it.[35] This, incidentally, was one of the many levitations which occurred out of doors.

So far we have discussed some of the phenomena attributed to saints from four different centuries: Benedict in the 6th, Clare and Francis in the 13th, Teresa in the 16th, and Joseph of Copertino in the 17th. Our next miracle-worker brings us much closer to our own times. Jean-Baptiste Vianney was born in 1786 and died in 1859, having spent the greater part of his working life as curé of the little village of Ars, which lies some twenty-two miles from Lyons, in the département of the Ain. So famous did this village curé become that by 1850 the number of visitors to his church was estimated at around 20,000 a year. The influx of penitents seeking counsel and absolution at his hands was so great that towards the end of his life he was compelled to spend 16 to 18 hours a day in the confessional. After his death his tomb became a place of pilgrimage, and in 1904, when the tomb was opened in preparation for the process of beatification, his body was found to be incorrupt (that is, to have resisted the normal processes of decay). Jean-Baptiste Vianney was beatified (given the title 'blessed') in 1905, canonised in 1925, and made patron saint of parish priests in 1929.

Examining the life of the Curé d'Ars we find the familiar pattern of a strict religious upbringing leading to an ascetic lifestyle, self-torture, and the eventual emergence of apparently paranormal phenomena. The 'disciplinary' practices of the Curé were perhaps not as horrifying as those of St Joseph of Copertino; but he certainly went without food for days on end, refused to sleep in a proper bed, wore hair-shirts and flagellated himself with whips made more painful by the addition of sharp iron points. 'It was pitiful to see the left sleeve of his shirt all cut up and dyed with blood', said one of his followers.[181] In later years the Curé became less excessive in his practices, and sometimes referred to his earlier terrible penances as 'my youthful follies'. Nevertheless, there is no doubt that he drove his body extremely hard, even into old age.

Many miracles, particularly miracles of healing, have been attributed to the Curé d'Ars. In this book we are mainly concerned with occurrences which seem to imply the action of unexplained forces upon matter, so we will pass over the alleged instances of ESP or thought-reading, and the healing effects which might be explicable in psychosomatic terms. Among the miracles which seem to be clearly physical in nature are two examples of the multiplication of food[181] and a curious 'earthquake effect' which is oddly similar to that reported as happening in the presence of Daniel Dunglas Home. A young man who spent a night in the Curé's presbytery reported as follows:

'I was unable to sleep. At about one o'clock I heard a violent shaking of the handle and lock of the front door. At the same time heavy blows were struck, as if with a club, against the same door, whilst within the presbytery there was a terrific din, like the rumbling of several carts.

'I seized my gun and rushed to the window, which I threw open. I looked out but saw nothing. For nearly a quarter of an hour the house shook – so did my legs.'[181]

One might attribute this phenomenon to earth tremors or other natural causes, were it not for the fact that a number of witnesses experienced it on various occasions, and always in the house where the Curé d'Ars was sleeping, never anywhere else in the village. When M. Vianney went to take part in a mission at St Trivier-sur-Moignans, for example, the house where he was staying shook violently and loud noises emanated from his bedroom. The frightened inhabitants rushed to the saint's room and found him in his bed which had been dragged, apparently by invisible hands, into the centre of the room. These and similar poltergeist-type phenomena were attributed by the Curé to the action of the 'grappin', his nickname for the Devil; nowadays we recognise them as belonging to a well-documented class of events which happen in the vicinity of certain persons, be they saints or sinners. Incidentally, it is *not* true, as some writers have maintained, that poltergeist phenomena are never harmful. Gauld and Cornell[58] describe a number of cases where quite serious injuries were inflicted on the victims. Potentially the most dangerous phenomena of all are the incendiary effects associated with some cases (11% of the Gauld-Cornell sample). The unfortunate Curé d'Ars did not escape this particular form of torment; to this day the visitor to Ars can see at the foot of the saint's bed a picture whose glass has been splintered by the heat of a fire, apparently started in the bed by the action of the *grappin*.

Although most modern Christians would take a different view, there was a strong tendency in previous centuries to regard the occurrence of paranormal phenomena as 'signs' or indications of especial sanctity. In fact, the evidence for St Teresa's levitations played an important part in the decision to canonise her. However, all the evidence suggests that it is not sanctity as such which leads to the production of these effects; rather, they seem to occur in connection with people who are in a highly abnormal condition of body or mind. Whether that condition is produced by the fasting and penances of Catholic sanctity, the obscene rituals of Witchcraft and Voodoo, exceptional emotional tensions within a family circle (as in poltergeist children), or simple breakdown of certain body systems in disease, seems to be irrelevant. Most of the miraculous phenomena attributed to the saints can be matched by similar, if not identical, phenomena in the annals of devilry, as we shall see.

In his book *Exploring the Occult*, Douglas Hunt has what must be one of the shortest chapters ever written. Headed 'Black Magic', it consists of only fourteen lines of print, and takes up less than half a page. Here is what Mr Hunt has to say about the Satanic art:

'No warning against any participation in real or alleged Black Magic can be strong enough. Have nothing to do with it, do not enquire into it, and shun like the plague anyone whom you know to be involved in it. Where it is an imitation of the genuine article – as in most cases – it is dirty, childish, and bestial. It can lead to nothing but a contemptible depravity. Where real power is involved the consequences to the operators are disastrous beyond the imagination.'[87]

Even a cursory examination of the literature will make it clear that Mr Hunt was not exaggerating. From the early Middle Ages right through into the nineteenth century come detailed descriptions of every conceivable kind of witchcraft, sorcery, devil-worship and necromancy. The effects of these practices were almost invariably disastrous, both to their practitioners and to those who came into contact with them. It is a long and depressing story of human folly. Exactly how mediaeval witchcraft came into existence is not clear, although various theories have been put forward. It is likely that there is an element of truth in all the theories, for witchcraft was by no means a coherent or homogeneous system. Included in it were elements drawn from the old pagan religions which went underground following the triumph of Christianity. There were also components derived from the magical practices of folk-lore, the charms and spells used by country folk to combat disease and promote fertility. Early heresies such as the various forms of Gnosticism played a part, and so did the importation of Arabic and Jewish magical practices brought back by soldiers returning from the crusades.

At first, the Church treated witchcraft fairly lightly, demanding only minor penances from those who were thought to be its devotees. However, by the end of the fifteenth century witchcraft was beginning to be treated very seriously indeed. In 1490 the *Malleus Maleficarum* was published, and became the standard handbook for witchcraft investigators. During the two centuries which followed many thousands of human beings were accused of witchcraft, tortured, and burnt at the stake in what must be regarded as one of the blackest periods in the history of the Christian Church. In their understandable zeal to stamp out the evil practices of the witches, Christians resorted to methods which were even more devilish than those of their opponents. Fortunately, the practice of torturing and executing witches began to decline at the end of the 17th century. In England the last proper witchcraft trials took place in 1712; however, a Witchcraft Act remained on the statute book, and was used as recently as 1944 to obtain a conviction against Mrs Helen Duncan, a fraudulent materialising medium.

Father Urbain Grandier was one of the most striking figures of seventeenth century France. Even as a boy he had shown himself to be well above his contemporaries in intelligence; as a man he was tall and handsome, with large dark eyes and a ready wit. After being trained by the Jesuits he was ordained priest in 1615. Two years later, when he was twenty-seven years old, he was appointed to the living of Saint-Pierre-du-Marché at Loudun, a town in the district of Poitou. Before long he was cultivating the friendship of some of the most influential members of Loudun society, including Jean d'Armagnac, the town governor, and Louis Trincant, the public prosecutor. Unfortunately, Grandier had certain defects of character which were to lead to his downfall and destruction in one of the most horrible outbreaks of witchcraft mania of the seventeenth century. The Loudun story has been told in great detail by Aldous Huxley,[88] here we can do no more than outline the sequence of events which led Urbain Grandier from his comfortable presbytery to the torture chamber and the stake.

Grandier, it seems, had a habit of loosing his shafts of wit at all and sundry, especially the well-to-do and the distinguished. Quite early on in his career he managed to insult the Prior of Coussay who later became Cardinal Richelieu, the most powerful man in all France. This was a dangerous enemy indeed! Grandier also became notorious for his amorous exploits, and his friendship with Trincant came to an abrupt end when it was discovered that the lustful priest had caused the daughter of the public prosecutor to become pregnant. These and many other incidents led to the formation of a small clique of men who hated Grandier and wanted to see him removed. Their chance came in 1632 with an outbreak of mass hysteria among the nuns of a nearby Ursuline convent. The whole thing seems to have started as a practical joke, with some of the nuns dressing up as ghosts and faking poltergeist phenomena in the dormitories. However, when exorcists were brought in from outside, the matter soon became anything but a joke. Subjected to the continual suggestions of the exorcists, the good sisters rolled on the floor, performed incredible bodily contortions and acrobatics, grunted like pigs, fought with each other, screamed obscenities, exposed their private parts, and invited by-standers to copulate with them. Contrary to Church law, the 'exorcisms' which provoked these amazing performances were often performed in public, and crowds flocked from miles around to enjoy the entertainment!

There was never any evidence that Urbain Grandier had even been near the convent where these occurrences were taking place; in fact, he had earlier declined an invitation from the Mother Superior to become the nuns' spiritual director. Nevertheless, his handsome features were well known all over Loudun, and it was not long before the possessed women, guided by the suggestions implanted by their exorcists, began to declare that it was Grandier who had bewitched them. The 'devils', speaking through the mouths of the writing sisters, called upon Grandier as their lord and master. He was arrested, subjected to a farcical trial, hideously tortured, and finally burnt at the stake in 1634, protesting his innocence to the last. If anyone thought that would be the end of the matter, they were very much mistaken. Grandier's death did not lead to the cessation of the phenomena, and the exorcisms continued for some years afterwards. Sister Jeanne, the Mother Superior, developed all sorts of strange symptoms. She developed a false pregnancy, and was tormented in the night by mysterious voices. Sometimes, invisible hands tore the sheets off her, and on several occasions she was thrown forcibly out of bed and beaten (one is reminded again of Suetonius's story). Eventually she turned to inflicting severe penances upon herself in an effort to drive the devils away.

Aldous Huxley was inclined to think that there were no genuine paranormal phenomena at Loudun. He pointed out that the tests for ESP devised by visiting lawyers and physicians invariably failed, and attempts to produce levitations and object-movements were also unsuccessful. However, that is only what one would expect. It is always difficult to obtain evidence of ESP under test conditions, and every investigator knows that a poltergeist will not normally perform to order. If this were not the case, then psychical research would be a much easier activity than it is! However, we do have the statements of eye-witnesses who claimed that they saw paranormal happenings at Loudun. Thus, Jacques de Nyau (called 'Nion' by Huxley) declared that on several occasions he saw the Mother Superior 'carried off her feet and suspended in the air at a height of two feet,' while Father Leriche said that he saw two other nuns levitate during their exorcism. Of course, they may have been mistaken; but their testimony cannot be lightly brushed aside.

Witchcraft mania was by no means limited to the Old World. One of the best documented examples was the outbreak which occurred at Salem, Massachusetts, in the year 1692, and which led to the deaths of twenty people. Professor Hansen has argued that some of the victims were indeed guilty of the crime of which they were accused: the practice of malefic witchcraft.[72] Even if that is true, it is certain that the *majority* were innocent. As at Loudun, the whole affair seems to have started as a childish game which quickly got out of hand. Two little girls aged 9 and 11, the daughters of a respectable clergyman, had been dabbling in occult experiments at the instigation of a slave woman called Tituba. The girls became hysterical, and the hysteria spread to other girls who came into contact with them. Soon there was a group of young ladies, ranging in age from 9 to 20, rolling on the floor and contorting their bodies in a similar manner to the nuns of Loudun. The girls experienced loss of memory, sight, hearing, and appetite, and suffered from terrifying hallucinations. A doctor brought in to examine some of the girls declared that 'the evil hand is upon them'. From then onwards it became a matter of seeking out the practitioners of the black arts, and determining which ones had bewitched the girls.

The phenomena at Salem were very similar to those recorded in poltergeist cases elsewhere: mysterious rappings, movements of objects, strange smells and levitations. However, the evidential value of the Salem phenomena is exceptionally high because Cotton Mather, the clergyman chiefly concerned with the case, took the trouble to obtain signed statements from eyewitnesses. Here, for example, is the testimony of one Samuel Ames:

> 'I do testify that I have seen Margaret Rule in her afflictions from the invisible world lifted up from her bed, wholly by an invisible force, a great way towards the top of the room where she lay. In her being so lifted she had no assistance from any use of her own arms or hands or any other part of her body, not so much as her heels touching her bed or resting on any support whatsoever. And I have seen her thus lifted when not only a strong

person hath thrown his whole weight across her to pull her down, but several other persons have endeavoured with all their might to hinder her from being so raised up, which I suppose that several others will testify as well as myself when called unto it. Witness my hand, *Samuel Ames*'

Several others did indeed confirm Samuel Ames' testimony:

'We can also testify to the substance of what is above written, and have several times seen Margaret Rule so lifted up from her bed as that she had no use of her own limbs to help her up, but it was the declared apprehension of us, as well as others that saw it, impossible for any hands but some of the invisible world to lift her. *Robert Earle, John Wilkins, Daniel Williams*.

'We whose names are underwritten do testify that one evening when we were in the chamber where Margaret Rule then lay in her late affliction, we observed her to be by an invisible force lifted up from the bed whereon she lay, so as to touch the garret floor, while yet neither her feet nor any other part of her body rested either on the bed or any other support, but were also by the same force lifted up from all that was under her, and all this for a considerable while. We judged it several minutes, and it was as much as several of us could do with all our strength to pull her down. All which happened when there was not only we two in the chamber, but we suppose ten or a dozen more whose names we have forgotten. *Thomas Thornton*

'William Hudson testifies to the substance of Thornton's testimony, to which he also hath set his hand.'[72]

Here, then, we have no less than six witnesses, all testifying to the levitation of Margaret Rule in the clearest possible manner. In the absence of photography, it is difficult to imagine how the evidence for any paranormal event could be much stronger. Professor Hansen considers the possibility that the witnesses were hallucinated as a result of suggestion, but he finds that this explanation is hardly consistent with the facts: '... they were not simply bystanders; they were engaged in violent physical activity, trying to bring her body back to the bed. Such activity would, ordinarily, tend to break the power of suggestion.' It is also worth adding, as Professor Hansen points out elsewhere in his book, that *lying* was regarded as both a serious sin and a punishable crime in Puritan New England; it is therefore highly unlikely that all these witnesses were in a conspiracy to deceive.

What conclusions can we draw from this brief survey of alleged PK phenomena in the Ages of Faith? Although many of the reports can be dismissed on the ground of insufficient evidence, there remains a small number which cannot be so easily discarded. In particular, the levitations of St Teresa, St Joseph of Copertino and Margaret Rule are well documented and witnessed by persons whose sanity and reliability there is no reason to question. In every case the levitated person was in an abnormal physical or mental condition, either as a result of intensive spiritual effort or as a result of 'demonic possession'. The force generated seems to have been considerable; thus, St Joseph lifted into the air a wooden cross which had resisted the combined strength of ten workmen, while Margaret Rule's witnesses had to exert all their strength to get her to return to a normal resting position. Therefore we should not assume that paranormal forces, if they exist, are always weak. If these accounts are to be taken seriously, they point towards the existence of a PK force which can, on occasions, be overpowering.

5 The Age of Enlightenment

As the seventeenth century gave way to the eighteenth, a radical change became apparent in the intellectual life of Europe. Slowly but surely the mental cobwebs left over from the Middle Ages were being swept away by the fresh winds of rationalism, and there was a perceptible shift in the attitude of educated Europeans towards the supernatural and the occult. In part the change was due to the rise of modern science, which had its beginnings in the sixteenth century, and began to yield its first convincing results in the seventeenth. The first stirrings began in 1541, when Copernicus upset the Church's applecart with his theory that the earth revolved around the sun. Ninety-two years later, Galileo was arraigned before the Inquisition for daring to support the Copernican theory with observations of his own. Then in 1687 came the masterpiece which Sir James Jeans has described as the greatest scientific work ever produced by the human intellect: Isaac Newton's *Philosophiae Naturalis Principia Mathematica*. As it were at a stroke, with a few simple, all-embracing principles, this Lincolnshire farmer's son united all the observations of the astronomers into a beautifully coherent theory of the universe, a theory which was to stand as the foundation of all scientific thinking for the next two hundred years.

Newtonian thinking had profound repercussions on both philosophy and religion. The universe revealed by Newton was essentially a mechanistic one; it ran like a great piece of eighteenth century clockwork, in strict obedience to the inflexible 'Laws of Nature'. In such a universe there was no room for capricious events of any kind. Miracles, whether allegedly produced by saints or witches, were strictly taboo; even God was not permitted to interfere with the universal mechanism. During the eighteenth century the proponents of the philosophical system known as *Deism* argued that God, having created the universe and established the laws by which it was to operate, then left it entirely to its own devices. In the words of one hymn-writer:

> Praise the Lord, for He hath spoken,
> Worlds His mighty voice obeyed;
> Laws which never shall be broken
> For their guidance He hath made.

The rise of rationalist thinking in Germany is usually known as the 'Aüfklarung' (enlightenment), and is chiefly associated with the names of Hermann Samuel Reimarus (1694–1768), Gotthold Ephraim Lessing (1729–1781), and Johann Gottfried Herder (1744–1803). Reimarus was a Deist, and therefore did not believe in the possibility of miracles. He regarded all the Biblical miracles as bogus. Only a small part of his work was published during his lifetime, but even that was regarded as highly scandalous. After his death, some of his writings were published by Lessing as the *Wolfenbuttel Fragments* (1774–8); they created an uproar in religious circles. No doubt in an earlier century Reimarus and Lessing would have been condemned to the stake, but by now the defenders of orthodoxy could do little more than howl their protests. In France, however, the Church still had some teeth left, and the Chevalier Julien de la Mettrie was forced to flee to Holland to escape the wrath of his opponents. His principal crime was the production of a booklet in which he supported a mechanistic theory of man, and denied the existence of the human soul.[138]

The new wind began to penetrate into every corner of the establishment. In England Hobbes' *Leviathan* was censured by name in the House of Commons, and its author prohibited from publishing his writings on ethics. Hobbes's works were considered to be atheistic, and his philosophy of psychological determinism was thought to undermine the fundamental principles of ethics. Hobbes was one of the earliest of the free-thinkers (he died in 1679), and the first philosopher to propose a theory of human behaviour based upon the principles of natural science; he may be regarded as one of the fathers of present-day psychological and social science.

Nowadays, whenever there is a serious discussion about

psychic phenomena, it is usually not long before someone
mentions the name of David Hume. He was born in Edinburgh on April 26th, 1711, of a very ancient and
distinguished family. At first his name was spelt 'Home', but
quite early on in his career the spelling was changed to its
present form. He was a brilliant child, and after matriculating
at the early age of twelve, he set out to study law. However,
by the time he was sixteen he had set his heart on becoming a
philosopher, and from then on he pursued that ideal with a
fixed determination. In 1734 he went to France for a time,
where he became involved with a Jesuit priest in an argument
concerning the reality of miracles. Hume was dissatisfied
with the orthodox view presented to him by the priest, and he
sat down to write a long philosophical essay on the subject.
Later, as his thought-processes matured, he expanded this
work to cover many of the problems of natural and revealed
religion, and the whole was published in 1748 under the title
Philosophical Essays Concerning Human Understanding. It is the
centrepiece of this volume – the famous essay on miracles –
which is frequently invoked nowadays in support of a sceptical attitude towards the existence of paranormal phenomena.

Like most thinkers of the post-Newtonian era, Hume
believed that Nature is governed by precise and unalterable
laws. Our knowledge of these laws is derived from the
uniform experience of mankind; therefore the evidence for
them is overwhelmingly strong. Thus, we *know* from the
common experience of mankind through the ages that fire
consumes wood, lead does not float in the air, and dead men
do not come to life again. There is, therefore, a uniform experience against every miraculous event, otherwise we
should not call it a miracle at all. No matter how many people
testify to the reality of a miracle, their evidence cannot be sufficient to overcome the collective experience of mankind,
which is against the occurrence of such events. For, said
Hume, 'it is contrary to experience that a miracle should be
true, but not contrary to experience that testimony should be
false'.

If we accept Hume's reasoning, no amount of evidence can
be sufficient to establish the reality of a paranormal event. No
matter how many reliable and intelligent witnesses testify to
the occurrence of the phenomenon, it will always be more

probable that they are mistaken or in collusion with one another to deceive, than that the fixed laws of nature have been breached. Even if cameras and automatic recording devices are used, there will still remain the possibility that those who set up and operated the machinery were conducting an elaborate hoax, for there is no piece of equipment which cannot be 'rigged' in some way or other. This kind of argument has been used repeatedly in the twentieth century as a way of discrediting the evidence for the existence of paranormal phenomena. [71]

As we have seen, Hume was a product of the Newtonian revolution, which portrayed the cosmos as a sort of gigantic machine, running according to inflexible laws. His thesis seems to rest upon two assumptions: (1) that there are such things as unalterable laws of nature, and (2) that the experience of mankind is uniformly against any breach of those laws. Neither of these assumptions is in accordance with modern knowledge. Twentieth century physics has shown that the so-called laws of nature are mainly statistical; material objects behave the way they do only because the probability of them behaving in other ways is rather small. With very small objects the probability of anomalous behaviour becomes much greater, and extremely bizarre events can sometimes occur in the world of micro-physics. As for the second assumption, the evidence assembled in this book is surely sufficient to show that the uniform experience of mankind is *not* entirely opposed to the occurrence of paranormal events. On the contrary, there is a great deal of evidence which suggests that, on occasions, such events do occur.

On the whole, the effects of eighteenth century scepticism were beneficent. Much of the fear and cruelty associated with the superstitious beliefs of the past was swept away. Witches were no longer tortured and burnt at the stake, largely because the educated classes no longer believed in the efficacy of witchcraft. From now on, those who dabbled in the occult were to be regarded as harmless eccentrics, tolerated with a supercilious smile by those who knew that there was no place for such things in the Newtonian universe. In future, paranormal occurrences were not to be fought against as manifestations of devilry; rather they were to be ignored, or else exposed as examples of human credulity and fraud.

It might be expected that in such a sceptical century reports of paranormal phenomena would become less common; and indeed, there do seem to be fewer accounts from the eighteenth century than there are from other centuries, before and since. Even so, the eighteenth century was not entirely lacking in miracles. At the church of St. Médard in Paris, for instance, there was an astonishing outbreak of mass hysteria following the death and burial of the Jansenist deacon François de Paris in 1727. Pilgrims came from miles around to visit his tomb. Some of them stayed to become *convulsionnaires*, throwing themselves into all sorts of strange postures and inflicting upon themselves incredible torments. Most of the phenomena attributed to primitive shamans, witches and spiritualist mediums were reported at St Médard: resistance to fire and pain, levitation, ESP, paranormal feats of strength and paranormal healings. One of the most astounding of the performers was young Gabrielle Moler, who became a convulsionnaire at the tender age of twelve and continued for several years. Her speciality was resistance to physical damage of any kind. She was jabbed with pointed rods, struck on the body with heavy mallets, chopped with sharp-edged shovels and her head placed in a fire; all, apparently, without the slightest damage being done to her person. To prove that the phenomena were genuine, spectators were invited to join in the attack for themselves, and no less than twenty-one witnesses, some of them persons of distinction, made signed statements testifying to the reality of the phenomena.

Sometimes one cannot resist the feeling that whatever powers lie behind such outbreaks must be possessed of a mischievous sense of humour. In 1732 one of the secretaries at the court of Louis XV, a certain M. Fontaine, became converted to Jansenism. The immediate consequence of his conversion was a weakening of his leg muscles so that at times they would not support the weight of his body. The following year he was invited to a dinner party which was attended by a number of distinguished personages. Suddenly, he found himself forced to get up and turn around on one foot. He began to rotate at great speed, to the astonishment of everyone present. Some of the observers timed these amazing gyrations, and found them to be about sixty to the minute!

The whirling continued for about an hour, during which time M. Fontaine was able to read a book aloud to the assembled company – no mean feat in the circumstances. The phenomenon recurred the following day, and twice every day for the next six months the extraordinary secretary demonstrated his revolutionary capabilities.

Poltergeists seem to be largely immune to the effects of scepticism, and there was no shortage of poltergeist cases throughout the eighteenth century. In 1706 there was an outbreak at St Maur, near Paris, where raps and other noises were heard, curtains drawn, and a bed levitated while the occupant was in it.[99] An exceptionally long-lived outbreak occurred at Amiens in 1732. It continued for fourteen years, and the phenomena included noises, lights, the movement of furniture and a general shaking of the whole house (the 'earthquake effect'). In London the famous Cock Lane ghost was the major sensation of 1762, attracting such distinguished visitors as the Duke of York, Lady Northumberland, Horace Walpole, Oliver Goldsmith and the irrepressible Dr Samuel Johnson. The phenomena centred around a twelve year old girl, Elizabeth Parsons, and included raps, scratching noises, and object movements. Eventually, one of the investigators told the girl that she would be punished if the raps did not occur, and shortly after this she was caught trying to produce them artificially with the aid of a piece of wood. From then onwards, those who had taken the Cock Lane phenomena seriously (including Dr Johnson) became the laughing stock of cartoonists and satirists of all kinds. However, there are many features of the case which have never been satisfactorily explained, and the evidence for paranormality was sufficiently strong to impress the critically-minded Andrew Lang.[99]

Undoubtedly the best known and best documented of all the eighteenth century cases is that connected with Epworth rectory in Lincolnshire.* This was the home of the Rev. Samuel Wesley, the father of some twenty children including the future founders of the Methodist movement, John and Charles. The trouble began in December, 1715, when mysterious groans and raps were heard in the dining room. Later there were the sounds of footsteps going up and down the stairs, and loud noises from locked and empty rooms. At

*Now in the county of Humberside.

first Mrs Wesley thought the phenomena were due to rats, and tried to get rid of them by having a hunting horn blown in every room of the house; unfortunately, this seems to have made matters worse. As the phenomena developed, doors opened and closed of their own accord, and on three occasions Mr Wesley found himself violently pushed by an unseen force. Sometimes small objects were seen to move, including a hand-mill which 'whirled about very swiftly', and a wooden plate which 'danced' upon the table. The phenomena became most violent when the family were saying prayers for King George I and the Prince of Wales; from this the Wesleys concluded that 'Old Jeffrey', as they nicknamed the ghost, must be a Jacobite. It is possible that two of Samuel Wesley's young daughters were the unwitting PK mediums in this case, for it was noticed that they would often sweat and tremble violently in their sleep just before an outbreak began.[27]

Although it may not be strictly relevant in a book concerned with PK phenomena, we cannot leave the eighteenth century without mentioning the development of Mesmerism. Franz Anton Mesmer (1733–1815) believed in the existence of an invisible energy which he called 'animal magnetism', and which could be passed from one person to another to promote healing. At first he practised his art around Vienna, but he encountered so much opposition from the orthodox medical profession that he was obliged to flee to Paris, where his healing séances became extremely popular towards the end of the century. Later the cult declined somewhat, but then in the early part of the nineteenth there was something of a revival, and for a time mesmerists were to be found practising in most of the countries of Europe and in the USA. Often these practitioners would report the occurrence of 'higher phenomena', that is, examples of telepathy, clairvoyance, or precognition, in their patients. There is a surprisingly large amount of evidence for the existence of ESP effects in the work of the early mesmerists, evidence which was largely ignored until the publication of Dr. Dingwall's scholarly four-volume work *Abnormal Hypnotic Phenomena,* in 1968.[37]

If the history of psychical research is anything to go by, Shakespeare's question 'what's in a name?' must be answered with the words 'a very great deal'. Mesmerism could not become respectable as long as it was linked with the discredited name of Mesmer, and the occult theory of animal magnetism. In 1843 Braid changed its name to *hypnotism*, and from then onwards it gradually gained acceptance until eventually it came to occupy a limited position in orthodox medical practice. Braid denied the existence of the 'higher phenomena' entirely, attributing them to 'hyperacuity of the senses', and he explained the hypnotic trance as a state of extreme suggestibility. In fact, such words have very little explanatory value, and there are still many aspects of the hypnotic state which we do not fully understand. Nevertheless, the change to a new, more 'scientific-sounding' terminology was effective in reducing the aggressive stance of orthodoxy towards mesmerism. It is interesting to compare this with Dr Rhine's attempt in 1934 to improve the academic respectability of psychical research by changing its name to parapsychology.

In spite of Braid, there were always those who continued to practise the older form of mesmerism. They did not die out, but in the first half of the nineteenth century became incorporated into the spiritualist movement. 'The mesmerists became mediums overnight', writes Pearsall, 'and the tricks of their trade were transplanted wholesale into the new craze.'[126] The scene was set for a return to occultism, this time on a greater scale than ever before.

6 The Phenomena called Spiritual

The nineteenth century was one of those great turning points in the history of mankind which occur, perhaps, only once in a millenium; for it was in the middle of the nineteenth century that the scientific approach to reality emerged to become a dominant influence upon human thought and progress. The scientific exploration of the physical world had been steadily advancing ever since the days of Galileo and Newton, but until the mid-nineteenth century it was largely the concern of a handful of leisured amateurs and academics. Now, for the first time, science began to impinge upon the life and thought of the common man. The Darwinian theory of evolution, published jointly by Darwin and Wallace in 1858, overturned the accepted religious teaching of the time, and showed that science had something important to say about the nature of man, and his position in the scheme of things.

It is perhaps not surprising that such a turbulent century should also give rise to a spate of new religions, emanating mainly from the New World. The Mormons, Jehovah's Witnesses, Theosophists, and Christian Scientists all made their debut during this century. One of the first of many new religions to arrive on the scene was *Spiritualism,* which traces its origin to an outbreak of strange noises in the household of a respectable Methodist farmer living in the village of Hydesville, New York State, in 1848. The family consisted of John D. Fox, his wife Margaret, and their daughters Catherine (Kate), aged 11, and Margaretta, aged 15. There is some evidence that earlier occupants of the house had experienced strange phenomena, and a previous tenant was said to have left because of 'mysterious noises'. In March 1848 the Fox family found their sleep being disturbed by inexplicable rapping noises occurring in the bedroom where the whole family slept. Matters came to a head on Friday, March 31st, when outbursts of rapping constantly interrupted the family's rest. Reading through the accounts of this period, one cannot resist the impression that the two girls were getting a great deal of fun out of the situation. Little Kate jumped up and down, clapping her hands and inviting the 'spirit' to knock in response, which it obligingly did. 'Do as I do, Mr. Splitfoot!' she called, and the raps responded accordingly. Mrs Fox then began addressing questions to the communicating entity, inviting it to reply by means of a simple code: one rap for 'no', two for 'yes', and three for 'don't know'. Using this code, the 'spirit' informed the family that it was the ghost of a pedlar who had been killed and robbed by a previous occupant of the house. The pedlar's body was supposed to have been buried under the cellar floor. Naturally, attempts were then made to locate the body by digging in the cellar, but these attempts seem to have been largely unsuccessful at that time. All that was uncovered were a few teeth, some fragments of bone, and a quantity of hair. However, many years later, in the November of 1904, part of one of the cellar walls of the house collapsed, exposing to view an assortment of vertebrae, ribs, arm and leg bones, a shoulder blade and a collar bone.

Whether or not the original rappings were associated with something which had happened in the house at Hydesville, they very quickly became attached to the persons of the two girls. When Kate went to stay with her widowed elder sister, Leah, the rappings went with her. When Margaretta went to stay with her brother David a few miles away, rappings broke out there also. What is more, the phenomena became increasingly violent. In Leah's house at Rochester objects were thrown around by unseen agencies, tables vibrated and moved around the room, and beds were overturned so frequently that the family had to sleep on the floor. So frightening did the phenomena become that all Leah's pupils left her (she was a music teacher). Within a few months of the original outbreak, the disturbances had changed their character, and the Fox family found themselves in the centre of a full-blooded poltergeist attack.

There are a great many features of the Hydesville phenomena which should be of interest to the modern psychical researcher. First of all, the case is extremely well documented, for many people came to visit the Foxes, observed the phenomena, and left careful and detailed descriptions of their experiences. Also, the sisters were called upon to submit to careful investigation by a special committee, which was appointed by the townsfolk of Rochester. The five worthy citizens who constituted the committee took Margaretta and Leah, without advance warning, to a hall, and later to the home of a private citizen. In both these places rappings were heard upon the walls, doors, and floors. The committee reported that it could find no normal explanation for the phenomena. Dissatisfied with this conclusion, the Rochester meeting then appointed a second committee consisting of five even more worthy citizens, hoping, presumably, that they would uncover evidence of fraud where the first committee had failed. However, the second committee came to the same conclusion as the first one, so it became necessary to appoint a third! The third committee was determined to outdo its predecessors in the rigour of its investigation, and leave no stone unturned in the search for fraud. First, a group of ladies were appointed to strip and search Leah and Margaretta. When the searchers were quite satisfied that the sisters had no conjuring devices concealed on their persons, they made them stand without their shoes upon large feather pillows placed in the centre of the room. The girls' dresses were bound firmly with handkerchiefs at the ankles, and all their friends and associates were excluded from the room. Nevertheless, even under these conditions the rappings were heard coming from the walls and the floor. Having completed all its experiments, the third committee reported that it too had found no evidence of fraud; whereupon the Rochester meeting broke up in confusion.

The fact that three groups of people, charged with the task of finding out how the trick was done, each failed to do so, is surely important when we try to assess the validity of these phenomena. Sceptics often portray the observers of a century or more ago as highly gullible people, possessed of a powerful will to believe. In fact, even before the foundation of bodies such as the Society for Psychical Research, there was no shortage of hard-headed investigators who were only too glad of an opportunity to expose a fraudulent medium. With regard to the Fox sisters it is surely relevant to ask: what conjurer could have performed similar tricks under such conditions, without being caught? Taken *without prior warning* to a room he had had no chance to prepare beforehand, stripped and thoroughly searched, with all possible confederates excluded from the room, and under the eagle eyes of *five* sceptical observers, each of whom was free to move around in any way he wished at any moment during the proceedings – *could any conjurer perform satisfactorily under such conditions?* It is a question we have to ask ourselves time and time again when we study the voluminous accounts of nineteenth century mediumship.

One of the most extraordinary features of paranormal phenomena in general is that they appear to be *infectious*. Thus, when Uri Geller appeared on our television screens during the 1970s, large numbers of people suddenly found that they also had the ability to deform metal objects in an apparently paranormal manner. The nineteenth century medium D. D. Home also seemed to have the ability to spark off PK activity in others. The evidence suggests that children may be particularly susceptible to this kind of 'psychic infection', and in the years following the Hydesville outbreak, many child 'mediums' appeared all over the United States. People who came to witness the phenomena of the Fox household, and even those who only heard about them, sometimes found themselves afflicted with similar happenings in their own homes. From such strange beginnings the Spiritualist movement spread like wildfire across the USA. By 1852 it had arrived in London, in the person of a New England medium, Mrs W. R. Hayden. She was welcomed with the greatest enthusiasm.

Sceptics and opponents of Spiritualism have made much of the fact that two of the Fox sisters, Margaretta and Kate, announced in later life that their phenomena had been fraudulently produced. The story is a sad one. By the time the 'confession' was made, both sisters were in their fifties, had lost their husbands, and had become alcoholics. Their mediumistic powers had declined, and they were living in a state of poverty. Furthermore, they had quarrelled with their eldest sister, Leah, who had tried to deprive Kate of the custody of her children. Eventually, in October 1888 Margaretta succumbed to the temptation of a large bribe, and announced at a public meeting in New York that the rappings had been produced by the cracking of knee, toe, and ankle joints. Her sister Kate apparently concurred in this confession. Margaretta gave a rather unconvincing demonstration of how the trick was supposed to have been done, the movements of her muscles being quite obvious to a doctor who was present on the platform. Shortly after this meeting Kate denied that she supported her sister's confession, and insisted that the original phenomena had been genuine. A month later Margaretta withdrew her confession, and the sisters revealed that they had been paid fifteen hundred dollars for making it. The 'confession' was to form the centre-piece of a book by Reuben Briggs Davenport, attacking the Spiritualist movement, and entitled *The Death-Blow to Spiritualism*.

Whatever view may be taken of Spiritualism as a whole, it is sad to contemplate the depths to which Kate and Margaretta Fox had sunk. The long years of excitement, of international fame and adulation by the Spiritualists, had taken their toll. The farmer's daughters who had once climbed to such giddy heights of public acclamation now found themselves shamed and discredited. The lexicographer Isaac Funk, who knew them well, said of Margaretta in her later years that 'for five dollars she would have denied her mother, and would have sworn to anything'. Within five years of the confession and retraction all the Fox sisters were dead, Kate having died at the early age of 55 and Margaretta at 60.

Whether the Fox sisters were charlatans or not, the spread of Spiritualism could not now be halted. With incredible rapidity it swept across all the civilised countries of the world, extending its influence into the homes of rich and poor alike. From the mid-nineteenth century onwards the holding of séances became a popular drawing-room pastime. It is said that even Queen Victoria was affected by the new craze, for in 1846 she presented a watch to a certain Miss Georgina Eagle 'for her Meritorious and Extraordinary Clairvoyance produced at Osborne House, Isle of Wight.'[126]★ After the death of Prince Albert in 1861, the Queen arranged for two members of her court to visit a medium anonymously; they subsequently reported that they had been greeted in the Prince's voice, and received from him a private

★Some authorities regard this as a forgery. See Somerlott[166]

message for the Queen. For many years the great physical medium D. D. Home toured the courts of Europe, performing before such elevated personages as Napoleon III and the Empress Eugenie, Czar Alexander II of Russia, and Kaiser Wilhelm I. There is a vast literature on Home, who has been called 'the Medium of Kings', and who was certainly one of the most fascinating characters of the nineteenth century.[21,41,35] Although he gave many hundreds of séances, Home was never once detected in fraud. Unlike the majority of physical mediums, he produced most of his phenomena in the light, and he was highly scornful of those practitioners who could only perform in darkened rooms, or with the aid of 'spirit cabinets' into which they could retreat at intervals. 'Where there is darkness there is the possibility of imposture,' he roundly declared, thereby causing much annoyance to many Spiritualists.

We shall return to Daniel Dunglas Home later, when we consider the tests performed upon him by Sir William Crookes, and examine the evidence for the authenticity of his phenomena from a scientific standpoint. Here we are mainly concerned with his impact upon the growth of the Spiritualist movement, which can hardly be over-estimated. Had it not been for Home, it is very doubtful whether Spiritualism would have gained such a powerful following among the landed gentry and the intelligentsia of the day. Home's phenomena presented a challenge which it was difficult to ignore, for they occurred under conditions which made them hard to explain in terms of any normal hypothesis. During Home's lifetime many famous people were converted to the Spiritualist cause. It is impossible to list them all, but as a sample we may mention Mrs Harriet Beecher Stowe (1811–1896), the anti-slavery campaigner and authoress of 'Uncle Tom's Cabin'; Alfred Russel Wallace (1822–1913), naturalist and co-author of the theory of natural selection; and Elizabeth Barrett Browning (1809–1861), wife of Robert Browning and a distinguished poetess in her own right.

In France, Spiritualism is usually known as *Spiritisme,* and derives largely from the writings of Léon Rivail (1804–1869), who later changed his name to Allan Kardec. Apparently the 'spirits' informed him that Kardec had been his name in a previous incarnation. In his book *Le Livre des Esprits,* which was published in Paris in 1857, Kardec brought together the concept of spirit communication and the ancient oriental doctrine of reincarnation. Largely as a result of Kardec's influence, French Spiritism has tended to follow an anti-Christian line, leaning more strongly towards the philosophical outlook of Hinduism and Buddhism. American Spiritualism, on the other hand, has often taken a Christian or semi-Christian form.

As the nineteenth century progressed the phenomena attributed to the spirits became increasingly bizarre. At first they communicated by raps, answering the questions put to them by means of a simple code. However, the raps soon gave way to phenomena whose sheer violence is staggering on any hypothesis. Heavy Victorian furniture was lifted into the air and hurled across the séance-room; in some cases the entire room vibrated as though in an earthquake. On some occasions the medium's body changed shape or floated in the air, musical instruments played without anyone touching them, and mysterious hands appeared and disappeared, apparently from nowhere. While there is no doubt that many of these phenomena were fraudulently produced, they were occasionally observed under conditions which make the fraud hypothesis difficult to sustain.

Reports of the elongation or contraction of the human body are often found in the Spiritualist literature, and are sometimes difficult to explain anatomically. Sometimes the entire body of the medium was distorted, sometimes only a part of it was affected. Furthermore, the phenomenon was frequently observed in a good light. Thus, at a séance held in 1870 one medium, F. Herne, was seen to become elongated by about eight inches, and another, J. J. Morse, underwent an extension of his right hand from $7\frac{1}{2}$ to 9 inches, followed by a contraction to $6\frac{3}{4}$ inches.[85] The following account of a similar occurrence with D. D. Home is reported by H. D. Jencken, barrister-at-law:

'I caused Mr Home to place his hand firmly on a sheet of paper, and then carefully traced an outline of the hand. At the wrist joint I placed a pencil against the "trapezium", a small bone at the end of the phalange of the thumb. The hand gradually widened and elongated about an inch, then contracted and shortened about an inch. At each stage I made a

tracing of the hand, causing the pencil point to be firmly kept
at the wrist. The fact of the elongating and contracting of the
hand I unmistakeably established . . .'[85]

Writing in the Journal of the American Society for Psychical Research, Helen Lambert described cases where
elongations and contractions occurred not only in the
medium but in some of the sitters as well. In one case a sitter's
arm was elongated to the extent of seven inches, the phenomenon being observed in full light. On another occasion, a
'badly frightened' sitter experienced a contraction of the
forearm, which only slowly returned to normal.[100] It may
well be that in some of these cases the observers were
mistaken in what they thought they saw; it is also possible
that some mediums are able to dislocate joints in such a way
as to produce small extensions or contractions of parts of their
bodies. However, there are a number of cases where explanations of this kind seem to fail. Thus, Lord Lindsay gave
evidence to the committee of the Dialectical Society that he
had measured the extension of Home's body and found it to
be eleven inches, which would seem to be well beyond
anything which could be achieved by muscular effort.

Among the early child mediums were the famous Davenport brothers, William and Ira, who were giving séances in
their native town of Buffalo, New York State, at the tender
ages of 11 and 13. Raps, levitations and the movement of
cutlery were all reported. Later the brothers toured the world,
giving demonstrations of their powers in England, Paris, St.
Petersburg, Berlin, and Brussels. In 1864 they were carefully
tested in the London home of the playwright Dion Bouci-
cault, where, in spite of being searched and then tied up, they
managed to produce some seemingly inexplicable phenomena. Ira was then twenty-five years old, and William
twenty-three. The following year they toured northern
England, and were roughly treated at both Liverpool and
Huddersfield, where angry crowds invaded the platform. It
was generally assumed that the Davenport brothers were
merely clever conjurers who were taking advantage of the
current interest in Spiritualism. Even so, no one seems to
have been able to *prove* that they were cheating, and the
brothers even won the grudging admiration of the great illusionist John N. Maskelyne, who was an inveterate opponent

of Spiritualism.

During the 1850s two wealthy farmers, Jonathan Koons and John Tippie, lived in the township of Dover, Ohio. A great variety of mediumistic phenomena occurred in both their households, including materialisations, the movement of objects, the playing of musical instruments, and the speaking of 'spirit voices' out of the air. It is said that crowds flocked from seventy miles around to attend the free séances which these gentlemen conducted. As with the Davenports, it is impossible to decide which, if any, of the phenomena were genuine, but it is worth drawing attention once again to the presence of young people in the household: Koons had eight children, and Tippie ten.[85]

One of the most interesting characters of nineteenth century England was the Rev. William Stainton Moses. He was born in 1839, and in his boyhood he suffered from occasional bouts of sleep-walking. During these somnambulistic periods he would occasionally write an entire essay, of which he had no recollection when he awoke. He took an M.A. at Oxford, was ordained priest in 1863, and worked for several years as a country curate. In 1870 he moved to London, where he took up a post as a teacher of English at University College School. It was about this time that he became interested in Spiritualism, and in 1872 he began to experience apparently paranormal events. These experiences continued intermittently for the next eight years. Moses had been engaged to give tuition to the children of a physician, Dr Stanhope Speer, and in 1872 a 'home circle' was formed, consisting of Dr and Mrs Speer, their son C. T. Speer, Mr F. W. Percival (a barrister) and Moses. At first the sittings produced only a few miscellaneous raps and table-tiltings, but later the entire gamut of Spiritualistic phenomena was observed. Many apparent communications were received, sometimes through Moses' own hand and sometimes through direct spirit writing. Raps were succeeded by loud pounding noises, furniture was thrown about, and the whole room vibrated. Moses was levitated on at least ten occasions, and various apports, including books, pictures, pearls, and precious stones, appeared on the séance-room table. Sometimes the physical phenomena occurred *outside* the séance-room, without warning, and in embarrassing circumstances. On one such occasion Moses was visiting the home of Serjeant E. W. Cox, the well-known barrister and founder of the short-lived 'Psychological Society of Great Britain'. Moses was sitting sideways at the dining-room table, reading *The Times*; Cox was opening letters. It was broad daylight. Suddenly, raps were heard from the table, and it began to shudder 'as if with an ague fit'. It swayed violently, then moved about three inches. The two men then stood upright, one on each side of the table and about two feet away from it. They held their hands over the table and it rocked violently, slid seven inches over the carpet, and rose three inches off the ground, one side first and then the other. Moses held his hand four inches from the table surface and asked it to rise and touch his hand three times. The table obeyed. Cox then asked it to rise and touch his hand; again, the request was granted. Cox pointed out that there were no other persons present in the room, and there was no cloth covering the table, so that it was perfectly possible to see underneath. The dining table was made of mahogany, and it was nine feet long and six feet wide. It stood on a Turkish carpet, which increased the difficulty of moving it. Cox subsequently found that it took two strong men to get it to move an inch. It seems that, unless one is prepared to call Serjeant Cox a liar, there is no way of accounting for this incident without invoking the action of a paranormal force.[113]

Was Stainton Moses nothing more than a clever conjurer? It is hard to believe that this is the true explanation of the many phenomena which occurred in his presence. During his lifetime no breath of scandal ever touched him, and those who knew him well testified to his complete integrity. He did not charge for séances, although presumably he made money out of publishing his volumes of *Spirit Teachings*. As an orthodox clergyman, he was converted to the Spiritualist viewpoint only very gradually, and he disliked the physical manifestations intensely. In fact, the reports on the physical phenomena were not published until after his death in 1892, so he can hardly be accused of gaining emotional satisfaction from the publicity which they attracted.

Very few movements have spread as rapidly as the Spiritualist movement did during the middle years of the last century. It was a phenomenal growth which, as Dr Gauld remarks, 'merits detailed investigation by a competent social historian'.[56] Yet equally remarkable is the speed with which the movement declined. Less than a hundred years later it had become nothing more than a minor cult among the many cults of the twentieth century. During its hey-day, Spiritualism attracted the attention of Kings, Queens, Dukes, Duchesses, great scholars and littérateurs, scientists, playwrights, lawyers, clergymen, and politicians; now, with a few notable exceptions, the intelligentsia give it a wide berth. Why did a movement which once seemed to hold out such great promises for mankind come to such a sorry state?

It is possible to point to a number of reasons for the decline. At the intellectual level, the rising tide of materialism left little room for anything of a transcendental nature in the minds of men. Then again, although the 'spirits' undoubtedly did their best, most of the communications which emerged from the séance rooms were trivial in the extreme. As Podmore remarked in reference to the *Spirit Teachings* of Stainton Moses, it was hardly necessary for a spirit to descend from the seventh sphere to preach views which could be heard from any Unitarian pulpit. However, there is no doubt that the greatest single factor was the widespread existence of fraud within the Spiritualist movement itself. Over and over again, with depressing regularity, the same pattern of events was repeated: a new medium appeared on the scene, produced brilliant phenomena, and became the idol of the faithful, only to be suddenly and rudely exposed by some sharp-eyed and sharp-witted investigator. Some of the mediums who were thus caught in trickery actually wrote their memoirs, explaining to the general public how they had deceived their gullible followers. Harry Price was actually able to obtain a catalogue issued in 1901 by Ralph E. Sylvestre & Co., of 25, Ashland Boulevard, Chicago, containing all manner of equipment specially designed for the use of fraudulent mediums. It ran to forty pages, and was issued for private circulation only. In his introduction to the catalogue, Mr. Sylvestre boasted that 'our effects are being used by nearly all prominent mediums . . . of the entire world.' The catalogue included such charming devices as: 'A Telescopic Reaching Rod. A very useful article for mediums working in the dark. They go in pocket and extend from four to six feet . . . will pick up or bring to you any ordinary small object, float a guitar, etc, $4.'[132]

To the sensitive mind, there is something peculiarly repulsive about those human parasites who make a profit by practising deceits of this kind upon the recently bereaved. It is not surprising, therefore, that the founder-members of the Society for Psychical Research became reluctant to have anything to do with physical mediumship. After Eusapia Palladino had been detected in fraud, Professor Henry Sidgwick referred indignantly to what he called her 'mischievous trade', and expressed his intention of ignoring her future performances. This is a very understandable attitude; indeed, 'mischievous trade' seems almost too mild a term to use for the activities of the fraudulent mediums who were ruthlessly exploiting human misery for their own ends. Nevertheless, from a purely scientific point of view (as distinct from a moral one) it seems possible that the stern line taken by Sidgwick and others may have prevented them from detecting the small grain of wheat among the chaff; or, to change the metaphor, they may have thrown out the baby with the bathwater. The only way to tell whether paranormal phenomena really do occur is by means of a rigorously impartial scientific investigation. In the chapters which follow, we shall examine paranormal physical phenomena from the point of view of the scientists who set out to investigate them.

7 Science Lends a Hand

It is commonly taken for granted that the serious investigation of paranormal phenomena began with the foundation of the Society for Psychical Research in 1882, and that before this time there were no truly scientific investigators. Such a view is very far from the truth. Paranormal phenomena have been reported in all periods of human history, and there have always been a few people who tried to establish the facts about them by calm, unprejudiced investigation and experiment. We have already seen how, in the sixth century before Christ, King Croesus of Lydia conducted an experiment in clairvoyance which was hardly inferior to some of those which have been performed in modern times (p. 41), and in the thirteenth century of our era St. Thomas Aquinas wrote extensively on the subject of ESP, particularly of the precognitive variety. He even considered the possibility of precognition in animals, a hypothesis which was not tested experimentally until 1968. Throughout the Ages of Faith, the Catholic Church was confronted with the problem of what to do about the numerous reports of miraculous phenomena which were said to occur in the presence of certain saintly persons, and it became urgently necessary to have some means of assessing the validity of these reports. Prospero Lambertini, a native of Bologna who was born in 1675, gave a great deal of attention to this problem. For some years he served as *Promotor Fidei* or 'Devil's Advocate', his task being to present every possible argument *against* the sanctity of a person under consideration for canonisation. This included the duty of trying to find natural explanations for any miraculous phenomena which were supposed to have occurred through the agency of that person. Lambertini was no gullible religious fanatic; on the contrary, his writings show him to have been a man of sound common sense and critical intellect. He was elected Pope in 1740, taking the title of

Benedict XIV.[82]

In England the founding fathers of the SPR were preceded by a number of individual investigators, some of whom showed considerable critical acumen. In the seventeeth century the diarist and antiquarian writer John Aubrey collected information concerning a case of alleged levitation in Scotland, and also made a study of the famous 'Drummer of Tidworth' poltergeist. His contemporary the Rev. Joseph Glanvill wrote a famous book in which he analysed the evidence for poltergeist phenomena, apparitions, and witchcraft.[60] Glanvill was rector of Bath Abbey, a prebendary of Worcester Cathedral, and chaplain to King Charles II. He was keenly interested in natural philosophy, and was one of the earliest members of the Royal Society. In the following century Daniel Defoe, author of the popular book *Robinson Crusoe,* explored a number of allegedly paranormal happenings, exposing some of them as fraudulent.

Of all these early psychical researchers, perhaps none is more surprising than Sir Francis Bacon, one of the outstanding figures of Elizabethan England.[10] He helped to establish the foundations of modern science by developing the technique of inductive reasoning. In a little known book *Sylva Sylvarum* (1627), Bacon suggested that many of those phenomena which are usually regarded as magical or occult might be amenable to experimental investigation. For example, he discussed the feasibility of using card-guessing as a means of studying ESP (or the 'binding of thoughts' as he called it), and he suggested that the success rate might be improved by using targets with an element of human interest. The ESP experiment would be more likely to succeed, he thought, 'if you tell one that such an one shall name one of twenty men, than if it were one of twenty cards.' He also considered the possibility of PK, or the action of 'imagination' upon matter, and proposed that it be tested by 'the casting of dice'. He thought it might be possible to demonstrate the effect of human mental activity upon the flight of birds and the growth of plants, and he suggested an experimental approach to the problem of paranormal healing, such as the charming away of warts by country folk. He claimed to have experienced the operation of telepathy in dreams, and advocated an experimental approach to that phenomenon also.

Although proverbially we are told that there is nothing new under the sun, Bacon's proposals appear startling when viewed in the light of twentieth-century developments in parapsychology, for he seems to have anticipated most of our modern procedures by about three hundred years. The use of card-guessing was suggested by Richet and Edgeworth about 1885, but it did not come into general use until the late 1920s. Dice-throwing as a means of investigating PK came in after 1934. The effect of thought processes upon the growth of plants was first studied by Paul and Marie Vasse in 1948, and the first controlled experiment in paranormal healing was performed by Bernard Grad and his co-workers in the early 1960s. As for the effect of human thought upon the flight of birds, that experiment still remains to be done, although positive results have been claimed for similar experiments with other animals.

In every century there has been a small but persistent trickle of reports testifying to the occurrence of PK-type phenomena, but in the nineteenth century the trickle became a veritable torrent. We have seen how, beginning at Hydesville in 1848, the Spiritualist movement spread with astonishing rapidity to all the countries of the western world, leading to a major epidemic of table-rappings, levitations, spirit voices, materialisations, and so on. Not surprisingly, the majority of scientists were highly sceptical, and most of them refused even to consider the reports of apparently miraculous occurrences which were being bandied about by the Spiritualists and their supporters. Such matters, they felt, were beneath their contempt. Nevertheless the reports continued to pour in, and a steadily increasing number of intelligent and well-educated persons with no particular religious axe to grind came forward to testify to what they had seen and heard. As the testimonies accumulated, it became increasingly difficult for scientific men to stand aloof. The paranormal was forcing itself upon their attention, whether they liked it or not!

One of the first scientists to respond to the challenge was Michael Faraday, whose brilliant work on electromagnetic induction led to the invention of the dynamo, the electric motor, and the transformer. Faraday had risen from very humble beginnings – he was the son of a blacksmith – to occupy a position of high eminence in the scientific establishment. Any pronouncement by Faraday, therefore, was apt to be regarded almost as revealed truth. It came as something of a surprise to his fellow scientists when, at the age of 62, Faraday revealed that he had been conducting experiments in table-tilting. In a letter to *The Times* (30th June, 1853), he claimed to have demonstrated that the table movements which were frequently reported during séances were caused by nothing more exciting than unconscious muscular action on the part of the sitters. By equipping a table with a moveable top attached to a dial, Faraday was able to show that a downwards pressure of the fingers could, in certain circumstances, be translated into a sideways movement of the table. This, he thought, was sufficient to account for the physical phenomena of the séance-room.

The sceptics breathed a sigh of relief. Science had accepted the challenge, investigated the phenomena, and shown them to be due to natural causes. In vain did the believers point out that Faraday's explanation could not possibly account for the numerous instances where tables moved without any human contact at all; nor could it account for the levitation of tables which were so heavy that the combined strength of all the sitters would not suffice to lift them. It seems that Faraday found the whole subject utterly distasteful, and only embarked upon his investigation in the first place because various colleagues had been pressing him for an explanation. It is a pity that this great scientist could not overcome his revulsion sufficiently to undertake an extensive investigation with a well-established medium. Had he done so, he might well have anticipated the later work of Crookes.★

In 1854 the Count Agénor de Gasparin published a two-volume work in which he described a long series of experiments at Valleyres, Switzerland. The experiments showed that objects could be moved by the unknown force, even when no human being was in contact with them. De Gasparin reported that his tables were raised in the air with heavy weights on them, they danced to music, and they spun around like a top. He made careful measurements of the vari-

★Crookes wrote in 1871: 'If circumstances had not prevented Faraday from meeting Mr. Home, I have no doubt he would have witnessed phenomena similar to those I am about to describe, and he could not have failed to see that they offered glimpses of natural action not yet reduced to law.'

ations in the weight of objects under the influence of the mysterious force. The following year Marc Thury, Professor of Astronomy at the University of Geneva, published a volume in which he analysed de Gasparin's work and reported some further experiments of his own. In addition to table movements, Thury observed the tilting of a piano weighing about three hundred kilograms. Later in the century, Lord Adare reported the total levitation of a piano in the presence of D. D. Home.[41]

De Gasparin and Thury were among the first investigators to attempt a scientific theory of PK phenomena. De Gasparin rejected the Spiritualist hypothesis, and attributed the object movements to the will power of the sitters, mediated in some unknown way. Thury did not rule out the possibility of spirit influence, but he thought that the human body contained some substance which he called 'psychode', and which was intermediate between mind and matter. This substance acted as a transmitter of the psychic or 'ectenic' force, directed by the will power of the person. Thury's concept of 'psychode' is an interesting early anticipation of the theory of *ectoplasm*, developed later by Richet.

Another scientist who disagreed with Faraday's interpretation was Dr Robert Hare. He had been Professor of Chemistry at the University of Pennsylvania and had a number of useful inventions to his credit, including the oxyhydrogen blowpipe which was used for welding metals and producing limelight for the music halls. Now in his seventies, Hare had lost none of his enthusiasm for scientific research. At first he was inclined to believe that all table-turning was due to deliberate fraud, unlike Faraday who believed that it was due to unconscious (but honest) muscular action. In order to test whether the hypothetical 'ectenic force' could pass from the medium's body into a physical object without direct pressure, Hare invented a piece of equipment consisting of a perforated bowl suspended in a glass vessel containing water. The suspension was made in such a way that the medium, while putting his hands into the bowl, could not exert any pressure on the containing vessel. The whole apparatus was placed on a wooden beam pivoted about a foot from one end, the other end being attached to a spring balance. Even if the medium *were* able to press downwards through the water, this would only cause the other end of the beam to rise. Therefore, if the far end of the beam were to *descend,* this would indicate the operation of an inexplicable force. Furthermore, the strength of the force would be registered by the spring balance.

Hare found several mediums who were able to bring about the descent of the beam without touching it, including one who caused the spring balance to register a force of no less than eighteen pounds weight. However, his greatest discovery was a boy who seems to have been what we would now describe as a 'poltergeist child'. In the presence of this youngster the apparatus registered a force of over forty pounds weight before collapsing completely! Hare communicated the results of his researches to a meeting of the American Association for the Advancement of Science in August, 1855, only to be shouted down for his pains. Nevertheless he continued to experiment, and the results of his investigations convinced him not only that the psychic force was real, but also that it could be manipulated by spirits. He therefore became a supporter of the Spiritualist cause. He also constructed a most ingenious contraption which was intended to make it easier for spirits to communicate through the table. Any upward movement of the table caused a wheel to revolve so that the letters of the alphabet, arranged round its edges like the numbers on a clockface, came opposite a fixed pointer. The wheel was pivoted on an axle projecting horizontally from the edge of the table, and was counterbalanced by a weight attached to a rope which ran round the rim of the wheel and was fastened to the floor on the other side. When the table was levitated the tight rope caused the wheel to rotate more or less, according to the height of the levitation. The medium sat on the opposite side of the table, so that he could not see what words were being spelt out in this manner. Using this equipment, Hare became convinced that he had proved that the messages were indeed derived from discarnate spirits and not from the unconscious mind of the medium.[74]

Theologians as well as scientists were deeply interested in the reports of paranormal phenomena which were pouring in from all sides during the middle years of the nineteenth century. Edward White Benson, who later became Archbishop of Canterbury, founded a Ghost Society at Cambridge during the years 1851–2, and among its members were distinguished biblical scholars such as J. B. Lightfoot, B. F. Westcott, and F. J. A. Hort. Some years later a similar organisation, the 'Phantasmological Society', was founded at Oxford, and in 1875 Serjeant Cox founded his 'Psychological Society' for the express purpose of investigating psychic phenomena. Many of these societies were short-lived (Cox's lasted only four years), but the fact that they were formed at all testifies to a widespread interest in investigating the para-normal at that time.

Of the many learned associations which flourished during the mid-Victorian period, one of the most prestigious was the London Dialectical Society. This was a rationalist debating society whose main purpose was to 'afford a hearing to subjects which are ostracised elsewhere', especially subjects of a metaphysical, religious, social or political nature. In 1869 this Society appointed a committee consisting of thirty-one men and three women, for the express purpose of enquiring into 'the phenomena alleged to be spiritual manifestations'. The committee was composed mainly of well-known pro-fessional people, and included the atheist Charles Bradlaugh. Among the scientists who were invited to join the enquiry were Alfred Russel Wallace, Thomas Henry Huxley and W. B. Carpenter. Of the three, only Wallace accepted the invi-tation; Huxley scornfully replied that he was no more interested in such phenomena than he would be in 'the chatter of old women and curates in the nearest cathedral town', while Carpenter sent the Society a brief summary of his theory of 'unconscious cerebration' which, in his view, was sufficient to account for all the phenomena which were not attributable to fraud.

The committee went about its task in a very business-like manner, collecting a great deal of oral and written evidence from persons who claimed to have witnessed the various phenomena of Spiritualism. It also divided itself into six sub-committees for the purpose of practical experimentation, and it is the reports of these sub-committees which constitute the most interesting part of the Society's work. Two of the sub-committees obtained no phenomena worth recording, while a third, the one which investigated D. D. Home, obtained only a few raps and movements. The other three all reported positive results, especially sub-committee No. 1, which conducted no less than forty séances in the homes of its own members. At the beginning, four out of the five members of this sub-committee believed that all the phenomena could be attributed to fraud or involuntary muscular action. They decided in advance that they would use no outside mediums, and that all their séances should be held in the light. Yet even in a well-lit room with only their own members present, clear-cut PK phenomena were obtained. One of the most interesting experiments was performed on December 28th, 1870. The members of the sub-committee turned their chairs so that the backs were pointing towards a heavy dining-table, and situated nine inches from it. They then *knelt* on the chairs with their wrists resting on the backs and their hands extended a few inches above the table. The reason for this kneeling posture was to make it impossible for anyone to get his foot under the table and move it surreptitiously. Under these conditions the table was seen to move four times, the distance varying from four inches to a foot. Later, the members moved their chairs further back so that they were a foot from the table, turned up the gas to make the room brighter, and knelt on the chairs in an upright position with their hands behind their backs. Even under these circumstances distinct movements of the table were observed by everyone present. After the experiment the table was carefully examined and even taken to pieces to satisfy everyone that there was no trick machinery involved. The members of the sub-committee were unanimously of the opinion that they had witnessed the operation of a force 'sufficient to set in motion heavy substances, without contact or material connection of any kind between such substances and the body of any person present'.

The final report of the Dialectical Committee came out in 1871. Its conclusion, although cautiously phrased, was a positive one; the Committee had obtained substantial evidence in favour of the phenomena, and it stated its clear conviction that they were worthy of more serious attention than they had hitherto received. Not surprisingly, this provoked something of a sensation, and the sceptics attacked the report vigorously.

In 1870 Mr William Crookes announced in the *Quarterly Journal of Science* that he was about to investigate the phenomena of so-called Spiritualism, and the announcement 'called forth universal expressions of approval'. One critic expressed 'profound satisfaction' that at last the subject was to be investigated by a man so thoroughly qualified as Crookes; another was 'gratified to learn that the matter is now receiving the attention of cool and clear-headed men of recognised position in science'.[106] These commentators seem to have taken it for granted that the results of Crookes' investigations would be negative; since, as they saw it, paranormal phenomena were impossibilities, it only needed a 'cool and clear-headed' man of science to make a thorough and impartial investigation for the error to be exposed. Once that was done, everyone would be able to sleep easily in their beds! It seems never to have occurred to them that the result of a cool and impartial investigation might be to endorse the reality of the phenomena.

William Crookes was undoubtedly one of the most brilliant scientists this country has ever produced. He was born in 1832, had little formal education, and never went to a university. At the age of sixteen he obtained a post as assistant to the great chemist A. W. von Hofmann at the Royal College of Chemistry in London, and before long young Crookes was conducting his own researches. His first scientific paper was published in 1851, at the early age of nineteen. From this promising beginning Crookes went on to become the Superintendant of the Meteorological Department of the Radcliffe Observatory, Oxford, and then Lecturer in Chemistry at Chester College of Science. In 1861 he announced the discovery of a new chemical element which he called 'thallium', and largely on the strength of this he was elected a Fellow of the Royal Society two years later. In the course of a long life (he lived to be 87), Crookes had many honours heaped upon him, including the Royal, Davy, and Copley Medals of the Royal Society, a Knighthood in 1897, and the Order of Merit in 1910. He was President of the Royal Society from 1913 to 1915.

Crookes' introduction to psychical research came at quite an early age. In 1853, when he was 21 and still working for Hofmann, he was introduced to Michael Faraday, who was then experimenting with his newly-constructed instrument for detecting unconscious muscular activity. Crookes discussed the device with Faraday, and even made use of it himself in some of his earlier experiments, although he soon came to the conclusion that there was more to table-tilting than could be accounted for in terms of unconscious muscle action. Later he began a series of systematic experiments with mediums in order to determine, once and for all, whether there was anything in the alleged phenomena which could not be explained in terms of known physical forces. Writers on psychical research have sometimes implied that Crookes' work with mediums consisted of an early, fairly scientific, series with Daniel Dunglas Home, followed by a later series with Florence Cook which was obviously fraudulent. This picture is a gross oversimplification. The truth is that Crookes applied himself to the study of mediumship with the same boundless energy that he brought to his electrical and chemical work. He held séances with many of the most important mediums of the day, including Stainton Moses, Miss Rosina Showers, Charles Edward Williams, Annie Eva Fay, Frank Herne, Nelson Holmes, and Kate Fox. After his death in 1919, Crookes' family set out to destroy all the records of his psychical experiments which were in their possession, so that only a portion of this vast work has survived. Fortunately, we still have records of the lengthy series of experiments he conducted with D. D. Home, Kate Fox, C. E. Williams, Florence Cook, and Mrs Fay, and a detailed study of these has been made by Dr. Medhurst, and Mrs Goldney.[107] Medhurst and Goldney refer to Crookes' 'prodigious' energy in pursuing these researches, and point out that in the period covering 1870–1875 he undoubtedly attended more séances with physical mediums than any other technically qualified investigator, before or since.

The first report of Crookes' experiments was printed in the *Quarterly Journal of Science* on July 1st, 1871, under the title: 'Experimental Investigation of a New Force'. In this paper Crookes described a number of experiments which he had conducted in his own home with D. D. Home. One of the occurrences frequently reported with Home was the playing of an accordion when no one was touching it, or when the medium or one of the sitters was holding it by a single hand.

To reduce the likelihood of fraud, Crookes devised a cage consisting of two wooden hoops, respectively 1 foot 10 inches and 2 feet diameter, connected by twelve wooden laths, each 1 foot 10 inches long. This made a drum-shaped frame, open at the top and bottom. Fifty yards of insulated copper wire was wound round the frame, so that each turn was less than an inch from its neighbours, and the horizontal strands were netted together firmly with string. This formed a mesh with spaces less than two inches by one inch in size. The height of the cage was such that it would just pass under Crookes' dining-table, leaving insufficient room for a foot to be pushed underneath the cage, or a hand to be introduced into the interior. Mr Home took hold of the accordion (a new one, specially purchased by Crookes for the occasion), and held it between the thumb and middle finger of his left hand, so that it hung down inside the cage. The cage was then pushed under the table, allowing only just enough room for Home's hand. Under these conditions the accordion was seen to move about, going round and round inside the cage, playing at the same time. Eventually the 'power' became so strong that Home was able to remove his hand from the cage completely, the accordion continuing to play on its own. These phenomena were observed in a room lighted by gas, and in the presence of witnesses who were able to move around freely and make direct observations of the apparatus and the medium. Among the witnesses were Crookes' brother Walter, Dr. William Huggins (an eminent physicist and Fellow of the Royal Society), and Serjeant-at-Law E. W. Cox.

In addition to the accordion experiments, Crookes' paper also described alterations in the weight of an inch-thick mahogany beam pivoted at one end on a firm table, and suspended at the other from a spring balance. When Home placed his finger tips lightly on the table end of the beam, the opposite end was seen to swing up and down, 'as if by successive waves of the Psychic Force'. The maximum increase in weight registered by the spring balance was six pounds. Once again, the experiments were conducted in a good light, with Dr Huggins sitting on one side of the board and Crookes on the other. The spring balance was fitted with an automatic register to record the maximum depression of the indicator.

As might be expected, the paper provoked a flood of corre-
spondence, and in July of that year Crookes forwarded an
account of his researches to the Royal Society, inviting the
two Secretaries to his laboratory to meet Mr. Home. One,
Professor Sharpey, declined without further comment. The
other, Professor Stokes, declared that he thought there was a
fallacy in Crookes' apparatus, and added: 'If I have time when
I go to London I will endeavour to call at your house. I don't
want to meet anyone; my object being to scrutinise the
apparatus, not to witness the effects.' Here, then, we have an
eminent physicist claiming to have demonstrated the existence of a force totally unknown to science, and offering what
amounted to a demonstration of that force, only to be
rebuffed by the Secretaries of that most famous Society
whose members are supposed to be pledged to the impartial
advancement of scientific knowledge! As far as is known,
Professor Stokes never found the time to examine Crookes'
apparatus, although he corresponded with him about it. One
is reminded of the savants who refused to look through
Galileo's telescope, lest they should see the moons of Jupiter
and have their whole geocentric concept of the universe over-
thrown.

On October 1st of the same year (1871) a second paper was
published by Crookes, bearing the title: 'Some Further
Experiments on Psychic Force'. In this paper Crookes set out
to answer some of the criticisms which had been made following his earlier work, and gave an account of his fruitless
attempt to engage the attention of the Royal Society. He then
went on to review the experiments carried out by de
Gasparin, Thury, and Hare, and described some more experiments of his own. In these, Crookes had made use of a
modified form of the apparatus previously employed by Hare
(see p. 83), in which the medium had no direct contact with
the wooden beam which was to register the psychic force.
Towards the end of this paper Crookes stated his conclusions
in the following strong words:

'These experiments *confirm beyond doubt* the conclusions at
which I arrived in my former paper, namely the existence of a
force associated, in some manner not yet explained, with the
human organisation, by which force increased weight is

capable of being imparted to solid bodies without physical contact. In the case of Mr. Home, the development of this force varies enormously, not only from week to week, but from hour to hour; on some occasions the force is inappreciable by my tests for an hour or more, and then suddenly reappears in great strength. It is capable of acting at a distance from Mr. Home (not unfrequently as far as two or three feet), but is always strongest close to him.' (Crookes' italics).[106]

Here, then, we have a very carefully worded and sober statement by a scientist renowned for his brilliant researches in other fields, whose whole scientific education had been (as he himself wrote) 'one continuous lesson in exactness of observation'. Nevertheless, it provoked a violent reaction from the biologist Dr. W. B. Carpenter, who launched a vicious personal attack on Crookes in an anonymously written article in the *Quarterly Review* (October, 1871). It will be recalled that Carpenter had previously refused the opportunity to make his own investigation when invited to do so by the Committee of the Dialectical Society.

Those members of the scientific establishment who found it hard to accept the results of Crookes' experiments with Home were even more aghast at the reports of his later experiments with mediums such as Miss Showers and Miss Florence Cook. In the same dignified phrases which he used in all his scientific writings, Crookes solemnly told of materialised spirits which walked around the séance room in a bright light, conversed with the sitters, allowed themselves to be touched, and even posed for photographs! Chief among these incredible beings was 'Katie King', who became the main 'spirit control' of Florence Cook from about 1871 onwards. 'Katie' first appeared as a full-form materialisation in 1873, and from then until her final appearance on May 21st, 1874, she was Crookes' star performer. Night after night she appeared in his laboratory, often in front of witnesses, and he took many photographs of her, using an assortment of five different cameras. Unfortunately, most of these photographs are now lost, although a few survive. Interesting as they are, the photographs do not enable us to tell whether 'Katie' really was what she claimed to be, or whether she was simply an accomplice dressed in a sheet.

A modern writer, Trevor Hall, has suggested that Crookes

was having an affair with Florence Cook, and used the séances as a cover for his amorous activities.[67] According to this theory, the 'Katie King' manifestations were faked by the pair of them working in collusion. Although this is certainly possible, it seems very unlikely that a man in Crookes' position would risk the loss of his scientific status by perpetrating such a monstrous fraud. Furthermore, Florence Cook was not the only medium who produced materialisations for Crookes; Rosina Showers produced a spirit form known as 'Florence', and Mrs Fay was able to produce materialised hands while she was connected in an electrical circuit intended to prevent any possibility of fraud. If Crookes was engaging in sexual activities with all these ladies (not to mention Daniel Home!) he must indeed have been highly promiscuous.

It would require a whole library of books to describe in full detail all the numerous researches which were made into the 'psychic force' during the second half of the nineteenth century. We have already considered the work done by Faraday, Hare, de Gasparin, Thury, and Crookes. In addition to these, it is perhaps worth mentioning the little-known work of Alexander von Boutleroff, Professor of Chemistry at the University of St. Petersburg and author of the *Lehrbuch der Organischen Chemie* (Leipsig, 1868). Boutleroff, like Crookes, experimented with D. D. Home and arrived at similar conclusions regarding the existence of a psychic force. Using a pivoted beam similar to that employed by Crookes, Boutleroff observed an increase in weight from 100 lbs to 150 lbs when Home's hands were placed upon it in such a position that any normal exertion of pressure would have led to a *decrease*. Boutleroff corresponded with Crookes, and supported him in his conclusions.

Another famous investigator of the time was the honourable Alexander Nicholas Aksakoff, who was a relative of Boutleroff by marriage. Aksakoff was one of the most distinguished members of the old Russian aristocracy. He was born in 1832, and in the course of an outstanding career rose to high office in the realm, becoming Councillor of State to Czar Alexander II. Psychical research was the dominating passion of Aksakoff's life. and he travelled all over the world in pursuit of the paranormal. He wrote a number of books on the subject, and translated others; he also experimented with most of the great mediums including Home, Elizabeth Hope (known as 'Madame d'Espérance'), Henry Slade, William Eglinton, and Eusapia Palladino. Aksakoff donated about £4,000 (a very considerable sum in those days) to the newly-formed Society for Psychical Research, and became one of its staunchest supporters. Later he edited the journal *Psychische studien,* and invented the word *telekinesis* to describe the movement of objects at a distance. This was a phenomenon which he had personally observed with a number of mediums. It is unfortunate that the name of this great pioneer, who died in 1903, is largely unknown to the present generation of parapsychologists.

In this chapter we have been mainly concerned with the work of those scientifically-trained persons who, in the years preceding the foundation of the SPR, had already carried out important investigations into the physical phenomena of mediumship. As we have seen, most of them came to the con-clusion that they had witnessed the operation of forces unknown to science, and in spite of persistent attempts to make them recant, they stuck to this opinion until their dying days. Anyone who takes the trouble to read through the vol-uminous reports produced by these nineteenth century researchers will inevitably find himself confronted by a puzzling dilemma. On the one hand there is the fact that most of the reports were compiled by men of unquestioned intel-lectual ability and scientific integrity, whose words would have been accepted without demur if they had been describ-ing events in any other field of human experience. On the other hand, the phenomena to which they testified seem so bizarre, so totally inexplicable on any reasonable view of reality, that it seems impossible to believe that they occurred exactly as described. Thus, Charles Darwin, writing to Lady Derby, confessed himself to be 'a much perplexed man', and added: 'I cannot disbelieve Mr. Crookes's statement, nor can I believe in his result'. In the same vein Sir Oliver Lodge, addressing the Society for Psychical Research in 1902, declared: 'It is almost as difficult to resist the testimony as it is to accept the things testified.'

This, then, is the central dilemma of psychical research, and it is no less acute today than it was a hundred and ten years ago, when Crookes began his investigation into 'the Phenomena called Spiritual'. In fact, during the intervening years many more people have witnessed the operation of apparently paranormal forces, so that today it is even more difficult to explain away the mass of accumulated evidence. We shall be considering some of the later evidence in the succeeding chapters of this book; meanwhile, it is perhaps appropriate to end this chapter with the words of Professor Challis of Cambridge, who in 1871 wrote as follows:

'In short, the testimony has been so abundant and consentaneous that either the facts must be admitted to be such as reported, or the possibility of certifying facts by human testimony must be given up.'[106]

8   The man who was called Mad

A remarkably stupid fellow: these were the words which Martin Gardner, one of the leading American science writers of our time, used to describe the nineteenth century German physicist and astronomer Johann Carl Friedrich Zöllner.[55] In making such a comment, Gardner was only reiterating the general verdict of posterity, which has dealt harshly with the reputation of the unfortunate Zöllner. Yet in his time, this man was regarded as one of his country's leading scientists. If he had restricted his investigations to the well-established areas of science, there is little doubt that his name would today occupy an honoured position in our text-books. However, Zöllner, like Crookes, dared to trespass into the forbidden territory of psychical research. As a consequence, the story was put around that he was insane, and after his premature death from a stroke in 1882, even his orthodox work was largely forgotten.

Johann Zöllner was born at Berlin in 1834, and was the son of a pattern maker who later became a cotton printer. Even as a boy, his ingenuity in constructing instruments and carrying out experimental work caused comment among his elders. When he was only nineteen his father's death compelled him to take over the direction of the factory, but he had no talent for administration or management, and soon returned to his scientific studies. He read physics at Berlin University, publishing a paper on photometric analysis while still an undergraduate. He also set up a small astronomical observatory in the tower of his father's factory in Berlin. In 1857 he went to Basel University, and in 1859 received the Ph.D. for his work on photometry. He invented several instruments which found extensive use in science, including a photometer for measuring the visual magnitudes of stars, a reversion spectroscope for measuring Doppler shifts in the spectra of fast moving objects, and a horizontal pendulum, which was widely used in geophysical research. In 1860 Zöllner described the optical effect sometimes known as 'Zöllner's illusion', in which a pair of parallel lines seem not to be parallel when crossed by a herringbone pattern of short diagonal lines sloping in opposite directions.

In science it is rather unusual to find a good practical experimenter who is also a brilliant theoretician, but Zöllner seems to have been an example of that rare combination. In 1865 he put forward a theory of stellar evolution, suggesting that the stars begin their lives as white-hot objects, slowly passing through yellow and red to extinction. He also wrote extensively on sunspots, solar rotation, and the theory of comets. By 1866 his scientific achievements had become universally known and admired, and in that year he was appointed Professor of Physical Astronomy at the University of Leipzig. Many scientific honours were heaped upon him, including membership of the Royal Saxon Society of Sciences, the Royal Astronomical Society of London, the Imperial Academy of Natural Philosophers at Moscow, and the Scientific Society of Psychological Studies in Paris. In many ways, Zöllner's theoretical speculations seem to have been years ahead of their time. For example, long before Einstein developed his famous equation $E=mc^2$, Zöllner was writing about the tremendous quantities of energy which, he believed, were locked up in ordinary matter:

'It is proved that the electrical energy present in the mass of one milligram of water (or any other body) would be able, if it could be suddenly set free, to produce the amount of motion which the explosion of a charge of 16.7 kilogrammes of powder in the largest of cannons now existing can impart to a shot of 520 kilogrammes.'

Fifty years before the first formulation of the general theory of relativity, Zöllner was already trying to develop a theory of the electromagnetic field based upon the geometry of space. Unfortunately the mathematical techniques needed to carry through such a programme were not yet available, so that the attempt proved to be premature. However, Zöllner was one of the first scientists to suggest that the observable world of three spatial dimensions may be merely a section of a much greater world of four or more dimensions. Today the concept of 'hyperspace' is almost a commonplace; theoretical physicists take it for granted, and even the science fiction writers have made good use of the idea. In the mid nineteenth century matters were very different, and Zöllner's speculations must have seemed wildly outlandish to his contemporaries. Nevertheless, it was not only Zöllner's metaphysical speculations and his involvement with psychical research which made him unpopular; he also made outspoken and tactless remarks about the state of contemporary science and scientists. Zöllner believed passionately in the effectiveness of scientific method, and he took the view that the true scientist should be cool-headed and impartial, setting himself above all purely personal vanity and ambition. He made no secret of his view that the blatant careerism of some of his fellow scientists was a major threat to the progress of true science.

Thoughts about the possible existence of a fourth dimension may well have been running through Zöllner's mind when, in 1875, he visited London and made himself known to Sir William Crookes. At this time Crookes had been studying the phenomena of mediumship for about five years, and had already obtained some remarkable results. Zöllner's enthusiasm for the subject was kindled by his discussions with the older scientist, for whom he had a tremendous admiration. Could it be possible that in the strange phenomena of the séance room lay the proof for which he had been seeking: proof of the reality of hyperspace? He returned to Leipzig determined to carry out psychical experiments in his own laboratory at the earliest opportunity. His chance came on 15th November, 1877, with the arrival in Leipzig of the famous American medium Henry Slade.

Like Zöllner, Slade has received rough treatment at the bar of history. Most writers, if they refer to him at all, do so in a scornful manner, assuming him to have been a cheat and a charlatan. However, when one examines the contemporary records a rather different picture emerges. In fact, many people tested Slade without discovering any evidence of trickery whatsoever. Slade was one of the earliest of the slate-writing mediums; in his presence 'messages' would appear on slates which had been carefully cleaned and marked beforehand. Robert Collyer, one of the most experienced of the American investigators, tested Slade and became convinced that the writing was not produced fraudulently. Even when Collyer brought slates of his own, and gave Slade no opportunity to tamper with them, he still obtained messages. Collyer was no Spiritualist, and did not believe that the messages came from departed spirits; even so, he was quite certain that what he had witnessed was no conjuring trick. Sergeant Cox was similarly impressed, and so was Carter Blake, former Secretary of the Anthropological Society of Great Britain.

The sceptic will no doubt argue that the academic distinction of these men gives no guarantee that they were immune to the wiles of the skilled magician; on the contrary, it is quite possible that the more sophisticated a man is, the more easily he can be deceived. However, Slade was also tested by professional magicians, men who were fully acquainted with all the tricks of the trade. They also failed to uncover his secret. One such person was Frederick Powell, a member of the American Society of Magicians, who examined Slade in 1881–2. Powell saw a matchbox disappear, furniture move at a distance, and a slate pull itself from his grasp and float around. Although Powell felt sure that there *must* have been trickery involved, he was unable to determine how the tricks were done. The most impressive testimony of all came from Samuel Bellachini, Conjurer to the Court of his Majesty the King and Emperor Wilhelm I at Berlin:

'I hereby declare it to be a rash action to give decisive judgment upon the objective medial performance of the American medium, Mr Henry Slade, after only one sitting, and the observations so made.

'After I had, at the wish of several highly-esteemed gentlemen of rank and position, and also for my own interest, tested the physical mediumship of Mr Slade in a series of sittings by full daylight, as well as in the evening, in his bedroom, I must, for the sake of truth, hereby certify that the phenomenal occurrences with Mr Slade have been thoroughly examined by me with the minutest observation and investigation of his surroundings, including the table, and that I have *not in the smallest degree* found anything to be produced by means of prestidigitative manifestations, or by mechanical apparatus;

and that any explanation of the experiments which took place *under the circumstances then obtaining* by any reference to prestidigitation, *to be absolutely impossible.*

'I must rest with such men of science as Crookes and Wallace, in London; Perty, in Berne; Butlerof, in St Petersburg; to search for the explanation of this phenomenal power, and to prove its reality. I declare, moreover, the published opinions of laymen, as to the 'How' of this subject to be premature, and according to *my* view and experience, false and one-sided. This, my declaration, is signed and executed before a notary and witnesses.'

(signed) SAMUEL BELLACHINI.

Berlin, 6th December, 1877.

This is an interesting document, from several points of view. Today it is quite common for conjurers such as James Randi to pour scorn upon the practitioners of the paranormal, and to ridicule the efforts of scientists to understand it. Here we have an extremely talented conjurer of an earlier generation admitting quite frankly that he cannot account for the phenomena in terms of his own art, and positively inviting the scientists to undertake an investigation!

Professor (later Sir) Ray Lankester was one of the most bigoted of the nineteenth century opponents of psychical research. He would never admit to even the remotest possibility of any of the phenomena being genuine, and did all he could to prevent his scientific colleagues from taking them seriously. Even telepathy, perhaps one of the least controversial of all the paranormal phenomena, was described by Lankester as 'a puerile hypothesis'. In 1876 Lankester decided to take the Spiritualists down a peg by bringing a prosecution against Slade under the vagrancy acts. Slade was convicted at Bow Street Court, London, of using 'subtle crafts and devices' to deceive Lankester and others, and he was sentenced to three months' hard labour. Two months later the Court of Appeal quashed the verdict on a technicality (the words 'by palmistry or otherwise' had accidentally been omitted from the indictment), and Slade fled to the continent. In the course of the trial, Lankester claimed that he had found writing on a slate *before* the spirits were supposed to have operated upon it, but he was quite unable to explain how the other physical phenomena were produced. The magistrate, Mr Flowers, seems to have taken the view that Slade *must* be guilty of fraud since, 'according to the well-known course of nature', there could be no other explanation. The defence had a number of eminent witnesses lined up, including Cox and Wallace, but they were allowed to call only four, Mr Flowers ruling that the evidence of witnesses who had not attended the same séances as Lankester was irrelevant. Taken all in all, the proceedings can hardly be said to have established Slade's guilt 'beyond all reasonable doubt', and the reporter from *The Times* described them as 'absolutely farcical'.[91]

By the time that Slade arrived in Leipzig, therefore, he was the centre of a heated controversy. His opponents pointed to the fact that he had already been tried and convicted of fraud by an English court; his supporters replied that the evidence brought against him could hardly be described as convincing, and there were a number of well-balanced and critically-minded observers who were prepared to accept his phenomena as genuine. In short, it was a situation which occurs quite frequently in psychical research: each side can make out a fairly convincing case for its own particular point of view, but neither is able to demolish completely the evidence supplied by its opponents.

At this time Zöllner had just celebrated his forty-third birthday, and was at the height of his powers. He was certainly not, as one of his detractors, Joseph McCabe, was later to claim, 'an elderly and purblind professor'.[39] He had more than thirty sittings with Slade, and brought in several of his colleagues to witness the phenomena. Among those who assisted in the investigation were Wilhelm Scheibner, Professor of Mathematics, Wilhelm Weber, Professor of Physics, and Gustav Fechner, Professor of Physics and pioneer of the new science of psychophysics. Fechner had had previous experience of this kind of enquiry, for he had worked with Baron Carl von Reichenbach on the investigation of a psychic known as 'Madame Ruf', who was able to produce oscillations of a compass needle. Although in his seventies at the time of the Slade experiments, there is no reason to suppose, as sceptics were later to claim, that Fechner was incapable of making accurate observations.

From the very beginning, quite startling and often violent phenomena were observed at Leipzig. On Friday, 16th November (the day after Slade's arrival in the city), Zöllner set up a séance in a room where Slade had never been before, the intention being to experiment with slate-writing. Professors Braune and Fechner were present, in addition to Zöllner and Slade. During the séance a pocket knife was hurled into the air, and a bed, which was behind a screen more than four feet away, moved outwards from the wall. Later that same evening the sitters heard a violent crack, 'as in the discharging of a large battery of Leyden jars', and a heavy wooden screen split into two pieces. The 'spirits' later apologised for this event, writing: 'It was not our intention to do harm; forgive what has happened'. Zöllner wrote a careful description of this event, pointing out that Slade was more than five feet away from the screen and had his back to it when the phenomenon occurred. The force required to split the screen must have been considerable; Zöllner calculated that it was of the order of 198 cwts, or about the strength of two horses! One of Zöllner's colleagues actually suggested that Slade must have somehow smuggled *dynamite* into the room to produce this effect.

Reading through Zöllner's account, one finds quite a close resemblance between the phenomena produced by Slade and those associated with D. D. Home. It is perhaps unfortunate that Slade has been largely forgotten whereas Home, even today, is frequently cited as the outstanding example of nineteenth century physical mediumship. Among the phenomena which Zöllner observed with Slade were violent movements of a bookcase, the overthrowing of a chair, the movement of a small table, and the ringing of a large hand-bell. The furniture movements all took place behind Slade's back, at a distance of at least five feet. Slade also made a compass needle move, and an accordion played when it was held by him in one hand. Later, the same accordion played when it was held in a similar manner by Scheibner, Slade's hands being all the while upon the table. Zöllner also observed the appearance and disappearance of materialised hands at some of the séances, and even succeeded in obtaining impressions of some of them in a jar of flour. Bizarre as such phenomena may seem, they were by no means uncommon among the nineteenth century mediums. The appearance of mysterious hands was a frequent feature of D. D. Home's séances,[192] and later of Eusapia Palladino's.

Of course, Zöllner's main preoccupation was his theory of hyperspace, and he set up a number of experiments specifically to test this idea. First, he took a hemp cord of length 148 cms and thickness about 1 mm., and tied the ends together with an ordinary knot. The loose ends projecting from the knot were then stuck onto a piece of paper with sealing wax, and sealed with Zöllner's personal seal. This was all done before the séance, and in the absence of the medium. Zöllner then hung the cord around his own neck, making sure that it did not leave his possession at any time before the séance began. During the séance he kept the seal all the time in front of him, with the rest of the cord hanging down upon his lap. *At no time was Slade permitted to touch this cord;* nevertheless, at the end of the séance it was found that four knots had been tied in it, the seal remaining unbroken. During the séance, according to Zöllner, 'Mr Slade's hands remained *all the time* in sight; with the left he often touched his forehead, complaining of painful sensations.'[191]

A similarly curious result was obtained with two bands of soft leather, 44 cms long and 5 to 10 cms broad, with the ends fastened together in the same manner as the hemp cord. The leather bands were laid separately upon the table, and Zöllner covered them with his hands. 'Slade sat at my left side, and placed his right hand gently over mine, I being able to feel the leather underneath all the time. Slade asserted that he saw lights emanating from my hands, and could feel a cool wind over them. I felt the latter, but could not see the lights. Presently, while I still distinctly felt the cool breeze, and Slade's hands were not touching mine, but were removed from them about two or three decimetres, I felt a movement of the leather bands under my hands. Then came three raps in the table, and on removing my hands the two leather bands were knotted together.' Zöllner added that the time the bands were under his hands was not more than three minutes.

These accounts certainly *sound* like the descriptions of rather clever conjuring tricks, although it is difficult to see how they could have been performed under the conditions reported by Zöllner. However, some of Slade's phenomena were well beyond the reach of any simple sleight-of-hand trickery. For example, on the 6th of May, 1878, at 11.15 a.m., Slade and Zöllner were sitting with their hands upon a card-table, in a room which was flooded with bright sunlight. A few feet away was a small round table made of birchwood; it was about 30 inches high, the diameter of the circular top was 18 inches, and the weight of the whole table was 9.9 lbs. After about a minute the round table was seen to be slowly oscillating, its top rising above the top of the card-table where the two men were sitting. Then the round table tilted over onto its side and came underneath the card-table, with its legs pointing towards Zöllner. 'Slade was about to take slate and pencil to ask his "spirits" whether we had anything still to expect, when I wished to take a nearer view of the position of the round table lying, as I supposed, under the card-table. To my and Slade's great astonishment we found the space beneath the card-table completely empty, nor were we able to find in all the rest of the room that table which only a minute before was present to our senses.' After searching the room for the missing table, the two men sat down again at the card-table. After about five or six minutes had elapsed, Slade asserted that he saw lights in the air, although Zöllner saw nothing. Then Zöllner suddenly observed, 'at a height of about five feet, the hitherto invisible table with its legs turned upwards very quickly floating down in the air upon the card-table.' The falling table struck both Slade and Zöllner on the sides of their heads, and Zöllner adds ruefully that he could still feel the pain of the blow some four hours after the event, which took place at about 11.30 a.m. The reader may like to consider what kind of conjuring trick could cause the disappearance of a solid wooden table and its re-appearance in mid-air some five minutes later, remembering that Slade had had no opportunity to equip the room with elaborate apparatus.

Zöllner made plans for four key experiments which, if any one of them were successful, would provide proof of the reality of the fourth dimension:

(1) He obtained two wooden rings, one made of oak and the other of alderwood, each turned in one piece. It is, of course, impossible for two such rings to become interlinked in our three-dimensional space without one or the other

being cut and rejoined. Zöllner hoped that the 'spirits' would join the rings by lifting them into the fourth dimension.

(2) He collected shells of various species and sizes, hoping that the spiral twist of one of them would be reversed. In our space it is impossible for a spiral object to turn into its mirror image; a right-handed corkscrew remains right-handed, no matter how we turn it. However, a being with access to a fourth dimension should find it a simple matter to reverse the direction of twist, simply by lifting the object into hyperspace, turning it over, and replacing it.

(3) A band without ends was cut from a piece of dried gut, of the type used in twine factories. The gut formed a continuous loop of length 40 cms and breadth about 5 mm. Should a knot be tied in it without any breakage of the loop, this would strongly indicate the use of an extra dimension of space.

(4) Zöllner made a hollow glass ball, totally enclosed, of diameter 4 cms. He also cut a piece of paraffin candle to such a size that it would just fit inside the ball. Should the 'spirits' succeed in placing the candle inside the ball, this would constitute an event which would be inexplicable in normal terms. Any attempt to place the candle inside by melting and resealing the glass would be bound to fail, since the heat required to melt the glass would inevitably melt the candle.

The design of these experiments shows the remarkable ingenuity of Zöllner's mind. In the event, none of them worked exactly as he had planned, but the first three did result in some remarkable experiences which were hardly less miraculous than those he had intended. On May 3rd, 1878, Zöllner sat at the table with two snail shells which he had bought that day from a dealer; their diameters were 43 mm and 32 mm respectively. At 8.30 p.m. Zöllner placed the larger shell over the smaller, completely concealing the latter from view. Slade was holding a slate under the table, and after a moment something clattered upon it. When the slate was removed, the smaller of the two shells was found upon it, having apparently passed through the solid table-top. 'Since both shells had lain before almost exactly in the middle of the table, untouched and constantly watched by me', said Zöllner, 'here was, therefore, the often observed phenomenon of the so-called penetration of matter confirmed by a surprising and quite unexpected physical fact.' At this point the reader is apt to become somewhat irritated with Zöllner; surely, he will argue, this is obviously nothing more than a conjuring trick? Probably the small snail shell was never underneath the large one at all. Perhaps Slade distracted Zöllner's attention for a split second, just long enough to enable the miracle-worker to palm the shell, and then triumphantly produce it later. There are innumerable ways in which such a trick could have been performed by a competent magician. This is fair enough; however, there was a surprising sequel. When Zöllner picked up the shell to examine it, he almost dropped it: it had become extremely *hot*. His friend Oscar von Hoffmann, who was also present at the séance, confirmed the high temperature of the shell. Now although it is easy enough to imagine how Slade could have palmed the shell, it is by no means easy to explain how it could have become heated to such a high temperature. Even Slade could not have had a lighted blowlamp or bunsen-burner under his waistcoat!

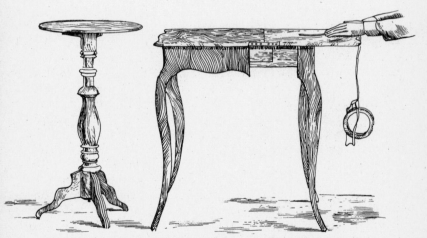

Fig. 3 Zöllner's experiment with two wooden rings, a continuous band of catgut, and a sealed loop of hemp cord – the first stage. (Redrawn from Zöllner,[191])

About a week later the two wooden rings and the continuous loop of gut were involved in an equally remarkable episode. At 7 o'clock in the evening Slade and Zöllner were alone in the sitting room, which was brilliantly lighted by the setting sun. The two wooden rings and the gut loop had been strung on a piece of catgut 1 mm thick and 1.05 metres long. The two ends of the catgut had been knotted and sealed, in the same manner as the hemp cord mentioned earlier. When Slade and Zöllner were both seated at the table, Zöllner placed both his hands over the upper end of the sealed catgut, the remainder hanging down in his lap, as shown in Figure 3. After a few minutes Slade asserted that he saw lights, and there was a faint smell of burning, apparently coming from under the table. When the two men stood up, they saw that the two wooden rings were encircling the leg of the round table, and the catgut was tied in two loose knots, through which the endless gut band was hanging uninjured (Figures 4 and 5).

Fig. 4 Zöllner's experiment – the second stage. (Redrawn from (Zöllner,[191])

While Zöllner was proudly showing the results of this surprising experiment to his friends, Slade fell into a trance. He informed the company that the 'spirits' had tried to tie some knots in the endless band, as requested, but had had to abandon the attempt because the band was in danger of melting from the great heat generated. On examination, a white spot was found upon the band, apparently caused by burning; when Zöllner took another piece of the same material and held it over a candle flame, he obtained precisely the same kind of spot. In his discussion of this phenomenon, Zöllner suggests that moving an object in the fourth dimension may generate heat in a similar way to the movement of a conducting body through a magnetic field.

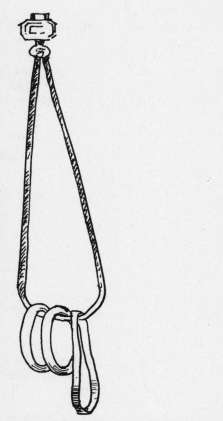
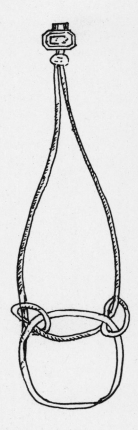

Fig. 5   Zöllner's experiment. *A* shows the position of the two wooden rings, the gut loop, and the hemp cord at the beginning of the experiment. *B* shows the interlocked gut loop and hemp cord at the end of the experiment. (Redrawn from Zöllner,[191])

What are we to make of the phenomena reported in Zöllner's treatise? Martin Gardner has no doubt that Zöllner, 'incredibly ignorant of conjuring methods', was simply duped, and refers to his book as 'unintentionally hilarious'. It is, of course, quite easy to dismiss the whole affair in this cavalier manner; it is much more difficult to explain *in detail* how the tricks could have been done. Some of the suggestions which have been made are quite ridiculous – we have already mentioned the sceptic who thought that Slade employed dynamite! Harry Price thought he could explain how sealed loops of string could be opened and closed again without detection:

'... the knot is a faked one in which is hidden a tiny threaded brass tapered socket. To one end of the cord is glued a tiny tapered brass screw. This end can be screwed into the knot at will, and as it buries itself in the knot, the deception is absolutely indetectable. I have a specimen which I have even loaned to people who have never found the secret. Yet, with hands behind my back, I was able to remove the ring from the cord – or put it on – in a few seconds.'[132]

This is typical of the sort of suggestion which is often made by conjurers when confronted with evidence for apparently paranormal events; for while it describes a perfectly feasible trick, it takes no account of the particular *conditions* under which the event occurred. The trick described by Price is only possible if the conjurer is allowed to use his own previously–prepared cord, whereas Zöllner makes it abundantly clear that in every experiment the materials were supplied by himself, and marked so that they could not be substituted. The cord in which the knots appeared was prepared and sealed with Zöllner's personal seal *in the absence of the medium*.

While it is possible that some of the minor phenomena described by Zöllner might have been conjuring tricks, when we come to the large-scale effects we pass beyond the scope of mere legerdemain. It must be remembered that Slade arrived in Leipzig entirely alone; he had no accomplices, nor is there any evidence that he brought any equipment with him. Yet in his presence a strong wooden screen was shattered from a distance, beds, chairs, and bookcases moved without contact, and a table vanished altogether, reappearing in mid-air some moments later. What is more, all these phenomena occurred in broad daylight. While it might be possible for a conjurer to produce such massive effects on a stage, surrounded with bulky and complicated equipment, there is no way in which they could have been produced in an ordinary living-room, under the conditions described by Zöllner. Some years later the American conjurer Harry Kellar gave a demonstration of slate-writing to the Seybert Commission, producing results 'far more remarkable than any which we have witnessed with mediums'. However, Kellar produced his 'phenomena' by means of a trap-door which he had had cut in the floor under the séance table, and an accomplice in the room below. To compare such trickery with Slade's effects is simply absurd; as Inglis points out: 'Slade gave séances wherever he happened to be, in private houses or hotel rooms; there could be no question of his having trapdoors cut wherever he went – and if he had, he would soon have been exposed.'[91] In attempting to decide between the hypotheses of trickery and paranormality we must take into account not only the nature of the phenomena, but also the conditions under which they were produced.

It seems that we are left with only two alternatives: either the phenomena produced at Leipzig were genuinely paranormal, or Zöllner himself was involved in the fraud. Although it would have been quite impossible for Slade to have 'rigged' the phenomena on his own, he could certainly have do so with Zöllner's help or connivance. This possibility cannot be ruled out, although the reader may think that a scientist of Zöllner's calibre, already internationally famous in his own sphere, would be unlikely to stoop to such a deception. He had little to gain, and everything to lose, by resorting to fraud. In fact, Zöllner's claims brought nothing but ridicule and ostracism from his scientific colleagues. Even if we accept the hypothesis that Zöllner was in the plot, there still remains the evidence of the other witnesses who tested Slade and became convinced of his paranormal powers. They include Edward Cox, Robert Collyer, Carter Blake, Baron von Hellenbach and, most significant of all, the court magician Bellachini. If there was a plot, it must have been a pretty extensive one.

Three years after Zöllner's death Slade arrived in Philadelphia, U.S.A., to be examined by the notorious Seybert Commission. This body had been created under the terms of the will of Henry Seybert, a prominent American Spiritualist. Its function was to make an impartial assessment of the evidence for Spiritualism, although most of its members seem to have been anything but impartial. Slade was able to produce some phenomena for the Commission, although nothing quite as startling as had occurred at Leipzig. Nevertheless, Slade left the enquiry with the feeling that he had been at least a modest success. He even wrote to thank the Commission for the courteous way in which they had treated him, and offered to return and give further demonstrations should this be required. However, the Commission's report condemned Slade's phenomena as 'fraudulent throughout', declaring that all the effects had been produced by sleight-of-hand and distraction of attention. Although no-one had actually caught Slade red-handed, various members of the Commission claimed to have seen suspicious movements of his hands or feet, and this was sufficient to convince a body of men who had in any case started out with the assumption that the phenomena were impossible. Their report, published in 1887, completely demolished Slade's reputation as a medium. He returned to London that same year, taking lodgings under the assumed name of Wilson. Slade was by now a broken man, and he became increasingly addicted to alcohol and morphine. He died of paralysis in a Michigan sanatorium in 1905.

Not content with the destruction of Slade, the Seybert Commission also set out to discredit Zöllner and his co-workers. Zöllner had died on April 25th, 1882, from a haemorrhage of the brain which occurred while he was having breakfast with his mother. This was several years before the Commission's investigations began, but they decided to see what information they could uncover regarding Zöllner. The Commission's Secretary, Professor Fullerton, went to Leipzig and subsequently issued a statement declaring that Zöllner had been mentally unbalanced at the time of the Slade experiments. Fechner, Weber, and Scheibner he dismissed on the grounds of age or physical infirmity (Fechner suffered from eye trouble). Thus, the impression was put around that the Leipzig experiments had been conducted by a group of infirm old men led by a lunatic. This spiteful campaign against a group of distinguished German scientists is one of the nastiest incidents in the history of psychical research. Zöllner's friends were furious at the suggestion that he was unbalanced; Weber and von Hellenbach were both prepared to swear on oath that he had remained perfectly sane until the day of his death. Later, Dr Isaac Funk wrote to the Rector of Leipzig University, who passed his enquiry on to the Professor of Statistics, Dr Karl Bucher. Bucher made his own enquiries, and wrote to Funk stating that: '. . . information received from Zöllner's colleagues states that during his entire studies at the University here, until his death, he was of sound mind; moreover, in the best of health'.[39]

The campaign against Zöllner was highly successful, and today his name is rarely mentioned in scientific text-books. Even psychical researchers have little to say in his favour, although he was undoubtedly one of the pioneers in their subject. Most modern books on psychical research do not mention him at all.* Yet in spite of this, Zöllner's name still occasionally draws the fire of the unbelievers, who seem unable to leave him alone! If his work is so obviously fallacious, why should this be so? For example, why should Dr Eric Temple Bell, writing a book on mathematics some 70 years after the death of Zöllner, find it necessary to refer to him as a 'misguided and deluded mystic'? Or why should Martin Gardner, writing in 1964, decide to waste his ink ridiculing the beliefs of a long-dead professor whose name is known only to a few scientific historians? Could it be that these sceptics have a sneaking feeling that perhaps Zöllner was not quite the fool he has been made out to be; that perhaps he really did observe phenomena which cannot be explained in terms of our normal concepts of space and time? Perhaps the tidy materialistic universe which we have all been conditioned to accept as reality is not quite as tidy as we think.

With the death of Zöllner, the day of the lone pioneer in psychical research came to an end. Although from time to time there would still be the occasional solitary worker pursuing his own particular interest, the mainstream of investigation was henceforth to follow the lines laid down by the organised societies. The first of these, the London-based Society for Psychical Research, was founded on February

*A notable exception is the excellent *Natural and Supernatural*, by Dr Brian Inglis.

20th 1882, just nine weeks before the death of Zöllner. It is to this corporate attempt to investigate the world of the paranormal that we must now turn our attention.

9 Mediumship and the SPR

'I say it is a scandal that the dispute as to the reality of these phenomena should still be going on, that so many competent witnesses should have declared their belief in them, that so many others should be profoundly interested in having the question determined, and yet that the educated world as a body should still be in an attitude of incredulity.' These words were spoken by Professor Henry Sidgwick in his inaugural Presidential Address to the Society for Psychical Research in 1882. The foundation of this famous society about a hundred years ago was a direct consequence of the steady accumulation of evidence for the reality of paranormal phenomena. A vast amount of research had been done by isolated investigators such as Aksakoff, Boutleroff, Cox, Hare, Crookes, de Gasparin, Thury, and Zöllner; as a result of their efforts there was already a strong case for the reality of at least some of the phenomena collectively described as 'psychical'. There seemed to be every justification for continuing the research effort in a more deliberately organised form. It was a time when mediumship of every variety was flourishing, and many intelligent people had become quite convinced that they had received evidence of the existence of another order of reality. As Medhurst and Goldney wrote, many years later: 'Remarkable things were happening in the second half of the nineteenth century, on one level or another. Either they constitute an extension, having far-reaching implications, of the field of phenomena recognised by physical science, or they represent an astonishing failure of human testimony.'[107] It was with the intention of deciding between these two alternatives that the Society for Psychical Research (hereafter referred to as the SPR) was founded in 1882.

There has been some disagreement among historians as to which persons should rightly be regarded as the founders of the SPR.[115] Certainly the Dublin physicist Sir William

Barrett played an important part, as also did the Spiritualist and journalist Edmund Dawson Rogers. However, the dominating influence in the early days of the Society came from a small group of Cambridge scholars, notably F. W. H. Myers, Edmund Gurney, and Henry Sidgwick. In general, their attitude towards the phenomena was cautious and mildly sceptical. While this undoubtedly enhanced the Society's reputation in the academic world, sooner or later it was bound to lead to conflict with the Spiritualists. In the early days Spiritualists played quite an important part in the work of the SPR; in fact, of the nineteen persons who constituted the first Council of the Society, thirteen were Spiritualists.[115] Later some of the Spiritualists, including the famous Stainton Moses, resigned in protest at what they considered to be the over-sceptical approach of the Cambridge group, thereby leaving the latter in full possession of the Society. Whether this was an entirely good thing for the SPR is a matter of opinion; but there can be no question about the tremendous amount of sheer hard work and enthusiasm which the Cambridge scholars put into their task. Today their achievements can be studied in the many volumes of *Proceedings*, in the two-volume treatise known as *Phantasms of the Living* (by Gurney, Myers, and Podmore), and in Myers' great masterpiece *Human Personality and its Survival of Bodily Death*. The sheer quantity of work represented in these volumes is astounding; it was also a remarkable innovation, for never before had the paranormal been subjected to such an intense and searching examination. As Dr Gauld wrote: 'To pass from even the ablest of previous works to *Phantasms of the Living* is like passing from a mediaeval bestiary or herbal to Linnaeus' *Systema Naturae*.'[56]

The enthusiasm of the SPR workers soon sparked off a similar response in other countries. In 1884 William Barrett toured the USA, with the result that the following year an American SPR was established under the Presidency of Professor Simon Newcomb. This Society was fortunate in having the support and encouragement of the great philosopher and psychologist William James, who was also President of the British SPR in 1894–5. In France Jean Meyer founded the *Institut Metapsychique International*, with Dr Gustav Geley as its first Director. Probably the *Institut's* most distinguished member was Professor Charles Richet, well known for his researches into the treatment of epilepsy and tuberculosis. In 1913 Richet received the Nobel Prize for his discovery of the phenomenon known as anaphylaxis.

During the last twenty years of the nineteenth century, therefore, psychical research gradually emerged as an organised branch of science. With a few notable exceptions, it commanded the interest and respect of the public at large and the academic community. In view of the split which was to come later, it is rather surprising to discover how close was the link between psychical research and academic psychology in those days. Among the early members of the SPR were A. A. Liébault and H. Bernheim of the Nancy school, Professor G. Stanley Hall of Johns Hopkins University, and of course William James, who was then at Harvard. In the years which followed, psychical research attracted the attention of many leading psychologists, including Janet, Freud, Jung, and McDougall. In the August of 1892 the Second International Congress of Psychology was held at University College, London, and attended by about three hundred psychologists from all over the world. The chairman of this distinguished assembly was none other than Henry Sidgwick, then in his second term as President of the SPR. Among the many papers read and discussed was Sidgwick's own report on the Census of Hallucinations conducted by the Society, and after the meeting, Sidgwick expressed his satisfaction that 'the severe taboo too long imposed upon the subjects with which we deal has been tacitly removed'. Alas, Sidgwick's optimism proved to be premature. As psychology became increasingly behaviouristic during the early years of the twentieth century, so its practitioners became less and less willing to involve themselves with the phenomena reported by the psychical researchers.

The principal aim of the SPR was to encourage the investigation of 'certain obscure phenomena, including those commonly known as Psychical, Mesmeric, or Spiritualistic'. Under this heading came a great variety of reported happenings, some of which, if taken at their face value, might seem to indicate the existence of a spiritual world in which human personality could survive after the death of the body. However, there were other pheneomena which could only be described as bizarre, comic, or even repulsive, and which seemed to point towards nothing of a particularly spiritual nature. This was especially true of many of the physical phenomena, most of which seemed merely ludicrous to the high-minded scholars and philosophers of the Cambridge group. After all, there is nothing particularly 'spiritual' about a table being hurled across a room, a person being levitated into the air, or a mysterious hand which pinches the sitters when no one is looking. Therefore it is not surprising that the Cambridge men, who were seeking for spiritual truths, should shy away from the antics of the physical mediums. This, together with the exposure of a number of obvious frauds, meant that by the end of the nineteenth century the leading members of the SPR had virtually lost all interest in PK-type phenomena. As Dr Inglis puts it: 'the Sidgwicks, Hodgson and Podmore had struck most of what had originally been accepted as psychic phenomena off the Society's visiting list.'[91] Podmore expressed the general feeling of the Cambridge group when he wrote:

'The accounts given by Spiritualists themselves, when they condescend upon detail, are sufficient to show that we need look for no other cause for the results described than trickery of the most trivial and vulgar kind – trickery for the most part too obvious to need a commentary.'[129]

This is, of course, a gross over-simplification. As we have already seen, there were in existence by Podmore's time innumerable accounts of PK phenomena which were not susceptible to such an 'obvious' explanation; Crookes' experiments with D. D. Home are but one example. Nevertheless Podmore's judgment, reinforced by most of the other British researchers, served to point psychical research away from the investigation of the physical phenomena. While in retrospect we may regret this narrowing of the Society's interests, it did have its advantages; in fact, at that particular stage in the development of psychical research it was probably a wise procedure. By ignoring the more bizarre activities of the séance room, the early pioneers were able to concentrate on establishing the occurrence of telepathy, and on investigating the evidence for survival after death obtained through the activities of so-called 'mental' mediums such as Mrs Piper. As we have seen, their achievements in these particular fields were considerable; indeed, the best scientific evidence which has ever been obtained for the reality of the human soul and its survival after the death of the body is to be found in the numerous publications of the SPR from 1882 to 1940. Anyone who is primarily interested in this aspect of psychical research must consult the original papers, or read one of the many popular accounts which have appeared from time to time. Here we must regretfully turn our backs on this wealth of material and return to the physical phenomena, which are the subject of this book.

Among the many strange characters that graced the nineteenth century Spiritualist scene, one of the strangest was Eusapia Palladino. There are various contradictory versions of her early life, but it seems that she was born in the village of La Pouille, southern Italy, on the 21st of January, 1854, her mother dying in childbirth. Eusapia's father was said to have been killed by robbers when she was only eight years old, and after that she was adopted into a family which was given to spiritualistic practices. Her mediumship first emerged at about the age of thirteen when, in the course of séances, various physical phenomena such as raps, lights, materialisations, and the movement of objects began to occur. According to her own account, Eusapia was at first rather frightened by these occurrences, and tried to escape the clutches of the Spiritualists who wanted to persuade her to become a medium. Nevertheless, in spite of her revulsion, she seems to have given quite a few sittings at this time. Later she moved to Naples, where she married a shopkeeper named Raphael Delgaiz. Although unable to read or write (she had had little or no education), Eusapia possessed sufficient business acumen to be able to run the shop quite effectively. As the years went by she also became increasingly famous (or notorious) as a medium.

Eusapia first came to the notice of a wider public as a result of the efforts of the Cavaliere Ercole Chiaia, a Neapolitan cavalry officer who held séances with her during the 1880s. In 1888 Chiaia wrote a letter to a Rome journal challenging the sceptical views of the psychiatrist and criminologist Cesare Lombroso, and inviting him to undertake research with Eusapia. Lombroso was a hard-baked sceptic and materialist who had made no secret of his view that spiritualistic phenomena were largely due to fraud, although he had come across some strange occurrences in the course of his practice. At the time when Chiaia's letter appeared Lombroso was Professor of Psychiatry at the University of Turin, and a greatly respected figure in the academic world. He agreed to investigate Eusapia, and in 1891 he embarked upon a series of experiments, accompanied by Professor Augusto Tamburini and several other scientists. Some very striking phenomena were observed, and the scientists, including Lombroso, asserted that they were completely convinced of the genuineness of Eusapia's phenomena.

Lombroso's conversion stirred the academic world into action, and in 1892 a commission was formed, headed by Professor Giovanni Schiaparelli, the well-known astronomer and director of the Milan observatory. Also serving on the Milan Commission were Giuseppe Gerosa, Professor of Physics; Angelo Brofferio, Professor of Philosophy; Charles Richet, Professor of Physiology at the Sorbonne; Dr G. B. Ermacora, physicist; Baron Carl du Prel of Munich; and Alexander Aksakoff, the Russian psychical researcher. The Commission held seventeen sittings with Eusapia, in the course of which they observed a variety of remarkable phenomena. In a cautiously worded report the Milan investigators expressed some doubts about the unsatisfactory nature of the controls which they had been able to impose upon the medium; nevertheless, they made it plain that they considered many of the phenomena to be quite inexplicable in terms of fraud. In a full light they had seen levitations of the table, object movements, and the alteration by 21 lbs of the medium's weight as she sat in a balance.

Following the successful outcome of the Milan investigations Eusapia was in great demand all over Europe, a situation which was to continue until her death twenty-six years later. Whereas D. D. Home had performed mainly before princes and noblemen, Eusapia performed chiefly for the scientists. Nicholas Wagner, Professor of Zoology at the University of St Petersburg, became impressed when he saw her at Naples; later, he invited her to Russia. In Rome she was investigated by the Polish scientists M Siemaradski and Dr Julien Ochorowicz, some of the séances also being attended by Richet, Lombroso, and Baron von Schrenck-Notzing.

The list of places where she performed is almost endless, and includes Paris, Warsaw, Genoa, Palermo, Turin, Cambridge and New York. Most of the committees which investigated her issued extensive reports, so that the literature on her mediumship is vast, ranging from several full-length books through a whole series of pamphlets and papers in most of the languages of Europe. Obviously, with such a wealth of material, it is not possible to give more than a very superficial account of Eusapia's activities in a book of this kind.

One of the most remarkable features of Eusapia's career was the number of eminent sceptics she managed to convert. We have already mentioned Lombroso, considered to be one of the most distinguished psychiatrists of his time, and regarded as the founder of criminology. Another eminent sceptic was Enrico Morselli, Professor of Pathology in the University of Genoa. He was not only one of the leading lights of Italian science; he was also a convinced materialist. For years he had been engaging in vigorous denunciations of the Spiritualist movement, and his scepticism was known to be so violent that he had been deliberately excluded from the Milan sittings in case his presence should inhibit the phenomena. However, in 1901 Morselli managed to get himself invited to a séance without the medium's knowledge, and he was sufficiently impressed with what he saw to make him determined to conduct his own experiments. He managed to win Eusapia's confidence, and in 1906 she gave a long series of sittings for him in his own laboratory at Genoa. As a result of these séances Morselli became completely convinced, declaring that: 'the phenomena of physical mediumship attributed to Eusapia are in the great majority of cases genuine'. He subsequently published a two-volume work on the phenomena, entitled *Psicologia e 'Spiritismo'* (Turin, 1908).

Eusapia Palladino provides us with a 'classic example of mixed mediumship' (Morselli's phrase). Given an opportunity, she would cheat quite shamelessly. She seems to have been totally lacking in moral scruples of any kind, and at the end of a séance she was quite likely to throw herself into the arms of the nearest male sitter with obviously amorous intent! There have also been suggestions that sitters' wallets and other personal belongings were apt to disappear 'mysteriously' in the course of some sittings. Eusapia was certainly a rough diamond, and it is not surprising that some of the refined gentlemen of the SPR found her company uncongenial. Eusapia made no pretence to be anything other than what she was; she herself warned her sitters: 'watch me carefully, or I'll cheat!' All this was very well known to the sceptical men of science who studied her phenomena; nevertheless, almost without exception, they came away totally convinced that *she could, at times, produce genuine PK phenomena.*

A very good example of this admixture of fraud and PK occurred in one of the Morselli séances. The medium was seated at the table with her back to the 'cabinet' (a curtained-off corner of the room), the sitters forming a chain around her. Suddenly Morselli called out a code-word, indicating to the others that he had seen Eusapia withdrawing one of her hands from the control of the sitters on each side of her. In fact, she had removed her left hand, and was reaching out towards a tin trumpet which lay upon the table. The professor thereupon seized the wandering hand firmly, the other sitters redoubling their vigilance. At that very moment, while Eusapia was firmly held hand and foot, the trumpet rose off the table and passed through the air between the medium and Morselli, disappearing into the cabinet. 'There is no doubt about the matter', wrote Morselli; 'this time the medium did not touch, and could not touch, the trumpet; and even if she could have touched it she could not have conveyed it into the cabinet, which was behind her back.'

Charles Richet was the only member of the Milan committee who did not sign the report endorsing the genuineness of Eusapia's phenomena; he was not certain in his own mind that all possibility of fraud had been excluded. However, in 1894 he arranged for the medium to give a series of séances on an island which he owned, the Île Roubaud, which is off the south coast of France, near Toulon. Since the only house on the island was Richet's, it seemed impossible for Eusapia to introduce a confederate. At this time the SPR in London had almost washed its hands of the physical phenomena; nevertheless Richet invited two of its leading lights, Lodge and Myers, to stay on the island with him, and assist in the investigation of Eusapia. They observed many phenomena including the movement of curtains, table levitations, the playing of musical instruments, and the appearance of materialised hands. As a result of the séances, Myers and Lodge became quite convinced that the phenomena were paranormal, and they immediately asked Henry and Eleanor Sidgwick to come and see for themselves. Sidgwick's attitude towards the physical phenomena is very clearly illustrated by a letter which he wrote at this time to a friend; referring to the invitation to visit the Île Roubaud, Sidgwick wrote: 'It will be rather a bore, and I fear, tiring to my wife: but we both feel that it has to be done.'[56] So far from regarding it as 'rather a bore', most psychical researchers nowadays would give their ears to have the opportunity of investigating a physical medium as powerful as Eusapia.

In the event, the Sidgwicks were impressed in spite of themselves. Although Eusapia was securely held, hand and foot, objects moved around the room and notes sounded on a piano some distance away. Later that year Lodge delivered a paper to the SPR in which he stated his firm conviction that many of Eusapia's phenomena were truly paranormal events, and the Sidgwicks rather reluctantly supported him. However, one member of the SPR hierarchy, the arch-sceptic Richard Hodgson, was not impressed. Hodgson was a complete unbeliever as far as the physical phenomena of psychical research were concerned, and he had distinguished himself by exposing a number of frauds, including those perpetrated by the notorious Madame Blavatsky in India. Seeing his most respected friends and colleagues becoming converted to the cause of Eusapia, Hodgson rushed into print. In the April, 1895, issue of the SPR *Journal* he published a detailed analysis of the sittings, claiming that there were a number of ways in which the phenomena could have been faked without the knowledge of the sitters. Richet, Ochorowicz, Myers and Lodge all disagreed with Hodgson, and each wrote a reply to his criticism. Eventually it was decided that the only way to settle the matter was by inviting Eusapia to come to England for further tests. She agreed to this proposition, and arrived in Cambridge on July 30th, 1895.

At first, everything seemed to go well at the Cambridge séances. Various phenomena were observed, some of them quite interesting although not as striking as those which had occurred on the continent. It is likely that Eusapia felt somewhat ill at ease in the presence of the English savants. Then, on August 29th Hodgson arrived hot-foot from America, determined to expose the Neapolitan woman, once and for all. He believed that the usual procedure of holding the medium's hands and feet as tightly as possible, and calling out the extent of the control to the note-taker, merely helped Eusapia to cheat by informing her when it was unsafe for her to do so. Therefore, he pretended to be thoroughly incompetent, and deliberately relaxed his control to see what she would do. Naturally, she cheated. A devastating report was issued in the SPR *Journal*, and the learned scholars breathed a sigh of relief. Now they could revert to their customary practice of ignoring the physical phenomena, and concentrating on what William James called 'the calm air of delightful studies': the investigation of telepathy and the other mental phenomena. Professor Sidgwick summed up his attitude to Eusapia in a few well-chosen words:

'Inasmuch as Eusapia Palladino has systematically practiced trickery for years ... I propose to ignore her performances for the future, as I ignore those of other persons engaged in the same mischievous trade.'

The Cambridge séances had, in fact, proved nothing, for it was already a well-known fact that Eusapia would cheat if she was given the opportunity to do so; indeed, she had herself made this perfectly clear. Whether the cheating was conscious or unconscious it is impossible to say; Eusapia claimed that it was her 'spirit control', John King, who compelled her to do it. The publication of the SPR's report caused an international outcry, for many famous scientists in other countries had by this time become convinced of the authenticity of the phenomena. Some of them pointed out that Hodgson's procedure of deliberately encouraging the medium to cheat was itself highly improper, for in all research of this kind the duty of preventing fraud lies with the experimenter, not the medium. Meanwhile Eusapia, apparently undeterred, continued to give her séances all over Europe, gaining more and more converts as she did so.

In 1908 the *Institut Général Psychologique* of Paris issued a two-volume report based on the results of four years' research with Eusapia. This was unquestionably the most exhaustive study of her mediumship so far made, and the team of scientists involved in the research was a formidable one. It included Richet, Pierre and Marie Curie, the philosopher Henri Bergson, the General Secretary of the *Institut*, M. Youriévitch, and the director of the Laboratory of Biological Physics, Jacques-Arsène d'Arsonval. The research team was headed by Jules Courtier, Professor of Psychology at the Sorbonne. Sophisticated monitoring equipment was introduced to eliminate the possibility of fraud; Eusapia's chair was suspended on a weighing machine, and the tables were wired up to recording apparatus so that the slightest movement would be registered. Everything which occurred during the séances was carefully recorded. Before the experiments began most of the observers, including Courtier, were sceptics; they were also fully aware of the possibility of fraud. Nevertheless, at the end of the series all the scientists were highly impressed. They had seen objects moving without contact in a clear light, heard musical instruments playing without human aid, and witnessed the levitation of a table – even, on one occasion, when an investigator was sitting on it! Their report, although cautiously worded, was positive; and it left the SPR in a very embarrassing position. Because of the high-and-mighty attitude of Sidgwick and some other members of the Society, the detailed research which might have been conducted in England had instead been conducted in Paris. The SPR leaders found themselves almost alone among international psychical researchers in their refusal to take the Palladino phenomena seriously.

Stirred into action by this international disapprobation, the SPR decided to take the unprecedented step of reversing its previously determined policy to have nothing to do with any medium who had been detected in fraud. As Mrs Sidgwick pointed out, Eusapia had already been examined by a larger number of scientific men than any other medium, and could produce 'a larger number of witnesses whose opinion would carry weight in other subjects'. Furthermore, some of her recorded phenomena could not be explained by her *detected* methods of trickery. 'In these circumstances the Council (of the SPR) came to the conclusion that as we do not maintain an obstinate attitude of incredulity, we should again make an attempt to collect material with a view to forming an independent judgment on the phenomena Eusapia presents.'[48]

They thereupon appointed three gentlemen, Everard Feilding, Hereward Carrington, and Wortley Baggally, to go to Naples and investigate Eusapia on behalf of the Society.

It would have been difficult to have found three men more admirably suited to the task of investigating a physical medium. Feilding was the second son of the Earl of Denbigh and had seen service in the Royal Navy; he was a sceptic as far as PK phenomena were concerned, and had exposed a number of fraudulent mediums. Carrington was the principal investigator of the American SPR; he was an expert conjurer, and had had a great deal of experience with fraudulent mediums of all kinds. In fact, he had written an entire book on the subject, describing in detail the various 'tricks of the trade'. Baggally, also an experienced conjurer, once claimed that he had investigated almost every medium in Britain without finding one who was genuine. It had often been argued that eminent scientists were the easiest of people for an accomplished conjurer to deceive; it therefore seemed reasonable that Eusapia should be investigated by experts in legerdemain and the techniques of deception rather than by experts in natural science. If she were indeed nothing more than a clever trickster, Feilding, Carrington and Baggally were eminently qualified to catch her out. As Dr Inglis drily remarks, they were the SPR's equivalent of a Fraud Squad!

When they arrived in Naples, Feilding and Carrington hired a suite on the fifth floor of the Hotel Victoria, and set about equipping part of it as a séance room. A corner of the room was curtained off to provide the 'cabinet', and various objects, purchased by the investigators, were placed inside it. Electric lighting of variable brightness was arranged overhead, and a stenographer was hired to make a detailed record of the proceedings. During the séances Eusapia sat outside the cabinet with her back to it, several feet away, while the investigators held her hands and feet. In the course of eleven séances the team recorded 470 separate incidents, many of them occurring in good light, and under excellent conditions of control. They included bulging movements of the curtain, the plucking of a guitar string inside the cabinet, the appearance of various grey objects looking like heads, lights, the untying of knots, and the levitation of the séance-table. Fully alert for any signs of trickery, the investigators noticed Eusapia trying to free her hands and feet from control on several occasions, but they also observed that these were the occasions when the phenomena were *weakest*. In fact, the best phenomena were obtained when the control of the medium was at its most rigorous. A good example of this occurred during Séance II. On this occasion the medium's legs were tied to the legs of her chair, her hands being controlled by Feilding and Carrington, and her feet in contact with their feet. The light in the room was at its maximum, 'bright enough to read small print'. After a number of tilts and partial levitations, the table finally rose completely into the air, in spite of Carrington's efforts to push it down. In fact, it levitated six times in succession. Later in the sitting Carrington glanced inside the cabinet and observed a small table moving of its own accord:

'While I was looking at the small table in the cabinet (the curtains having been accidentally parted, allowing me to see the whole table) it made a series of little jumps in a direction *away* from the medium, and back into the cabinet. I could see that there was no contact between the medium's foot and the table, while a thread, if pulled, would have had the effect of pulling the table in the opposite direction, *i.e.* towards the medium. About six or seven little jumps of this kind were made, bringing the small table again right into the cabinet. The light was particularly good, at this time, and I could clearly see the whole of the table as it was moving.'[48]

The lengthy report produced by Feilding, Baggally and Carrington is a masterpiece of its kind, giving a careful and detailed minute-by-minute account of the séances, with separate notes and comments on each séance by each of the investigators. Its conclusions were sensational. The three wise men of the SPR had been badly shaken by what they had observed. Carrington, the arch-exposer of mediums, wrote that, as a result of the sittings '... I have to record my absolute conviction of the reality of at least some of the phenomena; and the conviction, amounting in my own mind to complete certainty, that the results witnessed by us were not due to fraud or trickery on the part of Eusapia.' He admitted, however, that it would be impossible to convey this feeling of certainty to anyone who had not been present at the séances. The team were unanimous in their conclusions:

the trivial and almost pathetic attempts of Eusapia to cheat by freeing a hand or a foot could by no stretch of imagination be made to account for all the striking phenomena which they had observed. As Feilding put it: 'My colleagues, then, having come to the deliberate opinion that a large proportion of the manifestations of which we were the witnesses in Naples were clearly beyond the possibilities of any conceivable form of conjuring, entertain no difficulty in saying so in precise terms.'[48]

The rest of Eusapia's history can be briefly told. In November 1909 she went to America, where she gave séances at New York, Boston, and Columbia University. The results were very variable. Sometimes quite brilliant phenomena were observed under good conditions of control. However, on several occasions she was caught attempting to free a foot or a hand, and wide publicity was given to these so-called exposures. In vain Carrington pointed out that many of the phenomena would have been impossible to produce physically even with both hands and both feet completely free, and the investigators themselves recorded a number of such incidents.[23] Nevertheless, once the label of 'fraud' had become attached to Eusapia, people's minds tended to become closed to any other possibilities. The American visit was not a complete failure, however, for Eusapia was able to obtain a glowing endorsement from Howard Thurston, one of the most famous magicians of the day. Thurston was the successor and former assistant of Harry Kellar, the magician who had given evidence to the Seybert Commission. In the May of 1910 Thurston and his assistant examined Eusapia, and observed the levitation of a table in good light and under rigorous control conditions. In a letter to the *New York Times* he contradicted the views of those scientists who had claimed that Eusapia performed her 'tricks' by means of a freed arm or leg, and added:

'I have been a conjurer all my life, and have always been enabled to expose all mediums producing physical phenomena in the past. I am so far convinced that this medium can produce genuine table levitations, however, that I hereby agree to forfeit $1,000 to any charitable institution named if it can be proved that Madame Palladino cannot levitate a table without resort to trickery or fraud.

I am convinced that the table was levitated without fraudulent use of her hands, feet, knees, or any part of her body, or by any mechanical contrivance. All legs of the table were clear from the floor, and we could see that no foot was placed beneath any one of them.

HOWARD THURSTON[23]

Needless to say, the challenge was never accepted, and no charitable institution was ever able to benefit from the alleged exposure of Palladino. Whether from the treatment she had received in America, or from the effects of advancing age, Eusapia's powers now began to decline. Feilding and Baggally had a further opportunity to study her in a series of séances given in Naples in 1908, under the direction of the Count and Countess Petrovsky-Petrovo-Solovovo; they found that there had been a considerable change in her. The attempted cheating was still there, but this time there were few genuine phenomena, and certainly nothing to compare with her earlier performances. She died on May 16th, 1918, at the relatively young age of 64. She had been a focus of controversy throughout the civilised world for the past 30 years.

Following the death of Eusapia, the leaders of the British SPR returned to their main interest: the investigation of the so-called mental phenomena. The majority of the Society's founder-members were now dead, Myers having died in 1901, Gurney in 1888, and Sidgwick in 1900. About the year 1905 the remarkable series of 'cross-correspondences' began, in which the deceased founders apparently communicated with the living through a variety of mental mediums, setting complicated literary puzzles for their earthly devotees to unravel. For many years after this the physical phenomena were forgotten, as the leaders of the SPR occupied themselves almost exclusively with the problem of life after death. It was the age of the great mental mediums, such as Mrs Piper and Mrs Leonard. As Dr Gauld has remarked, 'the psychological interest of this material is very great; but whether for the SPR it was altogether good to be dominated by a group of elderly and closely linked persons whose immediate interests were in communications from their own deceased intimate friends might be doubted.'[56] Certainly it was to be many years before the leaders of the SPR could be persuaded to take any further interest in PK phenomena.

1. Mind over Micro-organism? The author attempts to replicate an experiment by Nigel Richmond in which he claimed to be able to influence the swimming movements of microscopic pond animals.

2. PK on plant life. Here the subject, John Heritage, attempts to influence the germination and growth of cress seedlings. The experiment was moderately successful, with a probability of the results being due to chance of about 1 in 500.

3. An electrically-driven dice casting machine, used for PK experiments at Duke University and elsewhere.

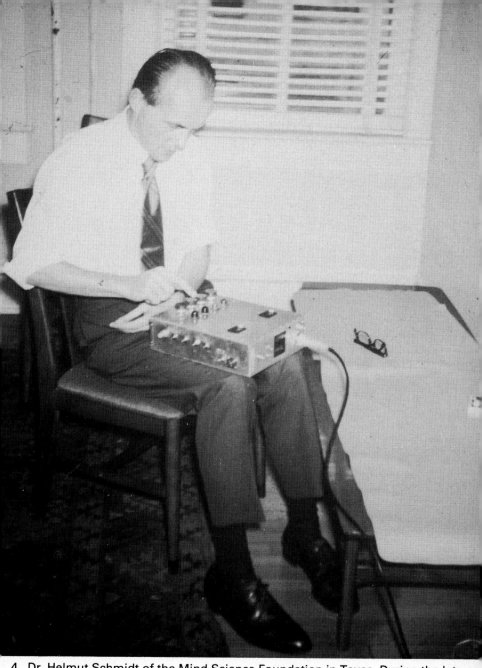

4. Dr. Helmut Schmidt of the Mind Science Foundation in Texas. During the late 1960s Dr Schmidt pioneered the use of random number generators for ESP and PK testing.

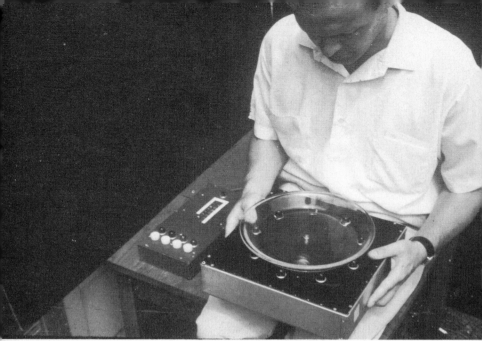

5. APK experiment using a binary random number generator. The subject, Anthony Gibbs, attempts to 'will' the light on the panel to move in a clockwise direction. To assist concentration, he simultaneously rocks a little ball around a glass pie-dish, imagining that it gives the light a flip each time it passes it.

6. A gerbil experiment, devised by the author. The human agent (concealed behind a screen) tries to 'will' the gerbil to jump onto one of the wooden blocks on the left or right of the target area.

Testing the Geller phenomenon: schoolboy subject Mark Briscoe strokes a piece of nitinol wire in an attempt to make it bend, and . . .

The nitinol wire rears upwards like a snake, to the obvious delight of the subject.

9. Mr Julian Isaacs of the Department of Applied Psychology at Aston University, Birmingham, lecturing on paranormal metal bending. Mr Isaacs is one of the very few scientists doing full-time research on parapsychology in Britain.

10. An apparatus devised by Mr Isaacs to detect very weak PK effects. The output from the sensitive detector (enclosed in the glass tube on the right) is fed through an amplifier to one of the pens on the chart recorder. The other pens are coupled to devices which register extraneous interference, such as sound vibrations or fluctuations in the mains voltage.

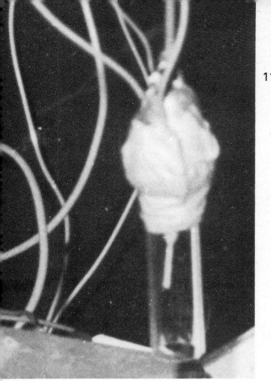

11. An enlargement of the PK detector in picture 10. Inside the glass tube is a piezo-electric crystal ('multimorph') embedded in epoxy resin. The slightest deformation of the crystal, brought about by a PK subject concentrating upon it, leads to the generation of a small electrical pulse which can then be amplified and displayed on the chart.

Another recent development in PK research has been the use of microcomputers. Here Karen Bowman and Duncan McInnes are testing their PK abilities on a Commodore PET 2001. The programme they are using was devised by Dr Richard Lowry of Vassar College, Poughkeepsie, New York.

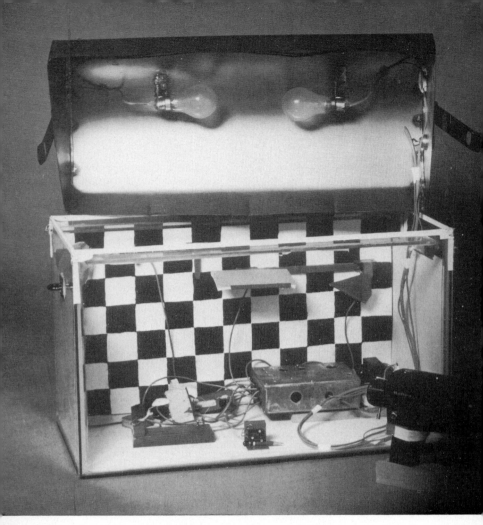

13. This picture shows a 'minilab' built by Julian Isaacs, and used to obtain eviden
    of large-scale PK effects. Various objects are sealed inside a glass-fronted tank,
    and kept under surveillance by means of a video-camera. In the presence of a
    suitable PK agent some of the objects may move, and their movements will be
    recorded on the videotape. Some American experimenters, notably W. E. Cox
    and J. T. Richards, have claimed considerable successes with minilab
    experiments.

10　PK in the Twentieth Century

The death of Queen Victoria in 1901 marked the end of an era in more senses than one. The nineteenth century had been an age of unprecedented expansion in all the fields of mathematics and natural science. In a well-known book,[9] Dr E. T. Bell refers to the nineteenth century as the 'golden age' of mathematics, the most prolific period in the entire history of the subject: 'No previous age approaches this period for the depth and tremendous sweep of its mathematics.' What is true of mathematics is equally true of science; one has only to think of the achievements of men such as Darwin, Faraday, Maxwell, Hertz, Mendeleef and Joule, to become aware of the great leap forward in our knowledge of the physical world which was accomplished by the scientists of the nineteenth century. Psychical research had been a part of that invigorating scene, although only a minor part. The founders of the SPR had certainly broken new ground in their attempt to apply the impartial investigative procedures of science to a field which had hitherto been mainly the province of faith or superstition. However, they had so far failed to carry much conviction with their colleagues in other branches of scientific endeavour.

As we have seen, many of the leading members of the SPR had arrived at the conclusion that most, if not all, PK phenomena could be attributed to fraud. Their views were not shared by researchers in other countries, where physical phenomena continued to play an important part. There was certainly no great shortage of physical mediums during the first quarter of the twentieth century. In Algiers, Professor Richet discovered 'a very intelligent and lively young lady' named Marthe Beraud, who produced apparent materialisations with the aid of an extraordinary substance which emanated from her body. This substance Richet termed 'ectoplasm'. Sometimes it appeared like a paste or jelly, at other times it seemed more like a white mist or smoke. Later, Marthe was very thoroughly studied by the great German neurologist and psychical researcher Baron von Schrenck-Notzing. He published detailed accounts of his séances with her, giving her the pseudonym 'Eva C.' After the outbreak of the First World War she was investigated by researchers of several nationalities, including Everard Feilding and Eric Dingwall from Britain, and Drs Gustav Geley and Camille Flammarion from France. Opinions about Marthe were very varied. Although she was subjected to some extremely rigorous control conditions, she was never actually detected in fraud. On the other hand, photographs taken during her séances show some extremely suspicious features, and many of her 'materialisations' look like paper cut-outs attached to her hair with some kind of pin or clip. Although several famous investigators, including Richet, Schrenck-Notzing and Geley, became convinced of her genuineness, it is difficult to feel much confidence in their conclusions. At this distance in time it is unlikely that we shall ever know whether Marthe was genuine, fraudulent, or a mixture of the two.

Another famous – or infamous – physical medium of the early twentieth century was Mrs Mina Crandon, known in spiritualist circles as 'Margery'. She was born in Toronto in 1888, and later married Le Roy Goddard Crandon, a surgeon and lecturer from Boston who had developed an interest in psychical research. Most mediums seem to develop their powers round about the age of puberty, but Margery was nearly forty when she began receiving apparent messages from Walter, a brother of hers who had been killed in a rail accident in 1911. As her mediumship developed, Margery began producing an astounding quantity of phenomena of almost every kind; in fact, she could be described as the most versatile of all mediums. Raps, lights, voices, mysterious odours, trance-writings in nine different languages, object-movements, apports, the passage of matter through matter, ectoplasmic projections and materialisations – the list is almost endless! In December 1922 the magazine *Scientific American* offered a prize of $2,500 to any medium who could produce 'a visible psychic manifestation' under specified test conditions, and Margery decided to enter for it. However, the outcome was unfavourable to her, only two of the six members of the investigating committee being convinced of the authenticity of her phenomena.

One of Margery's staunchest supporters was William H. Button, a lawyer who was President of the American SPR during the early 1930s. He had read about Zöllner's work, and was particularly interested in obtaining evidence for the existence of a fourth dimension. Button reported several experiments in which Margery's spirit guide, 'Walter', apparently transferred objects into or out of sealed boxes. For example, on June 17th, 1932:

'A pasteboard candy box was most securely taped and as thoroughly marked inside and out. Fig. 1* shows this box before it was opened and illustrates the thoroughness with which the box was sealed and the variety of the markings on it. The writer had some days previously placed a marked half dollar in the box – the markings verified by Mr Litzelmann. At the sitting the box was shaken by every sitter and each verified the fact that some rattling object was inside. The coin was shortly placed in the writer's hand and immediately identified by Mr Litzelmann and the writer. The sealed box was then shaken by each sitter in turn and each verified the fact that it was empty so far as sound indicated. Walter then announced that he proposed to bring to the writer a present which he had procured in Canada and would put it in the box. Shortly thereafter at Walter's direction the box was again shaken by each sitter and all agreed that it contained some hard object, according to the sound. The box was retained in the writer's possession under lock and key until the next day when it was photographed by Mr Thorogood and opened in the presence of Mr Thorogood and Mr Adams. There was taken out an English penny. So far as determinable no sitter had seen it before. There was no tampering with the box. The tapes had not been moved. The markings inside the box were disclosed.'[22]

'Walter' also succeeded in interlinking two solid wooden rings, a feat which Slade's spirit communicators had failed to accomplish (see pp 103–4). Button and his fellow sitters were so delighted with this that they decided to notify Sir Oliver Lodge of the results. Lodge suggested that the test could be made even more stringent by using rings made from two different kinds of wood. If a pair of such rings were successfully

*Not reproduced here

interlinked, it would be impossible for the sceptic to claim that they had been carved from a single solid block. Lodge therefore had two rings made, one of teak and the other of hard pine. He photographed them, and sent them to Boston. During a séance with Margery the rings became interlinked, and for some time they were kept in a glass case and shown to visitors as 'the greatest psychic exhibit in history'. Several other pairs of rings were also linked in the same way, and for a time it seemed as though the ultimate proof of the reality of a higher world had been achieved. Maurice Barbanell concludes the story:

'Then a series of strange events occurred. Whether these were due to joking on Walter's part or not I cannot say, but it seemed as if he were playing games with the interlocked rings. Sometimes, in the séance room, sitters would see the rings looking as though parts of them had been eaten away. At other times Margery Crandon saw sawdust lying on the table and part of the pairs missing. Then the ring would be found broken or separated. Finally, there remained only the exhibit in the glass case.

'When Hannen Swaffer visited the Crandon home, Button went to produce the prize exhibit. Alas, he found one of the rings broken as the result of a crack which he maintained could not have been accidentally made. This mysterious happening led Button to argue that there was "a law of frustration" at work.'[2]

Later developments in the Margery mediumship make a fascinating human story, unfortunately much too complicated to relate here.[179] Many famous men became embroiled in the controversy, including Sir Oliver Lodge, Sir Arthur Conan Doyle, W. B. Yeats, Harry Houdini, William McDougall, Frederick Bligh Bond, and J. B. Rhine. In Britain, the SPR held itself aloof from all the arguments, although Dr Dingwall did hold some séances with Margery in London. He found himself unable to come to any clear-cut conclusions regarding the nature of the mediumship. In America the atmosphere was much more heated, and charges and counter-charges flew thick and wild. Eventually the disputes led to a complete split in the ranks of the American SPR. By 1924 those who believed that Margery was genuine had gained complete control of the Society, and those who felt that standards of scientific integrity had been compromised resigned and founded a rival organisation, the Boston Society for Psychic Research. Eventually, definite proof of Margery's trickery was obtained in the form of an alleged 'spirit thumb-print', which turned out to be the thumb-print of the medium's dentist, a man who was still very much alive! The ensuing scandal almost destroyed the American SPR; fortunately it survived, and some years later it was restructured along more scientific lines. Today, the ASPR ranks as one of the world's most important and highly respected organisations in the field of parapsychological research.

Dr Dingwall described the Margery mediumship as 'the most remarkable hitherto recorded', and ranked Margery alongside Home, Moses, and Palladino as showing 'the extreme difficulty of reaching finality in conclusions, notwithstanding the time and attention directed to the investigation of them.' Such a judgment is hardly fair to Eusapia Palladino, whose phenomena were far more impressive from an evidential point of view than anything produced by Margery. One has only to compare the conditions under which the two mediums operated to see the difference. Whereas Eusapia's séances nearly always took place in the light, Margery operated under cover of darkness (a practice which would have provoked a scornful rebuke from D. D. Home). Also, Eusapia submitted herself for testing by numerous men of science who were permitted, within limits, to choose their own conditions. Margery never operated except in the presence of her husband, who acted as her manager and dominated the entire proceedings. It was Dr Crandon who decided who should be admitted to the séances, where they should sit, and so on. If a sitter showed undue scepticism, he was liable to be shown the door! Whereas Eusapia converted many famous scientists who had hitherto been sceptical about the reality of PK, most of those who investigated Margery came away convinced that they had been imposed upon, even though initially they had held views which were favourable towards the phenomena. Thus William McDougall, Walter Franklin Prince, J. B. Rhine and Louisa Rhine were all convinced that Margery was a fake. In retrospect, the most that can be said in her favour is that she *may* have produced some genuine phenomena during the early days of her mediumship. There are certainly puzzling features about some of the experiments which were performed with Margery, as can be seen from the account of Button's sealed box experiment.

We find ourselves on rather firmer ground when we turn to the mediumship of the Schneider brothers, who flourished about the same time as Margery. Their father, Josef Schneider, was a linotype compositor who lived at Braunau-am-Inn in Upper Austria. His wife gave birth to twelve children, of whom six survived. They were all boys, and were named Karl, Hans, Fritz, Willi, Franzl, and Rudi, the latter being the youngest. Four of the boys were said to possess mediumistic ability, although Karl and Hans possessed it to only a slight extent. The other two, Willi and Rudi, soon achieved international renown as physical mediums. The early stages of the Schneider mediumship were studied by Captain Fritz Kogelnik, the retired commander of an Austrian warship. He observed object movements and materialisations in the presence of Willi. Later, Willi was adopted by Schrenck-Notzing, who invited many eminent scientists and literateurs to visit his mansion in Munich, where he had set up a laboratory for psychical research. Thomas Mann, the novelist and future Nobel Prize Winner, described a séance in which a handkerchief which had been lying on the carpet 'rose, hovered in the air, flew at a sharp angle to the edge of the table and then fell to the ground again.'[172] Later he saw a bell which had been placed in the centre of the room begin to move and ring of its own accord. Mann was quite convinced that what he had seen was a genuine manifestation of the paranormal. In 1922 two British researchers, Harry Price and Eric Dingwall, visited Munich and witnessed what Price later described as 'a wonderful display of phenomena, produced in really excellent red light.'

Willi's mediumship first emerged about 1918, when he was fourteen years old, and it seems to have reached its peak about two years later. By 1925 it had begun to decline, and the boy's interest turned to other things. However, this was by no means the end of the Schneider mediumship, for Willi's younger brother Rudi was ready to step into his shoes. Rudi's mediumistic ability first came to the fore in 1920 when he was aged 11. During one of Willi's séances Rudi entered the room, apparently in a state of trance, and then became possessed by 'Olga', the spirit who was supposed to speak through Willi. From then onwards 'Olga' became Rudi's control, while Willi acquired another one known as 'Minna'. Needless to say, few psychical researchers took these spirit controls at their face value; it was generally assumed that they were nothing more than secondary personalities of the medium. To the investigators, the interesting phenomena were not the whisperings of 'Olga' or 'Minna', but the startling PK phenomena which accompanied them.

As Willi's mediumship declined, so Rudi's developed. Eventually the younger brother became the most famous medium in the world. Dozens of books, papers and articles of various kinds have been written about him, and in recent years a very detailed and scholarly analysis of his mediumship has been made by Anita Gregory.[63] Unfortunately, only a part of Mrs Gregory's work has so far been published.[64] Although from time to time various persons suspected that Rudi was cheating, no one ever caught him in the act, except for one incident which we will mention later. Like Willi, Rudi was more or less 'adopted' by Schrenck-Notzing, who subjected him to some of the most rigorous controls ever imposed upon a medium. The Baron had invented a kind of 'electric chair', with contacts for the head, arms, hands, seat and feet; if at any time during the séance any part of the medium's body ceased to make contact with one of these, a red indicator light immediately revealed the fact. There were also metallic socks and gloves which were to be worn by both the medium and the persons on each side of him; these formed part of an electrical circuit which again would indicate any suspicious movements. Schrenck-Notzing planned to have a long series of séances with Rudi using this method of control; unfortunately his plans did not come to fruition, for the great Baron died suddenly in the January of 1929.

Immediately he heard of Schrenck-Notzing's death, Harry Price hurried to Munich to try to persuade Rudi to come to England. Price was a flamboyant, publicity-conscious freelance psychical researcher who had set up his own laboratory in Kensington, calling it the 'National Laboratory of Psychical Research'. As a result of his popular writings, Price came to be more closely associated with psychical research in the mind of the British public than almost anyone else. In recent years the historians of psychical research have made many attacks on him, accusing him of practising cunning deceptions in order to boost his own image in the eyes of the academic world.[64,68] He is said to have faked many of the phenomena at Borley Rectory, the haunted parsonage which provided him with material for two of his most popular books. Naturally, Price's supporters (for he still has a few!) have strongly contested these attacks, and the matter can by no means be regarded as settled. The reader who is interested in these squabbles can only study all the available literature, and try to make up his own mind. Although Price was certainly no angel and could be devious and even deceitful at times, it does seem that the case against him has been rather over-stated. There is, in fact, no substantial evidence that he ever faked psychical phenomena, although his reporting of them was sometimes inaccurate.

Rudi Schneider came to London in April, 1929, and produced 'the most brilliant and convincing phenomena under unimpeachable conditions.'[132] Price used a system of control similar to that devised by Schrenck-Notzing, but he carried it even further: he provided *all* the sitters, controllers, and medium with metallic gloves and socks forming part of an electrical circuit. Unless each participant kept a tight hold on his neighbour's hands, and his feet in firm contact with the metal plates attached to the floor, an indicator light would be extinguished. Such conditions virtually ruled out all chance of fraud, either by the medium or a confederate. Delighted with the phenomena obtained under these conditions, Price invited a number of eminent scientists and philosophers to attend and see for themselves. They included Lord Rayleigh, Professor A. O. Rankine, Dr William Brown, Dr C. E. M. Joad, Professor F. C. S. Schiller, Professor Nils von Hofsten, and Professor A. F. C. Pollard. The following year Price's book *Rudi Schneider* was published, strongly endorsing the genuineness of the mediumship.

The following year Rudi went to the *Institut Métapsychique* in Paris, where he was tested by Dr Eugene Osty and his son Marcel. Since many of Rudi's phenomena involved the tele-kinetic movement of objects, Osty conceived the brilliant idea of using a network of infra-red beams to guard the object which was to be moved. This is essentially the system used to protect jewellery and other valuable objects when they are on exhibition; if anyone reaches through the invisible beam to catch hold of the object, an alarm is set off. Thus, it would not matter whether the fraud was perpetrated by Rudi himself, using a freed arm, by one of the sitters (an accomplice), or by some mechanical contraption such as a reaching rod: *any* interruption of the beam would immediately be recorded. In the event, the beam *was* interrupted during the Paris séances, but not by anything visible. When 'Olga' tried to lift a handkerchief lying on a table some distance away, the automatic alarm system was triggered, and a photograph immediately taken by means of a flashlight. To the investigators' astonishment, when they developed the photograph they found nothing whatever on the plate that could account for the interruption of the beam. Subsequent experiments showed that whenever 'Olga' tried to move anything, a partial interruption or 'occultation' of the infra-red beam occurred, although there was nothing visible to the human eye in its path. Later experiments conducted in London confirmed these findings, and showed that approximately 15% of the energy of the infra-red beam was absorbed by the unseen entity. Another curious feature was the fact that the occultations often varied in time with the medium's breathing, which was abnormally fast during séances.

We must now turn to the one occasion on which Rudi was said to have been caught cheating. On 28th April, 1932, a séance was held at Price's National Laboratory in London. During the séance a flashlight was set off twice in succession. The resulting photographs showed that Rudi had apparently freed his left hand from the controller (Price), and was reaching backwards to lift a handkerchief which lay upon a small table a few feet away. Instead of publishing this photograph straight away, Price kept it a secret until March 5th the following year, when he publicly denounced Rudi as a fake. Mrs Gregory has shown quite convincingly that Price was motivated by his jealousy of other researchers, particularly Lord Charles Hope, who had had the temerity to arrange sittings with Rudi without asking Price's permission. There was, in fact, a lot of bad feeling between Price and various members of the SPR, engendered by clashes of policy and temperament which had occurred over the years. There can be little doubt that Price used his exposure of Rudi in order to discomfort his enemies, and that he did this with a ruthless disregard for its possible effects upon the young medium. However, Mrs Gregory goes further than this, and suggests that Price actually faked the incriminating photographs, an interpretation which has been questioned by Dr Gauld.[57] It is perhaps more likely that Rudi did indeed have an arm free at that séance, perhaps by accident, and that the photographs happened to provide Price with just the ammunition he needed to sustain his accusation of fraud. Whatever the truth about this particular event, it cannot alter the fact that Rudi produced superb PK phenomena over and over again, under rigorous control conditions and under the watchful eyes of experts from many different countries. Since his death in 1957, Rudi Schneider's reputation has grown rather than diminished, whereas Harry Price is now very much out of favour among psychical researchers. The infra-red occultation phenomenon, independently observed in three different laboratories by different teams of experimenters, is itself unique in the annals of psychical research, and still awaits interpretation by some aspiring theorist.

It is unfortunate that Harry Price seemed unable to see the value of independent confirmation of results. Whenever he obtained control of a medium, he always tried to keep that medium for himself, hoping, presumably, that the fame and glory attendant upon a successful investigation would fall upon Harry Price! Fortunately he did not succeed in monopolising the services of Rudi Schneider, although he could not conceal his animosity towards others who investigated the youth, especially Osty and Lord Charles Hope. With Stella Cranshaw matters were very different, for in this case Price had complete control of the mediumship from beginning to end. Stella, whom Dr Tabori nicknamed 'the gentle maiden', was a 23-year-old nurse when she first encountered Harry Price. They met in a railway carriage on the way from London to Pulborough. In the course of their conversation, Stella mentioned that she had experienced a number of strange and puzzling phenomena for several years past. Sometimes small objects, such as matchboxes, would move when she put out her hand to touch them; sometimes there would be unexplained flashes of light. Occasionally she would experience a cold breeze, although she was sitting in a room with all the windows and doors tightly closed.

Price was excited by this information. He had always wanted to have his very own medium, someone whose gifts could be developed right from the start under his own control. He took a room in the old offices of the London Spiritualist Alliance in Queen Square, equipped it as a séance room, and invited Stella to come to London for a series of sittings. These began on March 22nd, 1923, and produced (in Price's words), 'the most unusual, beautiful, and convincing phenomena.'[133] Among the sitters at some of these séances were the famous medium Mrs Eileen Garrett, Dr Dingwall and Dr V. J. Wooley of the SPR, and (on one occasion) the Hon. Everard Feilding. After thirteen sittings Stella discontinued the series, but she eventually agreed to take part in a further series of eighteen sittings in 1926, and a final series of nine in 1928, shortly before her marriage to Leslie Deacon. As far as is known, she never again performed as a medium after 1928, so that our entire knowledge of her mediumship is derived from the reports of the three series of séances which she gave under the sponsorship of Harry Price. Fortunately, these do include the testimony of a number of eminent observers who were invited to the sittings. For the final series, Price invited Professors Julian Huxley and E. N. da C. Andrade, and also Dr R. J. Tillyard, an Australian entomologist who subsequently wrote an account of Stella's phenomena for the scientific periodical *Nature* (July 31st, 1926).

A striking feature of the Stella séances was the sharp falls in room temperature which were recorded, usually when object movements were about to occur. On one occasion a fall of more than 20 degrees Fahrenheit was registered. Normally, the presence of a number of people in a room causes a slight *rise* in temperature, and it is very difficult to see how this cooling effect could have been faked. As Sir Oliver Lodge remarked, 'It is easy for hocus-pocus to send a thermometer up; but it is by no means easy to send it down.' The cooling effect has also been observed with other mediums; Sir William Crookes noticed that cold draughts preceded the occurrence of PK effects with D. D. Home, and likened them to the feelings obtained when 'the hand has been within a few inches of frozen mercury'. Eusapia Palladino produced cold breezes which seemed to emanate from a spot in the centre of her forehead, and Zöllner reported a cold wind over his hands when the 'spirits' were trying to tie knots in a leather band (see p. 102). However, the Stella séances seem to have been the first investigation in which instrumental methods of recording temperature changes were used.

Violent telekinetic phenomena were also observed during some of the Stella séances. These included the movement of a heavy oak table weighing $43\frac{1}{2}$ lbs. During the third séance, a hexagonal table made of deal was shattered into a state which Price described as 'little more than matchwood'; it seemed 'as if a succession of lightning discharges (but without the flashes) had struck the table'. Here one is forcefully reminded of the incident of Professor Zöllner's screen, split by a force which was compared with 'the discharging of a large battery of Leyden jars (see p. 101). At some of the Stella séances, actual flashes of light were observed, usually of an 'electric blue' colour, and on one occasion a kind of mist or vapour was seen to pass in front of Mrs Garrett's hand. Whether or not this latter phenomenon can be regarded as a manifestation of 'ectoplasm', it is certainly very similar to some of the misty emanations which were described as occurring during the Rudi Schneider séances.

One's opinion as to whether or not the Stella phenomena were genuine must inevitably depend upon one's opinion of Harry Price. Whatever may be said about that extraordinary personality, there is no doubt that he kept the interest in PK phenomena alive in Britain at a time when the SPR had virtually abandoned its investigations in that field. Rudi Schneider was the last one of the great physical mediums to attract the interest of serious scientists; he gave his final séances in 1937, and from then onwards the physical phenomena were largely ignored by scientists in Britain and elsewhere. Harry Price died in March, 1948, having failed to obtain the academic recognition which he so much coveted. Meanwhile a new generation of psychical researchers was appearing on the scene, their minds filled with thoughts of graphs, statistics, and probability computations. The enormous masses of data collected by such heroic workers as Crookes, Zöllner, Schrenck-Notzing, Richet, Feilding, Carrington, Lombroso, Osty and many others was either ignored, or dismissed as valueless. Books on psychical research written during the post-war period were invariably disparaging towards the physical phenomena; if they mentioned them at all they left the reader with the (perhaps comforting) feeling that he need not unduly concern himself with that particular aspect of the paranormal. Thus, the results of many hundreds of carefully conducted experiments were rendered 'null and void'. As Dr Eisenbud put it: '. . . in parapsychology, we "undo" a fact by recognising it in a dim sort of way while putting it as fast as possible into the fading and innocuous past, making effectually as if it had never happened.'[45]

The tendency to reject or smother uncomfortable evidence in this way is a perfectly natural one; 'the mind confronted with an obviously absurd isolated fact merely rebels', wrote Everard Feilding. However, we are no longer dealing with an isolated fact, or even a handful of isolated facts; we are dealing with an enormous number of interlocking observations made by a body of men of unquestioned sanity and integrity, many of whom were initially highly sceptical towards the phenomena in question. The tacit ignoring of such a vast amount of information may explain why psychical research has so far failed to make much progress towards a suitable theoretical interpretation. If we were not permitted to make use of many of the facts discovered in the chemical laboratories, would we be able to formulate a satisfactory theory of chemical combination? Of course, we need a set of criteria to enable us to distinguish the genuine from the false; but when every possible precaution against fraud has been taken and the phenomena still occur, it is surely folly to ignore them on the grounds that they do not fit in with our preconceived ideas. To quote Dr Eisenbud again: 'It is disheartening to see how many cases have gone into virtual oblivion and have been lost to us both in our image of what parapsychology is all about and in our theoretical doodlings because we have allowed ourselves to become speciously one-sided in our criteria of credibility – have in effect tacitly allowed these criteria to develop by default.' It is disheartening, indeed.

11 PK and the Laws of Chance

The founding of the SPR in 1882 had given a tremendous impetus to the scientific study of the paranormal; however, by the end of the 1920s this impetus seemed to have largely petered out. Spiritualism, which had provided so much of the subject matter for the nineteenth century psychical researchers, was now in decline. Materialistic philosophies were in the ascendant, and the ability of science to account for an increasing number of phenomena in purely physical terms became daily more obvious. Yet it was not only the change in the intellectual climate which discouraged the psychical researchers; there were also signs of disillusionment from within the movement. Many of the great mediums had been detected in fraud at one time or another, and many researchers came to believe that those who had *not* been detected were simply the cleverest among a class of people who regularly practised the arts of deception for financial gain or personal glory. In America the Margery scandal rocked the ASPR; in Britain psychical researchers were becoming increasingly suspicious about the activities of Harry Price and his protegé Rudi Schneider. On the continent of Europe most of the great psychical researchers were either dead or very old: Schrenck-Notzing died in 1929, Geley in 1924, and Flammarion in 1925. Charles Richet, the great father-figure of European parapsychology, survived until 1935, when he died at the ripe old age of 85.

Obviously, psychical research badly needed an infusion of new ideas, techniques and personnel, and this came in 1927 with the arrival of two young biologists on the doorstep of William McDougall, Professor of Psychology at Duke University, North Carolina. In a gesture which McDougall later described as 'magnificently rash', Joseph and Louisa Rhine had thrown up their careers in biology to devote themselves to the study of paranormal phenomena. Under McDougall's guidance they were soon hard at work, and in 1934 the world's first officially sponsored Parapsychology Laboratory was established at Duke under the directorship of J. B. Rhine. The techniques developed in that laboratory are now used all over the world; there are many accounts of them available to the interested reader, so I shall not attempt to describe them here.[139] For our purpose it is sufficient to emphasise that within a few years of the foundation of the Parapsychology Laboratory, Rhine and his co-workers had altered the entire outlook of psychical research, providing it with a brand new terminology and a new public image. From henceforth the subject was to be known as 'parapsychology', and its principal activity was to be the laboratory investigation of extrasensory perception (ESP) and psychokinesis (PK). Both of these latter terms were invented by Rhine, presumably to avoid the occultist implications of older terms such as 'clairvoyance'. It must be remembered that Rhine's earlier experiences with mediums (especially the notorious Margery) had left him very disillusioned with Spiritualism and all its offshoots. He wanted to steer parapsychology away from the mumbo-jumbo of the darkened séance-room, with all its obvious opportunities for fraud. For his experimental subjects he chose ordinary people (usually students) rather than professional mediums, and he made them perform simple repetitive tasks under laboratory conditions.

Rhine began testing his subjects for PK ability in the early months of 1934. By that time he had already completed six years of research into ESP, using the five-symbol card tests which were soon to become the principal weapon in the parapsychologists's armoury. His monograph reporting the results of that research was due to be published in March, and would confront the scientific world with some of the most convincing evidence for the reality of a paranormal phenomenon that had ever been obtained.[142] However, all the work done so far at Duke had been concerned with ESP; there had been no research into the alleged physical phenomena of psychical research. What was required was a simple laboratory test for PK, equivalent to the card-guessing tests which had proved so successful for the study of ESP. The basic idea for such a test came one day when Rhine was watching a young gambler casting dice and trying to influence them by will-power. Rhine realised that such a procedure could easily be adapted to provide a suitable technique for the investigation of the 'mind-over-matter' effect. He therefore began conducting dice-throwing experiments with his students, and keeping careful records of the results.

A variety of procedures were used in those early PK experiments. Sometimes a pair of dice would be thrown together with the intention of getting a score of eight or more ('high dice'), or a score of six or less ('low dice'). On other occasions varying numbers of dice would be thrown with the intention of scoring on a particular face (say, sixes or ones). Whichever procedure was used, it was a fairly simple task to assess the results mathematically. Standard statistical techniques could be applied to determine whether or not the results were likely to have occurred by chance. As the experiments proceeded, it soon became clear that chance coincidence could *not* be the explanation of the astonishingly high scoring rates which were being obtained. It certainly seemed as though the intentions of the subjects were somehow influencing the fall of the dice, but could there be an alternative explanation? Rhine proceeded to tighten the experimental conditions in order to eliminate all possible explanations other than psychokinesis.

One of the most obvious counter-hypotheses was that of *dice bias*. It is likely that there is no such thing as a perfect diè, all dice being slightly biased in one way or another. Rhine therefore had his subjects aiming for high scores on some occasions and low scores on others, using the same dice in both cases. If the dice were biased in favour of sixes, then sixes ought to keep on coming up, even when the subject was aiming for a low score. If the dice produced a preponderance of high numbers when the subject was aiming high, and low numbers when he was aiming low, this would strongly suggest that the subject's intentions were influencing the dice.

Then there was the problem of skilled throwing. Could the subject be affecting the dice by the way he cast them, perhaps without even realising that he was doing so? Rhine solved this problem by introducing machines to cast the dice. A number of dice were placed inside rectangular cages made of wire-gauze or perspex, and the cages were slowly rotated by an electric motor. As the dice fell down the cage they were set spinning by a series of baffles set into the wall of the cage. All that the subject had to do was to sit back and concentrate on the tumbling dice. By this means the dice were cast without anyone having any conceivable muscular control over their movement.

The dice-throwing experiments continued for eight years, with the researchers checking and re-checking every imaginable counter-explanation to the PK hypothesis. Rhine was rather reluctant to publish his results, even though they appeared to contain very strong evidence for the reality of PK. His work on ESP had aroused a considerable amount of controversy and even hostility in some quarters, and he was reluctant to spring another startling claim on the scientific community before it had properly digested the first one. Then, in the summer of 1942 he decided to start a full-scale re-examination of all the results obtained so far with the dice-throwing technique. It was the result of this re-examination which finally convinced Rhine that he had obtained indisputable proof of the reality of PK, and led him at last to the decision to publish.

The re-examination came at a time when the Second World War had brought the work of the Parapsychology Laboratory almost to a standstill. All but one of Rhine's graduate students had been called up for military service. For the tedious task of analysing the records Rhine enlisted the help of the remaining graduate, Miss Betty Humphrey, and they embarked upon a detailed statistical examination of 24 separate PK projects which had been carried out since 1934. They decided to divide each record sheet into four quarters and study the distribution of hits in each quarter of the page. They found that 18 of the 24 projects had been recorded in such a way as to make this possible, giving them a total of 27,000 runs of 24 dice-falls each on which to perform the analysis.

The results were quite remarkable. The investigators found that the same hit-pattern had occurred in almost every case. The greatest number of hits had occurred in the first column of each page, and more hits had occurred in the top half of the page than in the bottom half. When divided into quarters, the record sheets showed the highest scoring rate in the top left hand corner, followed in order by the bottom left

and the top right. The lowest rate of all was found in the
bottom right hand corner of the page. The odds against such a
distribution occurring by chance in the eighteen separate
projects was about a hundred million to one. Furthermore,
there seemed to be no way in which this curious distribution
could be explained in terms of dice bias, or in terms of any of
the other hypotheses which had been suggested as alternatives to PK. Even the suggestion that the experimenters
might have cheated was ruled out, since none of the original
experimenters had the slightest idea that their results would
later be subjected to this kind of analysis. Rhine was jubilant.
'Here were data embedded in the PK records like fossils in the
strata of the earth', he wrote. They could be repeatedly
examined by any qualified person until no room for disagreement remained.'[143] The first qualified person to make an
independent analysis of the records was Lieutenant J. G.
Pratt, one of Rhine's former students then on leave from the
Navy. He confirmed the original findings and discovered
that the U-curve effect extended even within the sets of runs
which made up the individual pages. In fact, there were U-
curves within U-curves. Such patterns, it seemed, could only
be accounted for in terms of the psychological effect of the experimental procedures on the subjects. After all, the *dice* could
hardly be expected to know whether they were at the beginning or the end of a run!

The first reports of the PK experiments were launched
upon an unsuspecting world in March, 1943, just nine years
after the first dice-throwing tests had been performed. They
were received with nothing like the violent response which
had greeted the first ESP reports. In 1943 the world was in the
middle of its second Great War, and few people had either the
time or the taste for academic wrangling. Nevertheless, a
number of researchers in several countries set out to replicate
the American experiments, to see whether significant scoring
could indeed be obtained with dice. As the results of these
confirmatory tests came in, it became evident that PK was
displaying the same erratic and unpredictable properties as
ESP. Some experimenters reported clearly significant results,
thus confirming the findings of the Duke laboratory; others,
no less diligent and committed, obtained no evidence of a
mind-over-matter effect whatever. In England, Denys

Parsons and Dennis Hyde each carried out PK tests with dice, and neither found any signs of the phenomenon.[89, 125] Several other British experimenters were rather more successful. J. Frazer Nicol and Whately Carington reported a dice-throwing experiment which gave odds against chance of about 300 to 1,[146] and Dr E. A. G. Knowles, an English engineering mathematician, found to her surprise that she obtained significantly above-chance scoring when she carried out dice-throwing tests with her students.[96] Another British experimenter, Dr Robert Thouless, reported a modest level of success in some experiments with coin-spinning and dice-throwing.[176,177] Some years later a French researcher, M. René Perot, obtained astonishingly high scores when his wife acted as subject (odds against chance of more than three thousand million to one) but totally insignificant scoring when he used himself or his friend M. Peyrelongue as the experimental subject. In comparing the results from all these different experiments, it becomes clear that the outcome of the tests was being determined by psychological factors rather than physical ones. There can be little doubt that the personality of J. B. Rhine and his infectious enthusiasm for this kind of research played an important part in ensuring the success of the Duke University experiments.

In August 1945 the SPR published several papers on experimental PK, including a detailed assessment of all the American work up to that date.[185] The assessment was written by Dr Donald J. West, a psychiatrist and criminologist who was Honorary Research Officer to the Society for many years. West found a number of defects in the American experiments, but his overall conclusion was in favour of the PK hypothesis:

'Without calling the experimenters liars, the case for PK does not seem to be challengeable; it is probably even more clear cut and conclusive than the case for ESP itself.'

A few years after these words were written two British experimenters, G. W. Fisk and A. M. J. Mitchell, published the results of a dice-throwing experiment which would certainly have been regarded as conclusive in any other branch of science. Ten subjects in various parts of the country threw dice in their own homes, aiming for targets which were displayed each day in Fisk's study at Long Ditton, Surrey. The subjects' task was apparently a dual one: to use ESP to find which die-face was the target, and then to influence the fall of the dice by PK. The overall result was clearly significant, with odds against chance of about 4,000 to one.[149] The most outstanding results were produced by Dr Jessie Blundun, a lady physician living in Devon. During the years which followed Fisk and West carried out a lengthy series of experiments with this lady, under very carefully controlled conditions. Her PK scores seldom fell below the chance level, and by 1958 her combined score on all the tests had risen to a level which represented odds of more than a million to one against the chance hypothesis.[50]

Experiments such as Fisk's, in which the subject apparently has to use both ESP and PK at the same time, are often just as successful as those involving PK alone. This suggests that the two faculties are in some way closely connected, that perhaps they are merely different aspects of the same underlying phenomenon. J. B. Rhine held the view that ESP and PK are different sides of the same coin: in ESP the external world operates upon the human mind, and in PK the human mind operates upon the external world. Which of the two effects we observe in any particular experiment depends upon the experimental design. In 1947 Dr R. H. Thouless and Dr B. P. Wiesner proposed that the neutral term 'psi' should be used to describe any interaction between the mind and the environment which does not involve the use of known physical intermediaries. They suggested that ESP should henceforth be known as 'psi-gamma' and PK as 'psi-kappa'. Although these last two terms have never really caught on, the word 'psi' has been universally adopted as a useful shorthand way of describing any paranormal effect.

Dr West's assessment of the case for PK as 'probably even more clear cut and conclusive than the case for ESP' was by no means a rash one. The case for the reality of laboratory-type PK rests upon the work of a considerable number of researchers in different laboratories and different countries. Some of these researchers (Dr Knowles, for example) were originally rather sceptical, and only became convinced when they found evidence of PK in their own data. It is true that, with the possible exception of Dr Blundun, there have been no persistently high-scoring subjects in PK research, corresponding to such ESP 'stars' as Hubert Pearce, Basil Shackleton, and Pavel Stepanek. On the other hand, evidence has recently appeared which indicates that in at least one of these cases – that of Basil Shackleton – the high scores were inflated through fraudulent manipulation of the data by the experimenter.[105] It is therefore important not to place too much weight upon evidence derived from a few individual special subjects. The strength of the case for PK rests upon the cumulative effect of a considerable number of successful independent replications of the Duke research. It is a case which is difficult to break unless we are prepared to assume that *all* the experimenters concerned were either grossly negligent or dishonest.

A good general account of most of the PK experiments performed between 1934 and 1969 has been provided by Dr Louisa Rhine in her book *Mind Over Matter*. During this time, many different kinds of PK experiment were tried, with the intention of discovering more about the nature of the phenomenon. Apart from the Rhines, the two most diligent experimenters were probably W. E. Cox, a mechanical engineer from Southern Pines, North Carolina, and Haakon Forwald, an electrical engineer from Ludvika in Sweden. Cox invented a number of ingenious devices to detect the PK effect on all sorts of moving objects, including cubes, coins, marbles, water-droplets, and electronically-controlled clocks. He also developed the 'placement' method of PK testing in which dice, or other objects, are thrown and willed to fall into a particular area of the table, rather than to fall with a particular face uppermost. The placement idea was taken up by Forwald, who produced a lengthy series of PK reports spanning almost twenty years. Forwald built his own apparatus, and tested the PK effect upon falling cubes made of a variety of materials including wood, paper, aluminium, Bakelite, and steel. Instead of merely counting how many cubes fell inside the target area, Forwald actually measured their lateral displacements, and attempted to calculate the strength of the PK force acting upon them. Later, he developed a theory according to which the PK influence somehow liberates energy from inside the material of the cube, perhaps in the form of neutron emission. However, this theory has not found much support among either parapsychologists or physicists.

During the 1950s several experiments were done to find out whether or not PK can affect living targets. Dr Paul Vasse of Amiens and his wife Christiane claimed to have influenced the growth of seedlings by concentrating upon them. Although the Vasses did not attempt to assess their results statistically, the photographs showed a very marked difference in growth between the treated and the untreated plants.[83] Later work along the same lines usually employed the now standard methods of assessment and control. Probably the best evidence for a PK effect upon plants comes from the work of Bernard Grad, a Professor of Psychiatry at McGill University, Montreal. In a lengthy series of experiments, Grad was able to demonstrate very convincingly that PK can be used to influence plant growth, and that the effect varies with different people. For example, in one series Grad compared the effects of three different subjects: a man who believed he had a 'green thumb', a depressive neurotic, and a depressive psychotic. Plants treated by the man with the 'green thumb' grew much faster than an untreated control group; those treated by the neurotic grew slightly faster than the control group; and those treated by the psychotic grew slower than the control group. In Grad's experiments the subjects did not actually come into contact with the plants, but held flasks of water which were subsequently used to water the specimens.[156] Although on a much smaller scale than Grad's, my own experiments also showed that two schoolboys were able to influence the growth and germination of seedlings, one positively and the other negatively.[135] It seems most probable that in such cases the PK effect is operating at the molecular level, affecting the speed of action of the various enzymes which bring about germination and growth.

One of the first attempts to influence the movement of an animal psychokinetically was made by Nigel Richmond. He claimed to have influenced the swimming movements of the pond animalcule *Paramecium* as he watched it through the microscope.[147] His experiment seems to have been very carefully conducted, and in 1969 I tried to repeat it using a similar pond organism.[134] In practice, I found that it was quite difficult to concentrate on the organism, record its movements accurately, and at the same time make necessary adjustments to the apparatus. In this case I obtained no evidence of a PK effect. Later, I changed to using rather larger animals such as woodlice and gerbils, whose movements were easier to observe and record. I also brought in other human subjects to act as the PK agents. Under these conditions I was able to obtain evidence for a slight PK effect between human and animal.[136,137.] Almost at the same time another experimenter, Louis Metta* of the Sorbonne, reported an experiment with moth caterpillars which was of very similar design to my woodlouse experiment. He also obtained results which strongly suggested the operation of a PK effect, although they could not be regarded as conclusive.[108]

Some scientists have designed experiments to find out whether animals themselves have any PK abilities, quite apart from the possible influence of human beings. In *Parapsychology and the Nature of Life* I reviewed these experiments, and came to the conclusion that the case for the existence of animal PK must be regarded as not proven.[138] Since then I have seen nothing which would lead me to alter that opinion. The few experiments which have yielded significant results could equally well be explained in terms of human influence, and in some cases this seems to be the *only* reasonable explanation. For example, Dr Schmidt did an experiment in which cockroaches were placed upon a metal grid wired up to an electrical device. The object of the experiment was to see whether the cockroaches could influence the output of a random number generator in such a way as to reduce the number of shocks which they received. To his surprise, the cockroaches received significantly *more* shocks than could be accounted for by chance.[159] It can hardly be supposed that cockroaches are masochistically inclined, and therefore used their PK to increase the number of shocks which they received. On the other hand, most humans dislike cockroaches, and it is therefore quite likely that Dr Schmidt or one of his assistants was influencing the machine in such a way as to increase the animals' discomfort.

The 1970s was a decade of very vigorous research in parapsychology. On December 30th, 1969, the American As-

---

*Pseudonym. French scientists seem to be more reluctant to let their association with parapsychology be known than are British or American scientists.

sociation for the Advancement of Science recognised the legitimacy of the subject by accepting the Parapsychological Association as an affiliate member. The decision was a controversial one, and there have since been several attempts to get it reversed. However, the fact that parapsychology now seemed to be accepted as a respectable branch of science did provide an important boost to the morale of the experimenters. On the technical side, the introduction of electronic randomising devices made many of the older methods obsolete, and opened up new lines of research and new theoretical perspectives. The chief architect of this particular development was the previously-mentioned Dr Helmut Schmidt, formerly a Senior Research Scientist of the Boeing Aircraft Corporation's laboratories in Seattle. He began publishing the results of his experiments in 1969. Schmidt's random number machines derive their randomness from one of nature's most fundamental processes: the disintegration of the atomic nuclei of a radioactive isotope. According to orthodox physics it should be impossible either to predict the moment at which a nucleus will disintegrate, or to influence it in any way. However, Schmidt's experiments showed very convincingly that what is impossible in terms of orthodox science is not necessarily impossible for *psi*.

In my previous book I described the early Schmidt experiments in some detail, so I shall not repeat the descriptions here. In brief, Schmidt was able to demonstrate that some human subjects can foretell which digits will be generated by the random number generator to an extent well beyond what could reasonably be attributed to chance. This, therefore, showed the reality of that form of ESP known as *precognition*.[157] Later, by using machines which were internally wired in a slightly different way, he was also able to demonstrate that some people can actually *influence* the output of the machine, thus providing evidence of PK.[158] Although this did not add anything to the knowledge of psi derived from card-guessing and dice-thowing experiments, it was very encouraging to have those early results confirmed by an electronic method which seemed to be virtually fraud-proof and error-proof.

However, Schmidt's work did not stop there. Having demonstrated the existence of the basic psi phenomena, he went on to design more sophisticated experiments to reveal how those processes operate. For example, he found that it did not seem to matter whether a random number machine was wired for precognition or for PK; the results were equally good in both cases. Even when the subject did not know which of his psi faculties was being tested, he still performed at about the same level. Schmidt tried switching the machine from one mode to the other in the middle of a run, and found that this made no significant difference to the scoring rate.[162] Later, he used two random number machines with different degrees of internal complexity; one generated numbers according to the output from a single radioactive isotope, while the other displayed the 'majority vote' of 100 digits generated by a very fast random number generator of the first type. Once again, he found that the internal design of the machine made no detectable difference to the scoring rate.[160] Psi phenomena, then, appear to be *goal-determined* processes; the important factor is the end to be achieved, and not the route by which it is achieved. This is in accordance with our experience of ordinary psychophysical events: we do not think out in great detail all the complex electrical and chemical changes which take place when we move the muscles of our arm; we simply 'will' it to move, and it does.

Those who tend to be sceptical about the reality of psychical phenomena are hardly likely to be pacified by the latest Schmidt experiments, which really stretch the reader's credulity to the limits. Schmidt decided to perform an experiment in which some of the targets were generated and recorded on tape *before* the experiment began. These pre-recorded targets were interspersed with the ones being generated by the machine while the PK trials were actually in progress. Schmidt found that his subjects obtained equally significant scores on both the ordinary targets and the pre-recorded ones, suggesting that PK can actually work backwards in time.[161] It seems almost unbelievable that a thought which is occurring in my mind *now* can somehow be the cause of an event which occurred yesterday, and yet that is what the Schmidt results seem to imply. In fact, such a time-reversed PK effect is no more surprising than precognition, which also seems to imply a reversal of causality. Schmidt and several other physicists have pointed out that modern interpretations of the Quantum Theory should lead us to expect something of this sort, strange as it may seem to our commonsense view of reality. We shall be considering the Quantum Theory in a later chapter; meanwhile, if the Schmidt results are confirmed, we may find ourselves having to agree with J. B. S. Haldane, who once wrote: 'I have the feeling that the Universe is not only queerer than we supposed, but queerer than we can suppose'.

12   The Return of the Physical

As we have seen, the long line of the great physical mediums (or at least those who were willing to submit themselves for scientific investigation) came to an end during the 1930s, Rudi Schneider and Mina Crandon being about the last to attract any attention from serious researchers. Physical mediumship hit the headlines for about the last time in 1944 when a materialising medium, Mrs Helen Duncan, was convicted at the Old Bailey of fraudulent practices, and sentenced to nine months imprisonment. The newspapers called it 'the trial of the century', and it was certainly unique in British legal history. The action was brought under the Witchcraft Act of 1735, and one of the principal witnesses for the prosecution was the flamboyant Harry Price, who was later to be accused of faking some of his own research.

By the early 1950s psychical researchers were highly sceptical about the existence of physical paranormal phenomena. Admittedly, there had been some very puzzling happenings recorded in the past, particularly with D. D. Home, Eusapia Palladino, and Rudi Schneider. However, since these things were no longer happening today, the most likely hypothesis seemed to be that those early mediums were fraudulent, even though their investigators had failed to uncover the fraud. Was it just a coincidence that physical mediumship disappeared at about the time when new technological advances made it possible to keep the medium under continuous observation and control? At its headquarters in Tavistock Square, London, the SPR installed an infra-red telescope, and offered a prize of £250 to any medium who could produce a physical phenomenon in the dark while under observation with this instrument: there were no claimants. Most researchers drew the obvious conclusion from this failure.

The mood of scepticism was only slightly disturbed by the reports of dice-throwing experiments emanating from the

USA. After all, there is no obvious connection between a slight statistical anomaly which reveals itself after hundreds of dice-throws have been completed, and the large-scale forces which were supposed to hurl heavy Victorian tables into the air. The most that could be said about the dice experiments was that they kept the options open; for if the human mind could influence the fall of dice, it was *just* possible that it might, on rare occasions, cause the movement of other objects. This was the viewpoint voiced by Dr West in his popular book *Psychical Research Today*, which was first published in 1954. At that time there were few psychical researchers willing to argue in favour of the authenticity of large-scale PK phenomena.

However, history sometimes has a nasty habit of repeating itself, and those sceptics who thought that modern technology had disposed of physical mediumship were to receive several rude shocks during the succeeding decades. Beginning in the mid sixties a series of new PK 'stars' began to appear, and before long, names such as Nina Kulagina, Felicia Parise, Alla Vinogradova, Matthew Manning, Ingo Swann, and Uri Geller began to be bandied about at parapsychological conferences. Those who had confidently believed in the ability of modern gadgetry to detect fraud found themselves in a difficult position; for when it came to the test, the modern investigators were no more able to discover the *modus operandi* of the phenomena than their forebears had been. In fact, exactly the same arguments, challenges and counter-challenges occurred all over again. There is a depressing family resemblance between the squabbles which arose over Uri Geller in the 1970s, and those which arose over D. D Home in the 1870s. The introduction of such modern aids as movie cameras and video recorders made no difference to the fundamental issues at stake; those who were temperamentally unable to believe in the paranormal remained sceptical, no matter how 'scientific' the evidence. The moral of the story is clear: there is no such thing as a perfect experiment, for it is always possible to find alternative, non-paranormal, explanations of whatever phenomena are observed. As a last resort, the sceptic can always argue that the entire proceedings were 'rigged' by one or more of the participants acting in collusion.

The first of the new stars to appear in the psychic firmament was Ted Serios, an erstwhile lift attendant in a Chicago hotel. During some *ad hoc* experiments on hypnosis it was discovered that Serios had the ability to cause pictures of unidentified places and scenes to appear on camera film. From then onwards, Serios gave demonstrations of 'psychic photography' to various individuals and groups in the Chicago area. Eventually, his talents came to the attention of Dr. Jule Eisenbud, a psychiatrist from Denver, Colorado, who carried out experiments with Serios for several years. Eisenbud was totally convinced that the Serios photographs were paranormal, and he published the results of his investigations in several technical papers and one popular book.[44] Other scientists who studied Serios were not so completely convinced, although no one discovered any evidence of fraud.[168] The procedures used by Serios varied, but in most cases the experimenter was invited to bring his own Polaroid camera (marked for identification if required) and point it at Serios with the lens focused at infinity. At a signal from the medium, the shutter was opened for the equivalent of 1/30th of a second at f11. The advantage of using a Polaroid camera was that the picture developed immediately, giving no opportunities for fraudulent manipulation in the darkroom. Between May 1964 and June 1967 over 400 apparently inexplicable images appeared on film exposed in this way, usually pictures of objects or buildings from unusual angles. Sometimes the film went completely black or white, with no discernable image at all; these 'blackies' and 'whities' were equally difficult to explain in terms of normal optics.

Paranormal photography was not exactly a new phenomenon. From the very earliest days of photography in the 1850s, there had been people who claimed that inexplicable images appeared from time to time on their negatives. During the hey-day of Spiritualism these 'extras' often took the form of human faces which were said to be likenesses of deceased persons, and at one time there were many studios specialising in 'spirit photography'. There can be no doubt whatever that many, if not all, of these spirit photographers were fraudulent, and some were successfully prosecuted in the courts. Along with other forms of physical mediumship, spirit photography declined sharply during the 1930s, and little has been heard about it since. In a pamphlet issued by the SPR in 1965, Simeon Edmunds attributed the decline in spirit photography to the fact that modern photographic technology has made the photographs harder to fake without detection, and he summed up the matter thus:

'Every spirit photographer who has been thoroughly and competently investigated has been proved fraudulent. No reliable record appears to exist of a definitely recognised spirit extra being obtained on any photograph under completely fraud-proof conditions... Therefore, while it cannot be proved that spirit photography is impossible, there appears to be no real evidence to warrant rational belief in such a phenomenon.'[43]

However, 'spirits' were not the only things that appeared on photographs. In the early years of this century a Japanese investigator, Tomokichi Fukurai, was experimenting with a clairvoyant when he discovered, apparently by accident, that she could imprint letters upon film. Fukurai called this ability 'thoughtography', and carried out many experiments which, in his view, demonstrated the reality of the phenomenon beyond reasonable doubt. For daring to publish such results Fukurai was maliciously abused and forced to resign his professorship at Toyko University; nevertheless he continued with the research and a full account of his work was published in English in 1931.[52]

When Ted Serios burst upon an astonished world in the 1960s, psychic photography was thought to have been dead and buried for the past 30 years. Psychical researchers greeted its renaissance with the gravest suspicion, and a somewhat sceptical, and in places sarcastic, review of Dr Eisenbud's book appeared in the SPR *Journal*. 'As to Ted Serios' strange "world",' wrote the reviewer, Colin Brookes-Smith, 'well it's certainly interesting – like toothache.'[18] Unhappily for the sceptics, the psychic photography of Serios proved to be more resistant to treatment than most forms of toothache. The attention of the critics naturally focused upon the 'gismo', a curious device consisting of a cardboard tube of about one inch in diameter and rather more than an inch in length. In many of his sessions Ted held the gismo in front of the camera lens, gripping it between his finger and thumb. Apparently this extraordinary practice in some way helped him to focus his thoughts upon the film. Although it was frequently examined before, during and after shooting, no image-forming devices were ever found inside the gismo. In some experiments the ends of it were taped over with black sticky-tape, but inexplicable pictures were still produced. Professor Rushton showed that it was possible to simulate Serios-photos by means of a piece of microfilm glued onto a prism attached to a small lens;[149] however, in all the hundreds of experiments carried out with Ted, no such device was ever discovered. More important, there were quite a number of occasions when such a gadget could not possibly have been employed, for example, when Ted was separated from the camera by distance or screening. On one occasion inexplicable pictures were obtained with Ted inside an electrically screened room (a 'Faraday cage') and the camera some inches outside it. There were also experiments in which Ted influenced a photoelectric cell and a video-camera from a distance.

Practically everybody who investigated Ted Serios was on the lookout for trickery, and it is remarkable that no one ever discovered a sign of it. In spite of their natural suspicions, some psychical researchers eventually became convinced that the phenomena were genuine (cf. Beloff[11]). Others preferred to suspend judgment. Meanwhile, astonishing rumours were beginning to circulate about the alleged psychokinetic ability of a middle-aged housewife living on the opposite side of the world. In June, 1968, western scientists attending a parapsychological conference in Moscow were shown a film in which Nina Kulagina caused various small objects to move without touching them. Later, copies of the film were brought back to the west for scrutiny, and several scientists were permitted to go to Russia and see the phenomena for themselves. Although they did not conduct any experiments under controlled laboratory conditions, what they saw was sufficient to convince several of the westerners that Nina had genuine PK ability.[95]

Nina Sergeyevna Kulagina was born in 1927, and by all accounts had a fairly rough upbringing. She was only fourteen when the Germans invaded her country, and although no more than a girl, she served as the radio operator of a tank during the siege of Leningrad. Having fought bravely for her country, she was eventually removed from the fighting when she sustained serious injuries during an artillery bombardment. As far as is known, she had no intimation of her paranormal abilities until the early 1960s, when she discovered that she could pick out the correctly coloured threads for embroidery without looking at them. At that time Russian scientists were investigating the curious phenomenon of 'fingertip sight' or dermo-optic vision, and the principal exponent of the faculty was a twenty-two year old woman known as Rosa Kuleshova. Nina Kulagina read about these experiments in a newspaper, and came to believe that she also possessed dermo-optic ability. She contacted Dr Leonid Vasiliev, who was a physiologist and psychical researcher of some repute, and offered herself as an experimental subject. It was in the course of Vasiliev's experiments that Nina's exceptional PK powers were discovered, although she may have had some inkling of them beforehand.[112,119]

The researchers found that Nina could produce quite a wide range of phenomena. Sometimes small objects such as cigarettes or matches would glide across the table-top towards or away from her; sometimes these objects would perform circling or jumping movements. She seemed to find it relatively easy to move tall thin objects standing on end, such as cigar containers made from a non-magnetic material. The experimenters were rather surprised to see cigarettes balanced on their ends gliding appreciable distances without falling over; attempts to simulate this effect by inserting a steel pin into the cigarette and using a concealed magnet were unsuccessful. Sometimes the objects moved were in the open, but on occasions Nina was successful in moving objects enclosed underneath glass or plexiglass covers. She was also able to set a compass needle rotating, start and stop a pendulum, and alter the beat of a disembodied frog's heart. One of her investigators, G. I. Sergeyev, reported that she was able to impress simple patterns upon photographic film, but the western observers were not able to confirm this effect.

Several experimenters reported feeling a sensation of great heat, even to the point of being painful, when Nina Kulagina placed her hand upon their forearms. Mr Manfred Cassirer of the London SPR and Dr Jurgen Keil of the University of

Tasmania both described this sensation; Mr Benson Herbert of the Paraphysical Laboratory and Dr Jarl Fahler of the Finnish SPR actually developed burn marks after being touched by Nina, and these marks were said to be visible for several hours afterwards.[95] These observations raise the interesting question of whether there is any connection between physical mediumship and those gruesome cases of spontaneous human combustion which have been described and collected by Michael Harrison.[75] Sensations of heat are also not uncommon in cases of psychic or 'faith' healing, so that there may be a further connection here. Unfortunately, it is rather difficult to separate purely physical effects from those which are psychologically caused, for the mind can mimic a great range of physical sensations and diseases. Although Dr Fahler experienced a feeling of heat when touched by Kulagina, a thermometer placed on his skin showed no rise in temperature, suggesting that the sensation may have been a purely subjective one. It is known that powerful suggestions can even raise blisters on the skin of sensitive subjects.

There is a tendency for those of us who live in democratic societies to imagine that totalitarian governments are necessarily more efficient than our own, although the facts often indicate just the reverse. After Nina Kulagina had become known to the west, a number of sensational articles and books appeared claiming that the Russians were years ahead of us in parapsychological research. Stories were circulated about mysterious government-funded laboratories behind the Iron Curtain, where incredible breakthroughs were taking place. Russians were supposed to be communicating telepathically with their nuclear submarines, and developing psychokinetic techniques for guiding and detonating inter-continental missiles! It is, of course, impossible to prove that such stories are false, but there is no real evidence to support them. What little we do know about parapsychology in the communist countries suggests that it is a minority interest, generally distrusted by the official organisations. Some Russian parapsychologists, such as Eduard Naumov, have suffered persecution because of their involvement with psi research and with western researchers.

One of the characteristic features of very powerfully gifted mediums is that they seem to be able to pass on their gifts to others, at least for a short time. Thus, Lord Adare recounted how, in the presence of D. D. Home, he found himself able to suspend a book in mid-air with only his right hand placed flat upon the top cover.[41] One who certainly 'caught' the psychic infection from Nina Kulagina (although she never met her) was Felicia Parise, a laboratory technician at the Maimonides Medical Centre in New York. Felicia had been a participant in some of the famous telepathy experiments which had been carried out in the Maimonides Dream Laboratory. She was present on one occasion when the laboratory staff were viewing the film which had been brought back from Russia, showing the exploits of Madame Kulagina. With true American patriotism, Felicia decided that what the Russian lady could do, she could do also! She went home and practised steadily for several months. For a long time nothing happened; then one day she had her first definite intimation of success when a small plastic bottle on which she had been concentrating moved a few centimetres. Encouraged by this, Felicia continued to practise, and submitted herself for examination by expert parapsychologists. A ciné film was made in order to record the phenomena, and a non-professional magician, N. Moses, certified that they were authentic.[95] Among the parapsychologists who examined Felicia were Dr Montague Ullman, President of the American SPR, Dr J. G. Pratt of the University of Virginia, and Mr Charles Honorton of the Maimonides Medical Centre. Although most of her demonstrations took place in her own home, Felicia was also tested under laboratory conditions by Graham and Anita Watkins.[86] She eventually discontinued the experiments because she found that she could not maintain her success rate without constant practice, and the effort to do so was both exhausting and time-consuming. However, she had at least shown that directly observable PK was not a prerogative of the Russians.

The New York artist Ingo Swann has been described as 'a large man, good-humoured, and extremely thoughtful and articulate'.[174] This is rather an unusual description for a psychic, many of whom tend to be unpredictable, temperamental and over-emotional. In his autobiography, Swann tells us that he had his first psychic experiences at the age of about four, following the traumatic experience of a tonsillectomy.[171] His PK abilities began to receive attention in the early 1970s, when Dr Gertrude Schmeidler of the City College of New York performed some ingenious experiments with him.[154] Three thermistors were set up in different parts of the laboratory and connected to a polygraph chartrecorder. One thermistor was designated as the 'target', and Swann was instructed on each trial to try to make the target thermistor either hotter or colder, according to a prearranged schedule. To make the task harder, the target thermistor was enclosed in a thermos flask and placed twenty-five feet away from the subject. Although the temperature changes which occurred were not dramatic (usually only a degree or so), statistical analysis showed that they were correlated with the target instructions to such an extent that they were unlikely to have occurred by chance. The analysis also suggested that the PK effect operated by increasing the temperature at one location and reducing it at another. Later, Schmeidler reported the results of a similar experiment, this time using 22 volunteer subjects.[155] This also produced some significant results, although it was not as successful as the Swann series. Schmeidler's research attracted much attention from parapsychologists, some of whom tried to repeat it, without success. Dr Brian Millar of Edinburgh University wrote a critique of the work, arguing that Schmeidler's use of vacuum flasks could have introduced thermal fluctuations which would simulate the alleged PK effects.[109]

Even if it could be confirmed, Swann's ability to influence temperature would not be new to psychical research. In the nineteenth century it was reported that D. D. Home was able to alter the reading of a thermometer by six degrees, and in this century the Danish medium Anna Rasmussen was said to possess the same ability. Cold breezes were frequently observed at séances in the early days of the Spiritualist movement, and temperature changes were occasionally recorded instrumentally. However, Swann could influence other things beside temperature, as was seen when he visited the Stanford Research Institute at Menlo Park, California.[120] He arrived there in June, 1972, to take part in a week of parapsychological experimentation under the direction of Drs Russell Targ and Harold Puthoff, two young physicists with an interest in the paranormal. At that time the Institute possessed a superconducting magnetometer, a complex piece of equipment capable of monitoring very weak magnetic fields. It was part of an apparatus which was being used by Dr Arthur Hebard to try to detect quarks, the particles which theoretical physicists thought might be the building blocks from which protons and neutrons are formed. The sensitive magnetic probe was located in a vault under the building; it was shielded by a magnetic shield made of mu-metal, an aluminimum container, some copper screening, and a superconducting niobium shield. Inside the apparatus a decaying magnetic field had been set up in such a way that it produced an oscillating signal on a pen recorder. Swann was confronted with this equipment, which he had never seen before, and invited to try to alter the magnetic field inside the apparatus by means of PK.

'Ingo looked somewhat shocked and dismayed to find that he was supposed to affect a small magnetic probe located in a vault below the floor of the building and shielded by a mu-metal magnetic shield, an aluminium container, copper shielding, and most important, a superconducting shield, the best kind of shield known' wrote Hal Puthoff.[174] However, Ingo focused his attention on the inside of the magnetometer and, after about a five second delay, the frequency of the oscillation increased to twice its former value, much to the astonishment of Dr Hebard. This meant that the magnetic field inside the vault was decaying at twice the expected rate. Hebard then suggested that Swann should try to stop the field change altogether. No sooner had he said this than the pen on the recorder ceased oscillating for a period of about forty-five seconds, after which Swann said he couldn't hold it any longer, and the trace returned to normal. Later, Swann told the experimenters that he had produced the effect by visualising the inside of the apparatus (which he had never seen), and he proceeded to give them a quite accurate account of the interior. Once again, it seems, ESP and PK had been shown to operate together, as different aspects of a single paranormal process.

It is no exaggeration to say that the publication of these and similar results completely altered the outlook of parapsychology during the seventies. Serios, Kulagina, Parise, Swann and others brought directly observable PK effects back into the focus of attention, and stimulated the re-examination of some of the earlier accounts. After all, if these things could happen now, in a world surrounded with all the paraphernalia of modern science, was there any reason to suppose that they could not have happened all those years ago? Psychical researchers with a penchant for the historical approach began to look again at the numerous reports which were gathering dust on their library shelves. Thus, George Zorab uncovered some new evidence which greatly strengthened the case for believing in the authenticity of D. D. Home's phenomena,[193] Anita Gregory produced a very thorough and scholarly re-examination of the mediumship of Rudi Schneider,[63] and the spiritualistic researches of Sir William Crookes were re-published with a new and up-to-date commentary.[106]

There was even a renewal of interest in the old Victorian pastime of table-tilting, although now it was stripped of its spiritualistic overtones. An English psychologist, Ken Batcheldor, believed that the raps and table movements described by so many of the early Spiritualists were due to a kind of collective PK effect produced by the sitters. As he saw it, the production of the effect depended upon the establishment of just the right psychological atmosphere within the group. In 1964 he began a series of experiments using groups of ordinary people, none of whom claimed to be 'mediumistic', and obtained what appeared to be genuine levitations of the table.[7] Batcheldor's methods were adopted by other experimenters, and in the early 1970s Colin Brookes-Smith performed an important series of experiments in which he used special tables incorporating strain gauges. These devices enabled him to record the movements of the table on datatape, and thus to discriminate between movements brought about by unconscious muscular action and those produced by PK.[19] Another important experiment was conducted at about the same time by Iris Owen and a group of psychical researchers in Toronto; they decided to 'conjure up' an imaginary ghost whom they called Philip. They invented a detailed life story for this non-existent character, and spent many hours discussing him and meditating. Eventually they obtained raps, table-levitations, and 'messages' from Philip, who seemed to take on a life of his own! These researches throw an important light upon the whole field of spiritualistic phenomena, and bring into sharp focus the difficult problem of deciding what is the exact origin of alleged communications from the dead.

The revival of interest in large-scale PK extended to those phenomena which occur spontaneously, as well as to those which occur under experimental or semi-experimental conditions. That age-old phenomenon known as the poltergeist came under renewed scrutiny, and was given a brand new scientific-sounding name: Recurrent Spontaneous Psychokinesis (or RSPK for short). Several excellent and scholarly works on poltergeists were published during the 60s and 70s, incorporating accounts of recent outbreaks as well as those from the past.[58,148,121] Gradually the findings of numerous investigators and experimenters, spread over a century or more, began to cohere into a substantial body of knowledge, the pieces of evidence supporting one another like the stones of an arch. It looked as though psychical research was at last beginning to develop into something which could truly be called a science.

Then, in the midst of all this renewed activity a new type of paranormal phenomenon appeared on the scene. In 1971 a New York parapsychologist, Dr Andrija Puharich, went to Israel to investigate the activities of a young man called Uri Geller, who was supposed to have the ability to bend pieces of metal merely by stroking them. Geller was also reputed to be able to read concealed messages and re-start broken clocks and watches. Puharich was quite impressed with what he saw, and in 1972 Geller was invited to the United States for further testing. There he gave demonstrations to various scientists, including the former astronaut Edgar Mitchell, and Drs Puthoff and Targ of the Stanford Research Institute. During October of the same year Geller visited London, where he demonstrated his abilities to Dr Ted Bastin, a Cambridge physicist who specialises in the quantum theory.

The young metal-bender made a sensational entrance into the British consciousness on November 23rd, 1973, when he appeared on BBC television in the *Dimbleby Talk-In* programme. Also present on the programme were Lyall Watson, a biologist and freelance writer, and John Taylor, Professor of Mathematics at King's College, London. The two scientists were mystified and somewhat shaken by what they saw. John Taylor appearing to be particularly overwhelmed. 'I felt as if the whole framework with which I viewed the world had suddenly been destroyed,' he later declared, 'I seemed very naked and vulnerable, surrounded by a hostile, incomprehensible universe.' After the programme he announced his intention of making a scientific study of the metal-bending phenomenon. His opportunity to do so came during the following year when, in the course of several visits to London, Geller performed for Taylor at King's College and also for Professor Hasted and his colleagues at Birkbeck College. Both groups of scientists were convinced that the phenomena were genuine. Taylor issued a statement which appeared on the title page of Uri's autobiography in 1975:

'I have tested Uri Geller in my laboratory at King's College, London University, with specially-designed apparatus.

The Geller effect – of metal bending – is clearly not brought about by fraud. It is so exceptional that it represents a crucial challenge to modern science, and could even destroy the latter if no explanation becomes available.'

The year 1974 was the time when Geller's popularity reached its peak. During that year he travelled all over the world, performing before teams of scientists in Britain, Denmark, the USA and Canada. A vast literature on the 'Geller effect' began to grow up, consisting not only of articles in popular magazines but also including some technical and scientific papers. However, Geller's success provoked an inevitable reaction, and 1974 was also the year in which the opposition to his wonder-working feats began to gather momentum. The principal antagonist was James Randi, a professional conjurer with considerable determination and a personality which was hardly less flamboyant than that of Geller himself. Randi set out systematically to demolish Geller's reputation, and poured scorn upon those other magicians and scientists who had become convinced of the reality of the metal-bending phenomenon. Randi's book *The Magic of Uri Geller* was published in November, 1975, and it was described by Colin Wilson as 'one of the unkindest books written by one celebrity about another'. Had it been an impartial assessment, the book might have made a greater impact than it did; however, it was so obviously biased that few psychical researchers could take it seriously. Many of the 'facts' published in the book were inaccurate, and in places Randi descended to cheap mockery of scientists such as Taylor, Targ, Puthoff, Honorton, and Krippner, all of whom had committed the unforgiveable sin of taking the Geller phenomenon seriously.[140]

The highly respectable scientific journal *Nature* seldom publishes reports on parapsychological research, so that something of a sensation was caused on October 18th, 1974, when it carried a paper by Puthoff and Targ of the Stanford Research Institute.[173] The two physicists did not report any metal-bending effects because they felt that their experiments in that field had not been sufficiently conclusive; however, they *did* report some very striking long-distance telepathy with Geller, Pat Price and other subjects. Unfortunately, standards of professional conduct and scientific ethics seem to count for little so far as the opponents of parapsychology are concerned, and the Targ-Puthoff paper was under attack even before it was published. The editor of *Nature* himself broke the rules by prefacing the paper with an editorial of his own in which he questioned the validity of the experiments and quoted some of the comments made by the paper's referees. This was strictly contrary to normal procedures, and many parapsychologists felt that it was highly unethical. Usually when a paper is sent to a scientific journal it is given to several anonymous referees, who are acknowledged experts in the field. The referees read the paper, and advise the editor on whether it is suitable for publication or not. Once a paper has been passed for publication, it is usually printed without further comment. I know of no other instance where an editor has accepted a paper for publication, and then prefaced it with a critique of his own.

Even more obviously out of the 'dirty-tricks' department were the tactics of the weekly magazine *New Scientist*. They were annoyed with Geller because he had cancelled an appointment to appear before a committee of scientists chosen by the magazine. According to Geller's manager, the cancellation was made because threats had been received from an anti-Jewish organisation, and it was felt that Geller's life was in danger. *New Scientist* thereupon appointed Dr Joseph

Hanlon, its Technology Policy Editor, to do a 'hatchet job' on Geller. In a fifteen-page article Hanlon attacked Geller and his supporters, describing various ways in which he thought the tricks could have been performed. The article contained full details of the Targ-Puthoff report, not due to be published in *Nature* until the following day, and also details of a confidential report by the Birkbeck College team which had somehow been 'leaked' to Hanlon. Professor Hasted, the leader of the Birkbeck investigators, later wrote a bitter letter to the editor, pointing out that his report had not been intended for publication, and that he had had no proper communication with Dr Hanlon. He also questioned whether a popular science magazine should take the initiative in setting up an enquiry of this kind.[69,77]

The Uri Geller story is a long and complex one which could only be adequately described in a full-length book. Nowadays it is customary for parapsychologists to bewail the fact that Geller will no longer perform for scientists; 'Geller has shown little interest in research', writes Dr Joseph Rush, 'preferring the role of public showman.'[98] This is a little unfair. In the years between 1972 and 1978 Geller was tested in at least 17 laboratories in eight different countries, so it can hardly be said that he has been unwilling to submit himself to scientific investigation. Furthermore, most of the scientists who experimented with him became convinced that he had abilities which could not be accommodated within the framework of present-day science. There is no doubt that Geller has sometimes used conjuring tricks in his public performances – indeed, he has openly admitted to having done so. The question is not whether Geller can perform conjuring tricks, but whether he has ever done anything which can be regarded as paranormal. Despite what Randi and other sceptics may say to the contrary, there is a considerable body of evidence which indicates that he has. Much of this evidence has been collected into a single volume by Dr Charles Panati,[124] and this is an important source-book for anyone who wishes to study the Geller phenomenon in depth. In this book it is possible to give no more than a mere sample of the vast mass of evidence available.

One of the best pieces of evidence for the paranormality of the Geller effect comes from the use of a metal known as 'nitinol'. This is an alloy of nickel and titanium which was developed during the 1960s by William J. Buehler of the U. S. Naval Ordnance Laboratory (since renamed the Naval Surface Weapons Centre) in Silver Spring, Maryland.[20] It has the remarkable property of 'remembering' a particular shape which has been impressed upon it at high temperatures. Suppose we take a piece of nitinol wire, bend it to a desired shape (say, a wave-form) and, while it is held in that shape, heat it to about 500° centigrade. After cooling the wire may be bent or twisted into any other configuration we wish, but as soon as it is placed in hot water (about 80°C) it will begin to return to the wave-shape which it received during the initial heat treatment. Nitinol has found a number of useful applications in industry and medicine. For example, it has been used to make the antennae of satellites. When the satellite reaches its position in orbit, the heat of the sun causes the nitinol antenna to unfold and blossom like a flower.[153]

In October, 1973, Dr Eldon Byrd of the Naval Surface Weapons Centre set out to see what effect Uri Geller might have upon nitinol. Byrd took a piece of nitinol wire about 5 inches long and 0.5 mm diameter and held it tautly between the index fingers and thumbs of both hands, taking care to keep it very straight. Geller put his thumb and index finger over the wire and rubbed it for about twenty seconds. When he removed his hand, the wire was seen to have a definite kink in it:

Byrd then placed the wire in boiling water, expecting that it would snap back sharply to its original straight configuration (this particular wire had been heat-treated to give it a 'memory' of straightness). However, instead of behaving as expected, the wire bent into a right angle. Byrd lit a match and held it over the kink, but the wire still refused to straighten. Geller had apparently altered its 'memory', a feat which normally would have required a temperature of several hundred degrees.

After Geller had gone, Byrd had an X-ray crystallographic analysis made of the wire, and found that the crystal sizes in the kinked section seemed to have increased slightly. He also submitted the kinked wire to several metallurgists at the Naval Surface Weapons Centre who tried to remove the kink by heating the wire with an electric current while it was under tension in a vacuum chamber. The wire was taken up to red heat until it became straight; however, as it cooled down to room temperature, the kink spontaneously returned. Not only had Geller altered the 'memory' of the wire, *he had impressed upon it a new 'memory' which the experts found themselves unable to remove*. Furthermore, attempts made by Byrd and others to simulate this effect by treating pieces of nitinol wire with heat and chemicals failed completely. The permanent kinking of the wire appeared to be a paranormal effect which could not be obtained in any other way. Later, Byrd carried out further nitinol experiments with Geller which confirmed his original observations. Whatever the sceptics may say, there seems to be no way of accounting for these very clear-cut laboratory results in terms of known scientific principles. Dr Byrd concluded his report with the words: 'Neither I nor other experts can offer any scientific explanation of how these deformations may have occurred under the conditions imposed.' His paper was issued with the official approval of the Naval Surface Weapons Centre, after it had been checked for technical accuracy, quality, and editorial competence, compliance with security regulations and professional ethics.

As it happened, I was able to observe an almost perfect replication of Dr Byrd's results during June, 1977, in the science laboratories at Leamington College. In conjunction with the chief technician, Mr Peter Davis, I had been conducting some experiments with a 13-year-old boy, Mark Briscoe, who claimed to be able to perform Geller-type feats with metal objects. We took a piece of 55-nitinol wire which had been previously given a straight 'memory', and taped one end firmly to a sheet of cardboard. Mr Davis then photographed the wire, which was lying quite flat upon the cardboard. Mark then proceeded to stroke the wire with his finger for about 10 minutes, watched carefully by both experimenters. We saw the wire begin to bend upwards and, much to our surprise, the greatest bending occurred *beyond* the point where the stroking was taking place. Eventually the wire assumed an S-shaped configuration, rearing up above the cardboard sheet like a snake about to strike. We removed the wire from the cardboard and attempted to straighten it by heating it under tension with an electric current. We found that at red heat and with sufficient tension it was possible to get the wire almost straight again, but as soon as the current was switched off, it returned to the kinked form. Four days later we tried once again to straighten the wire, but it still refused to be straightened, even when heated to about 600°C. Eventually it snapped, leaving us with two pieces of wire which were still not straight!

On January 19th, 1974, the *Daily Express* carried an attack on Geller by the journalist Don Coolican, who stated that he could repeat all of Geller's allegedly paranormal feats after only one lesson from Professor Kelson of Tel Aviv University. Professor Kelson is an expert on conjuring techniques. At the time when he wrote the article, Coolican had not actually met Geller, but later he flew to Copenhagen, intending to expose the wonder-worker in a face-to-face confrontation. He took with him a photographer, Harry Dempster, and a journalist colleague, Andrew Fyall. Geller was thoroughly searched, his pockets emptied, and his sleeves rolled up above the elbows. His hands and arms were then thoroughly scrubbed, in case he had any chemicals on his skin. Fyall and Dempster kept close watch to ensure that there were no distractions. Coolican then selected a heavy key which he had brought with him, and asked Geller to make it bend without it leaving the journalist's hand. Coolican kept a tight grip on the key while Geller lightly touched the tip of it. After about twenty seconds the key bent in Coolican's hand, and *continued to bend after Geller moved several feet away*. The key was then sealed in a thick envelope and placed in Coolican's pocket, but it still went on bending. Coolican said that he could feel the movement caused by the key's bending, even through the envelope, On January 25th the *Daily Express* published a complete retraction of Coolican's original opinions.

The laboratory work of W. E. Cox has been mentioned in previous chapters. Not only is Cox an experienced researcher of many years' standing, he is also a semi-professional magician and an associate of the Society of American Magicians. On April 24th, 1974, he approached Uri Geller in a very critical frame of mind, having come prepared with various pieces of equipment. Geller was shown a flat steel key of the safety-deposit box type, much too hard to be bent by hand. The key was placed on a glass-topped coffee table and lightly stroked by Geller, using his right forefinger. Cox kept his own forefinger on the wider end of the key, and watched the proceedings carefully, using a small mirror which he held in his left hand under the edge of the table. The key bent upwards through an angle of 12¼ degrees, although Cox detected no signs of trickery. Later he handed Geller a Hamilton pocket watch and asked him to try to get it going. Cox had previously tampered with the watch by setting the regulator arm at F (fast) and inserting a piece of bent aluminium foil so that it impeded the movements of the balance-wheel. Geller knew nothing about the foil, but Cox told him that he had fixed the watch so that it would not work. After holding the watch to his ear and shaking it slightly, Geller cried 'It's ticking, it's ticking!' Cox then immediately opened the two back covers of the watch (the second cover was extremely tight and could only be opened with difficulty). He found that the aluminium foil had been severed and had moved out of the balance-wheel, while the regulator arm had moved a total of 40°, its extreme limit. Cox added 'I have failed to conceive of any means of deception in these tests, nor have other magicians whom I have consulted'.[28]

In view of the cumulative evidence from experimenters such as Targ, Puthoff, Byrd and Cox, it is extremely unlikely that all of Geller's phenomena were due to fraud. However, even if that were the case, it would make very little difference to parapsychology, for the 'Geller effect' has long since outgrown Geller. At the time when Geller exploded onto the television screens of Europe and America, thousands of people began writing to the television companies and to the newspapers claiming that metallic objects were bending in their own homes. Usually these events occurred while the family was actually watching Geller on the TV screen, although sometimes they happened an hour or two later. In January, 1974, the German newspaper *Bild* invited its readers to places pieces of cutlery and broken clocks or watches on a copy of *Bild* at a certain time when Geller was to concentrate on these objects. No less than 2,550 reports of allegedly paranormal events were received as a result! The reports were made available to the veteran parapsychologist Dr Hans Bender, who is renowned for his work on poltergeists and similar phenomena. Bender and his co-workers selected 80 of the reports for detailed study, and published their conclusions in the *Zeitschrift für Parapsychologie*.[14] At about the same time an English teenager, Matthew Manning, discovered that he too could produce Geller-type effects on metal. At the age of eleven Matthew had been the victim of poltergeist attacks which at one time threatened to ruin his school career. Later, he found that he could produce a wide variety of paranormal phenomena, including automatic writing and drawing. His metal-bending ability was examined by Dr George Owen of the New Horizons Institute in Toronto, and Dr J. L. Whitton, consultant psychiatrist at the Toronto Hospital. Whitton studied the electrical rhythms of Matthew's brain using an electroencephalograph. He reported the existence of an unusual electrical pattern, which he called a 'ramp function', which occurred while Matthew was producing PK effects on metal.[104]

Towards the end of 1975 another metal-bending star appeared, this time in France, Jean-Pierre Girard came forward in response to an appeal for persons who thought they might have Geller-like powers to submit themselves for scientific investigation. Girard made no secret of the fact that he was a trained conjurer, but claimed that he could also produce genuinely paranormal effects. He was investigated by Charles Crussard, metallurgist and research director of the Péchiney Company, which is one of the largest private companies in France. After an intensive investigation, Crussard produced a preliminary report on 116 experiments in which Girard had caused inexplicable deformations of metallic objects, including the bending of a stainless steel bar enclosed inside a glass tube. There was also evidence that Girard had somehow altered the configuration of the atoms of which the stainless steel was composed, converting it from the form known as austenite to the form known as martensite. This shift in atomic configuration is reminiscent of Geller's effect upon nitinol. Unless one is prepared to accuse Crussard of lying, it is an inescapable conclusion that Girard did, on some occasions, manifest a genuine and quite dramatic PK effect.[29]

In order to eliminate the possibility that Girard was using conjuring techniques, Crussard enlisted the help of an expert conjurer known as 'Ranky'. Ranky was a member of the executive committee of the French Magic Circle and a specialist in the production of pseudo-psychic effects; yet neither Ranky nor anyone else was able to detect any signs of cheating by Girard. In his own report Ranky wrote: 'In my capacity as an illusionist I am able to assert that I can think of no trick which could have been used by Girard to deceive under the protocol which was imposed upon him.'[141]

Crussard submitted a carefully written paper on his experiments to Nature, but once again that journal showed that it had no intention of treating parapsychological work with the impartiality expected in other fields of science. Instead of subjecting the Crussard paper to the usual refereeing procedures, the journal decided to launch its own investigation. In May, 1977, editor David Davies flew to Grenoble accompanied by Dr Chris Evans, a well-known arch-sceptic and author of several articles attacking parapsychology. Surprisingly enough, Girard succeeded in producing a few PK effects even under the watchful eyes of these two, and Evans seems to have been impressed in spite of himself. 'Girard is quite the best I have ever seen', he wrote; 'if this was fraud, it was very clever – not the sort of thing Geller or I can do.'[70] To admit the reality of PK was, of course, anathema to these men, but they had seen things which were clearly inexplicable in terms of the known laws of nature. What should they do? They decided to send for James Randi, whose fanatical opposition to the entire concept of the paranormal would, no doubt, bolster up their own crumbling disbelief. Three weeks later Davies and Evans returned to Grenoble accompanied by the powerful figure of Randi, and insisted on a further demonstration. For three hours Girard tried valiantly to produce a PK effect under the hostile stare of Randi; not surprisingly, he failed to do so. Needless to say, the Crussard paper was never published.

Fortunately, Professor Bender does not need to get his reports into Nature; he has the good fortune to work for a parapsychological institute which publishes its own journal. In 1976 Bender and Vandrey published an account of their metal-bending experiments with a 35-year old Swiss artist and graphic designer known as Silvio Mayer.[13] Their attention had been drawn to Silvio by a magician, Rolf Mayr, who had tested him and failed to catch him out in any fraudulent manipulations. The Freiburg researchers were able to obtain permanent records on film and videotape of apparently paranormal deformations of metallic and plastic objects. Physicists from Berne and Munich were brought in to assist in the experiments, and they found that Silvio was also able to alter the current flow through an electrical resistance. None of the experimenters found any evidence of cheating.

Ever since the earliest days of psychical research it has been known that children and adolescents often make good subjects for experimental work, possibly because they tend to be less inhibited and are more spontaneously enthusiastic than adults. The association of poltergeist phenomena with the presence of an emotionally disturbed adolescent is well known, and in the early days of the spiritualist movement there were innumerable child-mediums plying their trade. Children have also proved to be effective as metal-benders, and since 1975 Professor Hasted and his co-workers at Birkbeck College have made many detailed studies of their abilities in this respect.[78,79,80,81] Following the Geller experiments, Hasted appeared on London television and appealed for children who thought they might possess metal-bending ability to come forward for testing. Since then he has discovered several who have turned out to be excellent PK subjects. Hasted arranged for a number of metal objects, usually latch-keys, to be suspended from the ceiling at varying distances from the subject. Embedded in each key was a resistive strain gauge which was wired up to an amplifier and a pen-recorder. The subject was told to try to make the keys bend without touching them; any slight deformation of a key would be automatically recorded by the instrumentation, even though it might not be large enough to generate a visible bend. In fact, macroscopic bends of the kind produced by Geller and Girard were not all that common, but Hasted was able to show that slight deformations occurred quite frequently, often happening simultaneously in several of the specimens. He has demonstrated the probable existence of what he calls a 'surface of action', which seems to extend outwards from the subject. Metal objects which happen to come into contact with this invisible surface experience paranormal bending forces, although the resulting deformations may not be sufficiently large to be visible to the naked eye.

It is something of a relief to be able to turn away from the endless publicity, the arguments, challenges and counter-challenges generated by the Geller phenomenon to study the cool scientific reports of Hasted and his colleagues. While others have expended much hot air and not a little printer's ink arguing about whether PK is *possible*, the Birkbeck team have got on quietly with the task of finding out something about it, using the only procedures which are likely to advance our knowledge. These are the techniques of experimental science. Looking back over the past decade, one cannot avoid a feeling of astonishment at the extent to which physical phenomena (and physicists) have returned to occupy a central position in psychical research. It does not seem to be all that long ago since parapsychologists were bewailing the shortage of good PK subjects; now we seem to have almost an *embarras de richesse!* One can only hope that the knowledge so painstakingly gleaned by the present-day researchers will not be laid aside and forgotten, as happened to the efforts of their predecessors in the nineteenth century.

13   PK in Everyday Life?

'Five senses; an incurably abstract intellect; a haphazardly selective memory; a set of preconceptions and assumptions so numerous that I can never examine more than a minority of them – never become even conscious of them all. How much of total reality can such an apparatus let through?'

C. S. Lewis, *A Grief Observed*.

So far we have been considering various kinds of PK phenomena which are supposed to have occurred in the presence of certain special people known as 'mediums' or 'psychics'. In most cases the phenomena have been observed in either a séance-room or a laboratory. The question now arises: assuming that such a power as PK really exists, why do we not see more evidence of it in everyday life? For example, if the human mind can really alter the odds in favour of certain numbers occurring during a dice game, why are such vast sums of money lost through gambling, and why do the owners of casinos invariably end up as extremely rich men? Surely, the sceptic will argue, however strong the laboratory evidence for PK and other paranormal faculties may be, it is belied by our ordinary, everyday experience of life.

However, it is quite possible that PK does operate in everyday situations, but that in most instances we fail to recognise it as such. For example, Michael Harrison gives an interesting description of a visit he once paid to the theatre, where he saw a performance by the great ballet-dancer Vaslav Nijinsky. The famous Russian seemed to have an uncanny ability to control the descents which followed his amazing leaps into the air:

'For it was not as Nijinsky leapt up that one saw the oddity – he was so obviously a strong man that "superhuman" leaps hardly astonished. It was as he came down – "like a gull landing", said Uncle – that one saw the strangeness: only in dreams could one have realised the possibility of controlling one's *fall*.'

Of course, there may have been an element of optical illusion in this experience, but it is also possible that PK was involved, although there is no way in which we can be certain. The passage provokes the interesting reflection that we simply do not know how many skilled activities actually incorporate a psi component. When one watches a skilled darts player, for instance, it is noticeable that he follows the flight of the dart with his eyes and body movements *as though* he were actually guiding it through the air. Of course, according to classical physics a man can have no further influence upon a projectile once it has left his hand, but one cannot help wondering whether in some cases there might not be an unacknowledged PK factor in skills of this type. Glen Barclay has suggested that some of the oriental martial arts, such as aikido and karate, may involve forces which cannot be entirely explained in terms of modern knowledge.[3]

Another topic mentioned by Harrison is the curious children's game in which a person is lifted into the air using only the tips of the little fingers. Harrison points out that if five children raise a ten stone person in this way, the force on each little finger is equivalent to that exerted by a 28 lb bag of potatoes! As far as I know, no physicist has ever given a 'normal' explanation of this phenomenon, which is also discussed by Colin Wilson.[187] Once again, one wonders whether PK may not play a part in this activity. Celia Green has recorded several cases in which adults claimed to remember levitation experiences which occurred to them spontaneously when they were children.[62]

As we know, many gamblers have an intuitive feeling that they can somehow influence the fall of the dice, and the reader will recall that it was this fact which gave J. B. Rhine the idea of using dice in his PK experiments. Casino owners are aware that there are certain people who are prone to have exceptional runs of 'luck'. Fortunately for the owners, such people are not very numerous! However, in recent years attempts have been made to increase the chance of winning by a careful application of the findings of parapsychological research and at least one successful attempt has been reported in the literature.[15,16] In 1966 a book was published which actually explained to the reader how to achieve success at the gaming tables by using his own paranormal faculties.[167]

The Geller effect is an example of a parapsychological phenomenon which seems to have no historical precedents, and for this reason many researchers were sceptical about it when it first appeared. Most of the other phenomena can be traced back through the ages in one form or another, but metal-bending was sprung upon the world for the first time during the 1970s. However, the argument from silence is always a dubious one. The fact that people did not report such experiences before 1970 is no guarantee that they did not occur, and we do not know how many bent keys and broken spoons have, in the past, been attributed to vandalism on the part of a person or persons unknown. A careful search of the literature reveals that there were, in fact, a number of occurrences reported which might have been similar to the Geller effect. For example, Raymond Bayless discovered an account of a nineteenth century poltergeist outbreak in which spoons were broken, or suddenly twisted out of shape in the diners' hands,[8] and Manfred Cassirer has drawn attention to an eighteenth century poltergeist which tormented its victims by pricking them with pins which were bent into fantastic shapes.[24] Perhaps I might add to the collection by citing a strange case which was first reported in 1936. Dr Nandor Fodor recounted '. . . an extremely curious story which I heard from a Major friend. In his family the ring of the firstborn was the focal point of a premonitory haunting. The tradition of the family ran that whenever the head of the family died, the ring worn by the firstborn son would split. This splitting of the ring is always an infallible omen of death. My friend showed me his ring. There was a thin cut in it, as fine and straight as if done by a razor blade. It came about this wise: He was summoned home where his father was seriously ill. An improvement took place. His death was not expected. My friend was looking at his ring with relief. It was whole. He took it off and placed it in the soap basin while he washed his hand. Reaching for the ring, he saw that it was split. He ran into his father's bedroom. At that moment his father expired.'[51]

An impressive feature of Uri Geller's performance is his apparent ability to alter the functioning of clocks, watches and similar devices. However, long before Geller appeared on the scene people were reporting what appeared to be spontaneous PK-type phenomena in connection with time-keeping devices. Sometimes a clock would stop, for no apparent reason, at a time which was later found to have coincided with some emotionally significant event such as a family death. J. B. Rhine became interested in such occurrences during the 1930s when one of his girl students told him that her father's clock had stopped at the exact moment of his death, although it was not run down or out of order. Many hundreds of similar cases are now on record, and Dr Louisa Rhine published a detailed analysis of some 178 examples in 1963.[145] One of the most amusing instances from the Duke University collection concerned a little boy who possessed a battery-operated toy gun. The gun did not fire projectiles, but made an 'ack-ack' noise when the trigger was pulled. One day the child was in tears because the gun would no longer work properly. He brought it to his father, who was the proprietor of a small country store, and asked him to mend it. In the shop at the time were the boy's mother, his 12-year old sister, and one of the customers. They all made fun of the father, jokingly telling him that he was not clever enough to repair the gun. After tinkering with the toy weapon for a few moments, the father announced that the gun was now fixed, 'and if you don't believe it, I'll shoot that clock right off the wall.' He pointed the gun at the electric wall-clock, and pulled the trigger. The gun ack-acked furiously, and *the clock jumped off the wall.* The witnesses all agreed that 'jumped' was the correct word. The clock did not merely fall but projected itself outwards a foot or so and then, as if suddenly released, fell straight downwards, just missing a shelf. When it reached the limit of the cord it swung back against the wall and smashed. There was no wind, and no traffic vibration which could account for this strange event. As the onlookers reported, 'everything was still, including us – for a long time.'[146]

Disappearance-reappearance events, sometimes known as teleportations or apportations, are another form of PK which may occur more frequently than we imagine. Many such events were reported in the spiritualist literature of the nineteenth century, although they seldom occurred under conditions which would satisfy a modern psychical researcher. Several examples have been mentioned elsewhere in this book: thus Zöllner reported the disappearance and reappearance of a table (p. 103), Button the movement of objects into and out of closed boxes (p. 131), and several people the apportation phenomena of Yogananda and Sai Baba (p. 32). Until quite recently most psychical researchers would have dismissed such accounts as mere anecdotes, of little or no scientific value. This was not an unreasonable attitude to take, since most of the reports were very old and frequently involved mediums who were known to have cheated on other occasions. Furthermore, apports are exceptionally easy to produce by conjuring. Even if the medium and the séance-room are searched beforehand, there are all sorts of places where small objects can be secreted away from the prying eyes of the investigator. Mediums have even been known to hide objects in the investigator's own pockets, recovering them later when required. Apports occurring in the séance-room must therefore be regarded with the greatest caution. Even so, the phenomenon cannot be ruled out altogether, and there is now some quite good modern evidence in support of the suggestion that apportation does occasionally occur. For instance, Professor Bender has described a poltergeist case in which a sphere of water was seen to appear in mid-air under the eyes of the plumber. The sphere then fell to the ground and burst, scattering its contents all over the surroundings. Apports of various kinds seem to be reported in about 20 per cent of all poltergeist cases.[58]

Professor Hasted has described several disappearance-reappearance events which occurred in his own home, and were observed by himself and by members of his family.[80] He also witnessed a very remarkable 'de-materialisation' event in the physics laboratories at Birkbeck College. On September 10th, 1974, Hasted placed his right hand, palm downwards, a few inches above a table on which was lying a cellulose capsule of the kind used to contain drugs. Inside the capsule was a vanadium carbide disc of diameter 2 mm and thickness 0.2 mm. Uri Geller passed his hand above Hasted's, and Hasted felt a warm sensation, 'as though I was experiencing strong diathermic heating.' The other scientists who were watching saw the cellulose capsule give a little jump, like a Mexican jumping bean. Geller then removed his hand, which had been at least ten inches above the table. When the capsule was examined, it was found that the vanadium carbide disc had fractured across the centre, and *one half of it had totally disappeared*. The capsule was still sealed, and there were no holes in it. Microscopic examination proved that there had been no substitution of the disc, and when two scientists tried to fracture a similar disc by holding it in a vice and bending it with pliers, it took them almost an hour to do so! In case the reader should think that this was a trick worked by Geller with the aid of an accomplice, it should be added that the only persons present apart from Geller and Hasted were the laboratory technician Nick Nicola, and scientists David Bohm, Ted Bastin and Brendan O'Regan. Hasted wrote: 'We were forced by our observations to the preposterous conclusion that a part of the foil had disappeared from inside the closed capsule, presumably reappearing somewhere else in the laboratory. It could not have passed through the wall of the capsule, since the latter was undamaged.'[80] The scientists never succeeded in locating the missing piece of foil.

Once again, we have no way of telling how often disappearance-reappearance events occur in everyday life. An object vanishes from a cupboard or from a particular room in a house; later we discover it somewhere else. When such events occur we invariably *assume* that there must be some 'normal' explanation. Perhaps some other member of the household moved the object, or perhaps we moved it ourselves in a fit of absentmindedness. In most cases we are no doubt quite correct in assuming that the event has a simple explanation; however, the point I am making is that *if* teleportations did occur, we would probably never even notice them. If an object is found to be displaced, each member of the family will tend to assume that some other member has moved it.

It so happens that I have come across several incidents which *could* be examples of disappearance-reappearance events occurring in everyday life. During the very hot summer of 1976 a friend of mine, Mr John Isaac, found his wallet missing from his jacket pocket. The wallet contained £35 and several important documents, including his driving licence. For six weeks he searched everywhere for the wallet. Several times a week he re-examined the jacket, inside and out, looking to see whether the wallet could have slipped inside the lining. Eventually, when he had almost given up all hope of ever finding the wallet, he decided that it was time to have the jacket cleaned. Before sending the jacket to the cleaners, he searched it once again. A few days later it was returned from the cleaners with an envelope containing his wallet, and a note indicating that the wallet had been found in the jacket pocket!

Of course, no serious scientist would regard such an incident as evidence for the reality of PK. I have described it here only to illustrate my thesis that paranormal events *may* be happening more frequently than we think, the majority of them passing quite unnoticed. If a saucepan falls off a shelf or a cracking noise comes from the furniture we generally ignore it. It is only when the events happen repeatedly in the same locality that we begin to get suspicious; we then attribute them either to trickery or to a poltergeist, depending on our particular threshold of credulity.

It is a well-known fact that we do not see the physical world as it really is, for the act of perception always involves an element of interpretation. The eye-brain system does not merely register the passage of events like a movie camera; rather, it organises the incoming signals into coherent patterns, interpreting them in accordance with past experience and physiological need.[65] It is important to realise that our sense organs were developed for biological survival, not to gratify our philosophical urge to understand the nature of reality. Out of the vast complexity of the 'real' world our senses abstract just those elements which are necessary for the survival of our species. Thus, we have no sense organs for detecting X-rays, ultraviolet light or neutrinos because these components of the physical world have no direct bearing on the problems of self-preservation and reproduction. The same is probably true of PK phenomena; the mind tends not to notice them because they cannot be fitted into its world-picture, and have no direct relevance to the task of survival. We all have an internal model of the world which has developed as a result of years of practical experience, and which is perfectly adequate for everyday life. According to our model, we live in an isotropic space of three dimensions in which objects retain their shapes and positions unless they are acted upon by some disturbing influence. Within this space, events are organised in a linear time-sequence which we imagine to be part of an absolute reality: past, present, and future. This is the way our minds interpret the world; *it is not necessarily the way the world actually is.*

Our minds, then, are pre-programmed to seek for explanations of events which are consistent with our internal world-model. If we witness an event for which no such explanation is possible, we tend to discount it, forget it, or pretend that it never occurred. The investigators of Eusapia Palladino observed this tendency in themselves. Feilding wrote:

'The ordinary effect of the sudden confrontation of a fairly balanced mind with a merely bizarre fact is a reaction: the mind rejects it, refuses to consider it. And the more bizarre the fact, the stronger the reaction. If the possessor of such a mind were, for example, in the course of a walk down Piccadilly, to see a policeman levitated across a motor omnibus, no permanent impression as to the mutability of the laws of gravitation affecting policemen would remain with him. The emotional certainty produced by his long continued previous experience that policemen do not do such things would be stronger than any degree of intellectual certainty that this particular policeman did, and would presently efface it. And so it was with ourselves.'[48]

G. N. M. Tyrrell discussed the problem of what he called the 'adapted mind' in his much neglected book *Homo Faber*[182]. He pointed out that the long ages of evolutionary development have caused our minds as well as our bodies to become adapted to the physical environment, so that we can only think in physicalistic terms. Although our bodily adaptations are fairly obvious, our mental adaptation is subtly hidden; nevertheless, it influences all our thinking in science and philosophy. Tyrrell believed that it was this mental adaptation which led so many people to reject the findings of psychical research out of hand. A person who was truly rational would surely weigh the evidence impartially before coming to a decision; in fact, many people react emotionally, condemning the research before they have even examined it.

Quite apart from the tendency of our minds to reject the evidence for the paranormal, there also seems to be a built-in tendency for the events themselves to try to 'cover their tracks'. This has been called the 'law of frustration' (Button) or the 'shyness effect' (Taylor), and it has been extensively discussed by Ken Batcheldor who has devised means for circumventing it.[7] In simple terms, it means that PK events tend to happen when no one is looking. Thus, it is rare for anyone to see a poltergeist missile actually in flight; usually one becomes aware of it by hearing the crash as it lands. Metal bending often occurs at the very moment when experimenter and subject are just about to give up, or their attention is diverted elsewhere. There have been strange cases of films sticking in the camera, or video-recorders breaking down, just at the crucial moment when a paranormal event is taking place. Of course, these occurrences provide excellent ammunition for the sceptic, who can turn them to his own advantage and use them to ridicule the researchers. Nevertheless, I believe this law of frustration is a real phenomenon, and not just a feeble excuse offered by experimenters who have failed to produce convincing results. It is quite likely that this troublesome effect is merely another expression of the tendency noted in the previous paragraph: the tendency of the mind to reject evidence of the paranormal. In PK events the inner self and the external world are, in some mysterious way, united; the behaviour of the physical world thus reflects the emotional states and attitudes of the human observer. This is why PK effects often 'dry up' in the presence of sceptical onlookers, and poltergeists sometimes cease to operate after an exorcism has been performed.

We began this chapter by posing the question: if PK phenomena are real, why do we not observe them more often in our everyday life? The answers I have suggested are as follows:

(1) PK may indeed play a part, unknown to us, in certain sporting and artistic activities where exceptional skills are displayed.

(2) PK events may occur more frequently than we imagine, but they are not recognised as such because of the possibility of alternative explanations.

(3) Even when events occur which are quite obviously paranormal, the mind tends to reject them because they cannot be made to conform to our internal model of reality.

(4) PK events have an inherent tendency to try to escape observation – the 'law of frustration'.

Perhaps, then, we ought to keep our eyes open for possible PK effects in the everyday world around us. I am not, of course, suggesting that we should revert to the beliefs of our ancestors, who saw sinister and occult significance in such commonplace events as the flight of an owl or the arrival of a comet. It would be folly to plunge back into that superstitious way of thinking. Nevertheless it is quite possible that, since the rise of rationalism in the eighteenth century, we have neglected certain features of reality simply because they cannot be fitted into a tidy materialistic framework. There is no need to fall back into superstition; but now that reason has triumphed, we can at least widen our perception of possibilities.

14 The Phenomena Surveyed

> "I can't believe *that*!" said Alice.
>
> "Can't you?" the Queen said in a pitying tone.
>
> "Try again: draw a long breath, and shut your eyes."
>
> Alice laughed. "There's no use trying," she said: "one *can't* believe impossible things."
>
> "I daresay you haven't had much practice," said the Queen. "When I was your age, I always did it for half-an-hour a day. Why, sometimes I've believed as many as six impossible things before breakfast."
>
> Lewis Carroll, *Through the Looking-Glass.*

In the preceding chapters we have examined a wide range of alleged phenomena in which the state of the physical world appears to have been modified by some unexplained influence, apparently associated with the presence of certain human beings. We now have to tackle the two most difficult questions which arise from this examination: first, we have to decide which, if any, of the reported phenomena are genuine; second, we have to attempt some sort of explanation which is compatible with logical and scientific principles.

In most, although not all, branches of science there is no real difficulty in deciding what are the facts requiring an explanation. This is because most scientific facts are established by experimental procedures which can be repeated by anyone with sufficient time, knowledge, and equipment. It has sometimes been argued that parapsychology can never be regarded as a true science until it produces an experiment which can be indefinitely repeated at will. However, one can think of several sciences in which strict repeatability is the exception rather than the rule. The meteorologist, for example, is entirely at the mercy of phenomena over which he has no control, and whose vagaries he can predict only within a certain margin of error; nevertheless, we do not deny him the right to regard himself as a scientist. Furthermore, psychology, that branch of science whose devotees have often been most critical of psychical research, is itself not free from the charge of unrepeatability. Nathaniel C. Smith has pointed out that psychological experiments are often not repeated at all, and when they are, they frequently fail to yield the same results.[163] On the other side of the coin, many parapsychological experiments have been successfully repeated on numerous occasions under well-controlled conditions. This can truthfully be claimed for metal-bending experiments, for example, and for PK experiments with dice and electronic machines.

As regards PK phenomena in general, the spectrum of belief runs all the way from total rejection in the case of a few die-hard sceptics to total acceptance on the part of some occultists and spiritualists. Neither the believers nor the unbelievers have a monopoly of rationality; both sides have frequently been guilty of an unthinking fanaticism which has led them to distort the facts in favour of their own particular interpretation. I have already mentioned James Randi's book on the Geller effect,[140] after it was published Targ and Puthoff found it necessary to issue an eight-page report in which they listed no less than 24 incorrect statements in the single chapter dealing with their experiments at the Stanford Research Institute. In fact, anyone who takes the trouble to do so can locate many errors in Randi's writing, most of them tending to discredit psychical researchers. The reader might like to try comparing Randi's description of the Zöllner experiments,[140] with the original account given by Zöllner himself.[191] As regards the experiment with the hemp cord, Randi tells us that Zöllner 'kept no record of how many cords were prepared', whereas Zöllner states quite specifically that *four* such cords were made. Randi also asserts that *Slade* 'finally sat at the table with the loop hanging into his lap, the seal under his thumbs', whereas Zöllner's account informs us that Slade did not even touch the cord, which was on the other side of the table. It was *Zöllner's* thumbs which were over the seal, and *Zöllner's* lap into which the loop of the cord was hanging. Obviously, these small points are extremely important when one is trying to decide whether Zöllner was merely the victim of a conjuring trick.

Although the presentation of deliberately falsified data is probably not very common, there is a general tendency for sceptical writers to omit facts which might shed a very different light on the phenomena which they are describing. Thus, *The Table-Rappers*, by Ronald Pearsall, concludes a brief account of the mediumship of Eusapia Palladino with the words:

'Eusapia was up against a new generation of researchers, Myers and Sidgwick were dead, and were replaced by W. W. Baggally and Everard Feilding. Baggally had been investigating physical phenomena for thirty-five years, and had found nothing but fraud. Feilding had been investigating for ten years, but he too had drawn a blank. Eusapia did not encourage them to change their minds. In 1910 she admitted to an American reporter that she had cheated, claiming that sitters had "willed" her to do so.'[126]

It is astonishing that this writer makes no mention whatever of the 250-page report produced by Feilding, Baggally and Carrington in which they asserted quite clearly that they *had* changed their minds, and that they were convinced that they had witnessed genuine PK phenomena in the presence of Eusapia. By omitting this important fact, the reader is presented with the exact opposite of the truth, and led to believe that there is nothing worthy of serious consideration in the reports of the Palladino mediumship.

It has often been said that academics in general, and scientists in particular, are especially easy to deceive, and that conjurers pretending to be psychics have often been able to impose upon them. There is certainly an element of truth in this suggestion, and it is certainly advisable for anyone who intends to carry out a psychical investigation to listen very carefully to the warnings given by professional magicians.* On the other hand, there have been many instances where fully qualified professional magicians have themselves investigated or observed paranormal events, and have come to the definite conclusion that what they saw could not be explained in terms of their own art. Usually this conclusion was arrived at with great reluctance, and only after consideration of every conceivable alternative. The following are the names of some of the magicians who have endorsed mediumistic phenomena in this way, the name of the medium being given in brackets:

---

*I cannot, however, agree with Prof. Eysenck when he writes: 'Investigators who cannot explain every trick performed by stage magicians should consider themselves barred from investigating alleged psi phenomena' (Encyclopaedia Britannica 15th Ed., Vol. 13 p.1003)

Frederick Powell (Slade)
Samuel Bellachini (Slade)
Harry Kellar (Eglinton)
Howard Thurston (Palladino)
'Ranky' (Girard)
Rolf Mayr (Silvio Mayer)
Leo Leslie (Geller)
Artur Zorka (Geller)
Abb Dickson (Geller)

The testimony of Artur Zorka is particularly impressive because of his qualifications. He is a professional magician and a member of the Society of American Magicians. In 1975 he was Chairman of the Occult Investigations Committee of the Atlanta Chapter of the Society, and had been voted "Magician of the Year" for 1974. Together with Abb Dickson (also an experienced professional) Zorka made an investigation of Uri Geller's alleged paranormal abilities during the summer of 1975, and produced a report which was entirely favourable to Geller.[124] As might have been expected, this created quite an uproar, and Zorka was accused of improper conduct in that he had released the report before it had been discussed by the Society as a whole. Be that as it may, the reader who is sceptical about the existence of the phenomena might well ask himself how Geller was able to perform his 'tricks' when, as in this case, he was locked in a room with no windows and under the professional eyes of *two* experienced magicians.

The possibility of fraud on the part of the medium or psychic has, of course, been recognised from the beginning, and in all the serious studies careful precautions have been taken against it. However, fraud on the part of the *experimenter* is a very different matter, and one which has only recently come into prominence in psychical research. In June, 1974, Dr W. J. Levy resigned his post as Director of the Institute for Parapsychology in North Carolina, after being caught in the act of faking one of his own experiments.[144] More recently, doubt has been cast upon the reliability of some of the work of the late Dr S. G. Soal, whose ESP experiments were once considered to be outstanding in both design and execution.[105] In both these cases there was clear evidence of data manipulation by the experimenter, and we have no alternative but to reject as unreliable work which emanates from any experimenter who has been known to act in this way. Experimenter fraud is by no means confined to parapsychology, for there have been several cases reported in well-established fields of scientific endeavour. However, fraud of any kind tends to have a much more destructive effect in parapsychology, since we are dealing with phenomena which are in any case elusive and difficult to replicate.

How, then, should we proceed? In view of the ever-present possibility of fraud or malobservation, some critics have proposed a course of action which would have the effect of paralysing the entire research effort. They argue that, before we make any attempt to explore the nature of psi phenomena, we must first provide a conclusive proof of their existence. We must threfore devote all our research activity to devising a completely fraud-proof and error-proof experiment. This particular demand has proved to be a red herring which has bedevilled the efforts of psychical researchers for many years. There is really no such thing as a completely 'safe' experiment, for no matter what precautions are taken, it is always possible for the out-and-out sceptic to suggest an alternative explanation. As a last resort, he can always claim that there was a massive conspiracy involving all the participants in the experiment! The search for the perfect experiment is therefore like the quest for the Holy Grail; the desired object seems always to be just ahead of us, but as we reach out to touch it we find that it eludes our grasp. Thus, valuable research time and energy is expended in following a will-o-the-wisp, while the basic task of designing experiments to tell us more about the *nature* of the phenomena is neglected.

Those who insist that we provide absolute proof of the existence of the phenomena before proceeding further have misunderstood the nature of scientific enquiry. Except in the fields of logic and pure mathematics there is no such thing as 'absolute proof', for all factual knowledge is provisional. We have to make the most reasonable assumptions from the data available, and go on from there. Rutherford did not try to 'prove' the existence of atoms before embarking on his experiments in radioactivity; on the basis of past experiments he *assumed* that atoms do exist, and planned his research accordingly. Copernicus and Galileo could not 'prove' that the earth goes round the sun, but it seemed to them a reasonable assumption to make, a good working hypothesis on which to build the science of astronomy. Similarly, we cannot claim that our experiments have proved that PK phenomena occur; we *can* claim that there is a vast mass of evidence, collected by a large number of observers and experimenters in many different countries of the world, which is most easily accounted for on the *assumption* that PK occurs. We can therefore take the existence of PK as a good working hypothesis, and proceed to plan our experiments and formulate our theoretical interpretations accordingly. There is no need to listen to the strident demands for 'proof' because, unlike some politicians and theologians, we make no claims for infallibility; we are content to remain mere explorers, investigating a little-known area of human experience.

The *Journal of Parapsychology* defines psychokinesis as 'a direct mental influence exerted by the subject on an external physical process, condition, or object.' Such a definition contains several unspecified assumptions. For example, it implies that all PK events can be traced to the mental activity of a single subject, human or animal, and it excludes the possibility that PK may be a field effect produced by the mental interaction of a number of subjects. It also seems to exclude the possibility that some PK effects may be due to the activities of people who are no longer living on this earth (the spiritualist hypothesis), and the possibility that other PK effects may be due to non-human intelligences such as demons or extra-terrestrial visitors. In order to keep all our options open, I suggest that we define a PK event as *any physical phenomenon which cannot be satisfactorily explained in terms of known physical forces, and which seems to involve the participation of some kind of mental entity or entities.* The first step towards a proper understanding of such events must be to collect as many examples as possible, and try to sort them into groups according to the characteristics which they display. For convenience, I have grouped the phenomena described in this book into eight major categories, which are listed below; the page numbers in brackets refer to descriptions of cases elsewhere in this book.

(1) *Changes in the shape or structure of physical objects*

This includes all those examples where objects are said to have become distorted, bent or broken through the operation of paranormal forces. The various manifestations of the Geller effect fall into this group, together with certain spontaneous events such as the exploding of Jung's breadknife (p. 13), the shattering of St Benedict's wine-flagon (p. 12), and the splitting of the Major's ring (p. 80). I also include the alleged changes in shape of the human body (p. 73) in this group.

(2) *Apportation phenomena*

This includes all those cases where objects are said to have passed into, or out of, a completely closed space. The space may be a room, a box, or as in the case of Hasted's experiment, a plastic capsule (p. 182). Some of Zöllner's experiments with Slade and Button's experiments with Margery fall into this category (pp. 103, 131); so also do some poltergeist phenomena.

(3) *Horizontal movement of objects (telekinesis)*

In many séances with mediums such as D. D. Home chairs, tables and other objects were seen to move across the room. Modern PK agents, such as Nina Kulagina and Felicia Parise, seem to have the ability to make small objects 'walk' across a table-top (pp. 160, 162).

(4) *Vertical movement of objects (levitation)*

The levitation of physical objects such as tables is sometimes reported in séances; however, the most frequently reported event in this category is the levitation of the human body (pp. 30–32, 48–50). The sheer quantity of such reports is quite surprising, and they come from all centuries and cultures. However, there do not seem to be many examples recorded in recent years.

(5) *Auditory effects*

Apparently paranormal raps, footsteps and other noises have been heard from time to time, both in formal séances and in spontaneous situations. It is always difficult to be sure that such sounds are genuinely paranormal, and not due to undiscovered natural causes such as rats. It is also difficult to know whether or not they are hallucinatory. The latter possibility can be eliminated if a tape-recorder is available, but it is not easy to catch such sounds on tape as they tend to occur at unexpected moments.

(6) Thermal effects

Some PK subjects can apparently influence the temperature of their surroundings (pp. 139, 163), and sensations of cold have often been reported from the séance-room. On the other hand, poltergeist missiles are often found to be hot, as also were some of the objects apported during Slade's mediumship (pp. 105–7). The phenomenon known as 'spontaneous human combustion' may be exaggerated and grotesque form of this effect; fortunately it seems to be a very rare event.

(7) Optical effects

'Spirit lights' were frequently seen at séances during the nineteenth century, although they are rare nowadays. It is quite likely that some of these effects were hallucinatory. However, it is also possible that some forms of PK involve electrical discharges which could on occasion produce luminous appearances. The 'psychic photography' of people such as Ted Serios (p. 158) may involve the bending of light rays, or even the creation of photons through the transformation of some other form of energy.

(8) Effects upon randomising systems

Until the advent of metal-bending, most laboratory work on PK was done with dice-throwing machines and electronic random number generators (see Chapter 11). There is now very strong evidence to support the belief that the human mind can cause a normally random system to deviate from randomness to a statistically significant extent.

These categories may provide a convenient framework for discussion, although they cannot be regarded as completely exhausting all forms of PK phenomena. The reader will notice that I have omitted certain kinds of phenomena; for example, there is no mention of 'ectoplasm' or 'materialisation'. This is partly because I am not convinced that the evidence for such phenomena is strong enough to justify their inclusion, and partly because, if they do occur, they would seem to be complex events which cannot be neatly fitted into any classificatory system. It should also be pointed out that the eight categories are not intended to be water-tight; as we learn more about the nature of PK some of them will turn out to be merely special cases of others. For example, paranormal raps may be caused by slight deformations of metal or wooden objects, of the type studied by Hasted; in that case, category (5) would become a sub-division of category (1). It is also possible that metal-bending is caused by the apportation of metal atoms from inside the crystal lattice to the outside; if that should turn out to be the case, category (1) would be subsumed under category (2). Eventually, we may expect that research into PK will reduce all the various types to a single basic phenomenon occurring at the atomic or subatomic level.

One of the ways in which science advances is by detecting relationships between apparently unconnected events. Thus, Newton took a great step forward when he realised that the force which draws small objects towards the surface of the earth is the same as the force which maintains the moon in her orbit. It is therefore quite reasonable that we should seek for common features in the various types of PK event. However, we must make sure that the common features really do exist, and are not merely figments of our imagination. Some parapsychologists have tried to 'jump the gun' by grouping together phenomena which seem to have little, if anything, in common. For example, I am doubtful whether anything is to be gained by describing poltergeist phenomena as 'Recurrent Spontaneous Psychokinesis' or RSPK events. Such a term implies that the forces operating in a poltergeist outbreak are the same as the forces which influence the fall of dice in laboratory experiments. While this *may* be the case, there is no real evidence to suggest that it is. In fact, no one has yet demonstrated that there is any connection at all between events in category (8) and the very considerable outbursts of energy which occur during poltergeist attacks and in some séances. Calling two things by the same name does not make them identical; it merely confuses thought. I suggest, therefore, that we should keep all our categories separate until the possible connections between them have been elucidated by research. That this may not be too far distant is suggested by Hasted's work; he has already linked PK at the atomic level with metal-bending, by his discovery that slight movements of the metal atoms occur even when there is no visible bend produced.

Meanwhile, the theorists have not been idle, and there have been many attempts to supply a theoretical background to the psi research.[188] Most of the attempts have resulted in theories or models which are only partially explanatory, and usually they work rather better for ESP than they do for PK. Some have postulated the existence of hitherto unknown particles, such as 'tachyons' or 'psitrons', with their accompanying fields; others have coined new words, such as 'bioplasmic interaction', which seem to do little except disguise our ignorance. Although one must admire the effort and ingenuity which has been put into many of these attempts, they can hardly be said to have resulted in a satisfactory explanation of psi phenomena. Professor Taylor's attitude was at least understandable: when he found that he could not explain psi in terms of the four known forces of nature, he abandoned his belief in the phenomena!

It should be clear by now that the occurrences which we have been considering throughout this book cannot be incorporated into our present-day world view. No minor tinkering around with the entities of modern physics is likely to lead to a satisfactory conclusion. ESP and PK present a challenge to our entire way of looking at the world; we find ourselves forced to examine afresh just what we mean by reality, and the way in which it impinges upon our consciousness. Psi phenomena are important precisely *because* they force us to make this re-evaluation; they compel us to ask basic questions which would not arise in the normal course of everyday life.

However, parapsychology is not the only area of science which is pointing us towards a fundamental reassessment. For more than half a century physicists have also been grappling with problems which, at times, seem weird and paradoxical. It cannot truthfully be said that these problems have been solved, but at least they are under consideration. In their search for a deeper understanding of the mysteries of space, time, and matter, some physicists have looked towards parapsychology, hoping that the two disciplines will cross-fertilise one another, and lead to fresh insights which will be of benefit to both. This seems to me to be one of the most hopeful and exciting trends in current thought.

In chapters 15 and 16 we shall examine some of the concepts which, although they seem strange to our 'commonsense' view of things, have nevertheless proved useful to the modern physicist. In the course of this examination I shall suggest ways in which these concepts might be useful to the theoretical parapsychologist.

15   More than Meets the Eye?

'However successful the theory of a four-dimensional world may be, it is difficult to ignore a voice inside us which whispers "At the back of your mind, you know that a fourth dimension is all nonsense." I fancy that that voice must often have had a busy time in the past history of physics. What nonsense to say that this solid table on which I am writing is a collection of electrons moving at prodigious speeds in empty spaces, which relatively to electronic dimensions are as wide as the spaces between the planets in the solar system! What nonsense to say that the thin air is trying to crush my body with a load of 14 lbs to the square inch! What nonsense that the star-cluster, which I see through the telescope obviously there *now*, is a glimpse into a past age 50,000 years ago! Let us not be beguiled by this voice. It is discredited.'

Sir Arthur Eddington: *Space, Time and Gravitation.*

Sometime around the year 300 BC an Alexandrian Greek known as Euclid published what has been described as one of the most widely read books in the world: the *Elements of Geometry*. In fact, it consists of twelve books in which a series of mathematical propositions are logically deduced from certain basic assumptions known as 'axioms' or 'postulates'. There is also a thirteenth book, but this is composed mostly of disconnected fragments, and it seems likely that it was left unfinished at the time of Euclid's death around 275 BC. For more than two thousand years Euclid's geometry dominated western mathematics, and it formed the basis of most of the geometry taught in our schools until well into the twentieth century. However, during the first half of the nineteenth century several far-sighted mathematicians began to challenge the supremacy of the Euclidian system, and thereby opened up new avenues of thought which have had a profound effect upon the science and philosophy of our age.

The main breach with Euclid occurred over the so-called 'Fifth Postulate', which concerns the properties of parallel lines. Suppose we have a pair of lines, AB and CD, intersected by a third line EF at points P and Q (see Figure 6). Then Euclid's Fifth Postulate tells us that if the angles QPB and PQD add up to less than two right angles, the lines AB and CD will meet if extended on that side.

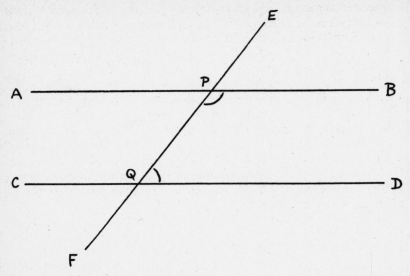

Fig. 6   Euclid's Fifth Postulate.

This all seems very obvious, but then, mathematicians are never satisfied with the merely obvious. They felt that somehow it should be possible to *prove* the Fifth Postulate, or show that it follows logically from simpler assumptions. This they tried to do, but in spite of many ingenious attempts, every effort ended in failure. Eventually, several people decided to see what would happen if they assumed the Fifth Postulate to be *untrue*, and discovered, somewhat to their astonishment, that entirely new systems of geometry could be constructed, systems in which the Fifth Postulate is no longer valid. Karl Friedrich Gauss (1777–1855) was probably the first to do this, but fearing ridicule, he kept the discovery to himself until others had come forward with the same ideas. Today the names most firmly associated with the non-Euclidian geometries are N. I. Lobatschewsky (1793–1856), Johann Bolyai (1802–1860) and G. F. B. Riemann (1826–1866). Lobatschewsky and Bolyai developed their geometries by assuming, contrary to 'common sense', that any number of lines can be drawn through a given point parallel to a given straight line (in ordinary geometry only one such line can be drawn). Bolyai was fascinated by the consequences which followed from this simple, if revolutionary, assumption. In 1823 he wrote to his father: 'I have made such wonderful discoveries that I have been almost overwhelmed by them ... *I have created a universe from nothing.*' A later mathematician, Howard Hinton, waxed lyrical over Bolyai's discovery:

'Nothing so triumphantly, one might almost say so insolently, ignoring of sense had ever been written before. Men had struggled against the limitations of the body, fought them, despised them, conquered them. But no one had ever thought simply as if the body, the bodily eyes, the organs of vision, all this vast experience of space, had never existed. The age-long contest of the soul with the body, the struggle for mastery, had come to a culmination. Bolyai and Lobatschewsky simply thought as if the body was not. The struggle for dominion, the strife and combat of the soul were over; they had mastered, and the Hungarian drew his line.'[84]

Depending on what assumptions are chosen to replace the Fifth Postulate, so various systems of geometry can be constructed, each one logically coherent and quite independent of the others. As we have seen, in Lobatschewsky's geometry an infinite number of lines can be drawn through any given point parallel to a given straight line; this kind of geometry is called *hyperbolic*. In Riemann's geometry there are no parallel lines at all, and this kind is called *spherical geometry*. There are many interesting differences between the various geometries. For example, in everyday (Euclidian) geometry the angles of a triangle always add up to exactly 180°, whereas in hyperbolic geometry they add up to *less* than this, and in spherical geometry they add up to *more*. Yet each one of these geometries is perfectly self-consistent, and there is no *logical* reason why we should prefer one rather than another. It is our bodily senses, not our reason, which tell us that the world is Euclidian.

There was a further extension of geometry which took place at about the same time as the non-Euclidean geometries were being developed. Just as our plain common-sense and everyday sensory experience tells us that the world is Euclidian, so it also tells us that the world is *three-dimensional*. All the ordinary objects around us seem to have length, breadth and depth, and the position of a single point in our world can be specified by just three numbers, known as its coordinates. However, there is nothing to stop the mathematician hypothesising spaces with four, five, six or even more dimensions, if he so desires. This extension of geometry to describe a multidimensional space was first carried out systematically by Hermann Grassmann (1809–1877) who published his work in 1844. Unfortunately his presentation was so obscure and the concepts so unfamiliar that most mathematicians simply ignored it. Later, other mathematicians developed similar ideas, and by the end of the nineteenth century the notion of a 'fourth dimension' had become quite commonplace, even among people who knew very little mathematics. Various popular writers assumed the task of bringing these novel ideas before a wider public. One of the earliest was the Rev Edwin A. Abbott, whose delightful little fantasy *Flatland* was published during the 1880s. In this book Abbott imagines a world composed entirely of two-dimensional people whose sensory impressions are limited to the flat surface in which they live. Since they cannot see into the third dimension, they are unable to imagine what a solid object would be like. Naturally, they believe that their world is the only one which exists. To a three-dimensional person, however, the world of the Flatlanders is totally transparent, for their 'walls' are merely lines on the surface, and they present no obstacle to perception from a higher space. If a three-dimensional being were to interfere in Flatland by lifting some object out of the surface into his own space, the Flatlanders would be astonished at what, to them, would be the complete disappearance of a 'solid' object. If the object were then replaced in their world, perhaps in a different location, they would probably describe the event as a 'teleportation' or a 're-materialisation'.

Of course, Abbott's *Flatland* is a kind of parable story in which the Flatlanders are really ourselves. We are born into a world of which we have no prior knowledge. Gradually, through the use of our eyes and our limbs we build up an internal model of a three-dimensional space in which the objects of our world appear to be extended. It is probably true to say that if it were not for the fact that we have two eyes set approximately three inches apart, we should never attain this conception of space, and there is some evidence that other animals actually see the world as *flat*. In any case, there is no logical reason for assuming that our intuitive notions about the nature of space correspond to reality; for all we know, the objects we see around us may have extensions in any number of dimensions where our senses are unable to penetrate. Just because we cannot see something does not mean that it does not exist.

Returning to Abbott's *Flatland*, we can use it to perform an interesting mental exercise. We can ask ourselves questions such as 'what would the Flatlanders observe if a three-dimensional being were to do such-and-such a thing to one of the objects in their world?' When we do this the results are quite fascinating; for in almost every case *we find that we are describing phenomena which have been reported time and time again in the annals of psychical research*. Extrasensory perception, materialisation, telekinesis, apports, levitation, teleportation – all of these phenomena could be produced quite easily in Flatland by a being who had access to a third dimension. By analogy, therefore, they could be produced in *our* world by a being who had access to a *fourth* dimension. As we saw in chapter 8, Johann Zöllner was the first to realise that the physical phenomena of spiritualism could be explained in this way, but he received nothing but ridicule for his efforts.

It is perhaps unfortunate that many people have confused the idea of a fourth dimension of space with the concept of time as it is interpreted in the Theory of Relativity. One still hears people referring to time as *the* fourth dimension, and this misunderstanding has been fostered by popular science writers and science fiction authors such as H. G. Wells. In fact, the Theory of Relativity does not regard time as a 'dimension' in the same sense as the spatial dimensions; rather, it abstracts *one particular aspect* of time (its duration) and represents this geometrically. Time enters into our experience in several different ways; one of these is the sense of 'becomingness', the progression through past and present into the future. On this particular aspect (sometimes referred to as 'time's arrow') relativity has nothing to say. In fact, the world of relativity is a *static* world in which events do not happen; they simply exist. Relativity represents only the metrical aspect of time; it is concerned with the measured time interval between two events. To see how this comes to be regarded as a fourth dimension we must digress slightly into the field of differential geometry.

In a three-dimensional Euclidian space the distance between two points is given by the formula:

$$(ds)^2 = (dx)^2 + (dy)^2 + (dz)^2 \qquad (1)$$

where dx, dy and dz are the differences in the x, y and z coordinates of the two points. The term $(ds)^2$ is known as the *metric* of the space. Formula (1) is easily derived, simply by applying Pythagoras' theorem to the coordinates of the points. In a four-dimensional space each point will be represented by *four* coordinates, which we will call x, y, z, and w. The formula for the metric then becomes:

$$(ds)^2 = (dx)^2 + (dy)^2 + (dz)^2 + (dw)^2 \qquad (2)$$

provided that the space is Euclidian. Now Einstein discovered that observers who are in motion relative to one another will not, in general, find the same result when they attempt to measure the distance or the time interval between two events. However, if they proceed to calculate a certain quantity, known as the 'interval', from their measurements, they will all arrive at the same answer. Although the individual measurements differ, the interval is *invariant*. The algebraic expression for this interval (which we will call *ds*) is as follows:

$$(ds)^2 = (dx)^2 + (dy)^2 + (dz)^2 - c^2 (dt)^2 \qquad (3)$$
$$\text{where c is the velocity of light}$$

Now there is a certain obvious similarity between equations *(2)* and *(3)* above, and in 1908 Hermann Minkowski suggested that Einstein's results could be represented by assuming that physical events occur in a four-dimensional continuum which he called *spacetime*, and whose metric is given by equation *(3)*★. Notice, however, that this is *not* the equation of an ordinary Euclidian 4-space; time, the so-called fourth dimension, enters the formula in a rather different way from the three space dimensions, making the spacetime non-Euclidian (or semi-Euclidian). If we prefer to have events represented by a more familiar geometry, we can replace measured time, t, with 'imaginary time', τ, where $\tau = \sqrt{-1} \times ct$.

★For mathematical convenience relativists usually reverse the signs in this expression to make ds^2 positive.

This will then give us a formula for the metric which is strictly analogous to equation *(2)*. We can, therefore, please ourselves how we represent reality geometrically. If we use real time measurements we shall find that the geometry is non-Euclidian, whereas if we convert our time measurements into imaginary times we can retain the geometry of Euclidian 4-space. Whichever we do, it is obvious that time is not simply another dimension like the three spatial dimensions, and relativity distinguishes them by referring to 'timelike' and 'spacelike' dimensions of the continuum.

A person making measurements of time and space intervals inevitably refers them to a particular set of axes – his personal 'coordinate system'. According to Relativity Theory, observers travelling at different speeds orientate their axes at different angles, so that they measure the events from different viewpoints. This leads to the well-known relativistic phenomena, such as distance contraction and time dilation. Each observer is, in effect, viewing the four dimensional world from a different viewpoint. As an analogy, we may think of a number of people looking at a solid object, such as a house, from different angles. Each person sees something different from the others, and to anyone unacquainted with the idea of a three-dimensional object the images would appear to be incompatible. However, once it is realised that the separate images are just different views of the same three-dimensional object, everything makes sense. It is only by postulating the existence of a three-dimensional world that we *can* make sense of the multitude of different ways in which physical objects appear to our senses. In a similar way, when we try to make sense of the various observations made by observers in relative motion, we have to postulate the existence of a Minkowski spacetime continuum.

All this is fairly straightforward. However, in 1915 Einstein published an extension of his theory to include the viewpoints of observers who are *accelerating* relative to each other. This is known as the General Theory of Relativity, the earlier form being known as the Special Theory. In General Relativity spacetime is regarded as *curved*, at least in the vicinity of large objects such as the sun, so that moving objects travel in curved paths. To describe a particular space as 'curved' is simply a colloquial way of indicating that its geometry is non-Euclidian. Riemann's geometry, in which the angles of a triangle add up to more than 180°, is actually the geometry which would apply in a 'Flatland' on the surface of a sphere. Two-dimensional creatures confined to such a surface would have no idea that they were living in the skin of a sphere; being two-dimensional they could not know what a sphere was in any case. However, if they started making measurements in their world they would soon discover that their geometry was Riemannian. In general, if we have a non-Euclidian space of n-dimensions, it is always possible to represent it as a curved 'hypersurface' in a larger space of $n(n + 1)/2$ dimensions. However, there is no *necessity* to do this; the existence of a non-Euclidian geometry does not necessarily mean that a higher space exists.

The mathematical treatment of a curved four-dimensional space is no easy matter, and Einstein had to learn an entirely new branch of mathematics – the tensor calculus – in order to do it. Our equation *(2)*, which gives the metric for a flat 4-space, is based on Pythagoras' theorem, which is no longer applicable if the space is curved. Instead, we have to use a much more formidable expression:

$$(ds)^2 = g_{11}(dx_1)^2 + g_{22}(dx_2)^2 + g_{33}(dx_3)^2 + g_{44}(dx_4)^2 \\ + 2g_{12}(dx_1)(dx_2) + 2g_{13}(dx_1)(dx_3) \\ + 2g_{14}(dx_1)(dx_4) + 2g_{23}(dx_2)(dx_3) \\ + 2g_{24}(dx_2)(dx_4) + 2g_{34}(dx_3)(dx_4). \qquad (4)$$

Here, the coordinates are represented as x_1, x_2, x_3, x_4 rather than x, y, z, and w, and the ten 'g's may be constants or functions of the x's. The g's collectively form what is known as the *fundamental tensor;* in any given situation, their values will depend partly on the kind of space we live in, and partly on our chosen coordinate system. By using some very beautiful and sophisticated mathematics, Einstein was able to develop a set of equations which enabled him to predict the path taken by an object moving in a gravitational field (i.e., a curved space), a prediction which turned out to be remarkably accurate. Since Einstein's death in 1955 theoretical physicists have discovered other fascinating possibilities concealed in his formulae, such as the possible existence of black holes and gravity waves. For our purposes, however, we need only note that, according to Einstein, a curvature of spacetime will appear to its inhabitants as a *force field* which causes moving objects to deviate from a straight line path.

What, then, is the world 'really' like? Is our universe Euclidian or non-Euclidian, and how many dimensions does it possess? The answer is that to some extent we can make it whatever we wish. Our only knowledge of the outside world comes to us via our sense-perceptions, which we organise into concepts such as space and time. We have already seen that spacetime can be regarded as Euclidian or non-Euclidian, depending on how we choose to represent time. The surface of a sphere can be regarded as a non-Euclidian two-dimensional world, or as a curved surface embedded in a Euclidian space of three dimensions. We can take our pick! However, as we try to incorporate more and more facts into our picture, so it becomes necessary to use an increasingly complex geometry. If we confine our observations to a relatively small region of space where there are no strong gravitational fields, and consider only the measurements of observers who are stationary with respect to each other, the geometry of Euclid will be perfectly adequate. The attempt to incorporate the views of observers who are in motion leads us into Minkowski spacetime, and the further attempt to deal with the observations of accelerated observers brings us into the curved spacetime of General Relativity. In each case *the incorporation of a wider range of observations leads to a more sophisticated geometry*. Now let us take a further step, one which has so far been rejected by orthodox science: let us try to incorporate the phenomena of parapsychology into an enlarged scheme of nature. If past experience is anything to go by, this will require a geometry which is even more complex than that of General Relativity. It is not surprising, therefore, that those few scientists who have attempted to follow this particular path have failed to carry conviction with their colleagues. [191,76,40,165]

If we are to attempt a theory of psi phenomena, how many dimensions shall we require? J. W. Dunne, who made an extensive study of precognitive dreams, put forward a theory of the universe which involved the existence of an infinite number of time dimensions. [40] However, Dunne's theory was strongly criticised by both philosophers and scientists. C. D. Broad showed that only *two* time dimensions are needed in

order to account for precognition.[17] Let us suppose, therefore, that we need one additional time dimension in order to
incorporate precognitive experiences, and one additional
spatial dimension in order to account for PK effects such as
teleportation. We then have a six-dimensional world in
which four dimensions are space-like and two are time-like.
This seems to be the very least we can get away with if we are
going to incorporate psi into our picture of reality. Since this
book is not chiefly concerned with precognition or the other
forms of ESP, the remainder of this chapter will be devoted to
an examination of the hyperspace theory as it could be applied
to PK events.

Let us begin by making the following two assumptions:
(1) All physical objects, including human bodies, are
extended in a universe of at least four space-like and two
time-like dimensions;
(2) Our brains and sense-organs are so constructed that we
can be aware of only one particular three-dimensional section
of an object at any one moment in the time-1 dimension.

Now consider a two-dimensional space or Flatland represented by the plane ZOX in Figure 7. To a being whose
perceptions are limited to this 2-space, the cylinder P will
appear to be a circle. Suppose that someone having access to
the third dimension OY tilts the cylinder into the position
represented by Q. To the Flatlander, his circle will seem to
turn into an ellipse. In fact, if the diameter of the original
circle was d, and the cylinder is tilted through an angle θ, the
Flatlander will now perceive an ellipse whose long axis is $d \sec \theta$,
and whose short axis remains unchanged at d. By analogy,
we can reason that if a four-dimensional object were to be
tilted out of its normal position in relation to our world, the
three-dimensional section perceived by us would change,
growing longer or shorter according to the extent and direction of the tilt.

Now in the records of nineteenth century mediumship
there are a number of cases in which objects, including the
bodies of mediums or sitters, seemed to be altered in size or
shape (p. 73). Some witnesses testified that they had seen part
of a limb shrink and then disappear altogether. Such phenomena could be easily accounted for by assuming that the object
was being slowly rotated into 4-space. The reader will readily

appreciate that if the cylinder shown in Figure 7 is rotated far enough it will eventually leave the XOZ plane altogether becoming invisible to the inhabitants of Flatland. Some such explanation might also account for the wooden rings which looked 'as though parts of them had been eaten away' during the Margery séances (p. 132). Apportation phenomena, in which an object enters or leaves a closed space such as a box or a room, also become quite understandable in terms of hyperspace. If space has four dimensions rather than three, there is no such thing as a 'closed' room in the strict sense of the word, since anything which is sealed against entry from 3-space is still open to the fourth dimension. An apport, therefore, is simply an object which has left 3-space at one set of spacetime coordinates and re-entered it at another.

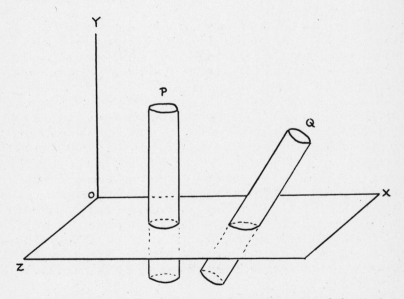

Fig. 7 Tilting an object in 3-space causes distortion of the section observed by beings confined to a 2-space such as the plane ZOX.

Telekinesis can be explained in a slightly different manner. Returning to Figure 7, suppose now that the OY axis represents a time dimension rather than a spacial one. The entire ZOX plane must be regarded as moving upwards in the direction OY. To the inhabitants of Flatland (i.e., the plane ZOX), the cylinder labelled P will appear as a *stationary* circle in their world, since each horizontal section of the cylinder lies at the same distance from the time axis OY. If the cylinder is now tilted into the position represented by Q the circle will become a *moving* one, for as the plane ZOX moves along the time axis OY, the successive sections of the cylinder appear further and further to the right of OZ. Thus, tilting the cylinder in a time-like dimension will cause the circle to move; it will also cause it to be elongated into an ellipse, as we noted before. This kind of distortion effect is already familiar to us from the Special Theory of Relativity, but there is a slight difference: in our diagram an object inclined at an angle to the time axis appears as a moving object which is *increased* in length, whereas in Relativity Theory a moving body appears to *decrease* in length (the Fitzgerald contraction). The discrepancy arises because in our diagram we have treated time as if it were merely an additional dimension of a Euclidian space. In fact, time measurements enter into the metric of spacetime with a negative sign (equation (3)), making the geometry non-Euclidian. When this fact is taken into account, the expansion shown in our diagram actually turns out to be a contraction. Returning to telekinesis, we may conclude that any tilting of a four-dimensional object in one of the time dimensions will appear as an unexpected movement in 3-space.

It is fascinating to note how almost the entire range of apparently chaotic PK phenomena can be brought within the scope of a few relatively simple assumptions involving higher dimensions of space and time. A very slight tilting of an object in a fourth spatial dimension will cause alterations in the shape and size of its three-dimensional section, whereas a similar slight tilting in a time dimension will bring about movement. Much greater tilting will cause the object to disappear altogether from 3-space, while a full rotation will cause it to re-enter 3-space at a different point. Thus, paranormal movements, changes in shape, appearances and disappearances are all neatly accommodated within the hyperspace theory.

The phenomenon known as 'materialisation' presents us with a rather different problem. Spiritualists use the word in two different senses. Sometimes it is used to describe the sudden appearance of an apport during a séance, a phenomenon which we have already accounted for in terms of the hyperspace theory. However, there is another kind of materialisation described, in which a mist or vapour appears and gradually thickens until it seems to resemble part of a human being. Sometimes the materialisation seems to be composed of a sticky substance, called 'ectoplasm' by Richet. There is no doubt that many of the alleged materialisations of the late nineteenth and early twentieth century were fraudulent but there were a few which may have been genuinely paranormal. During the mediumship of Rudi Schneider, for example, competent witnesses observed a kind of creeping mist which changed shape as it moved, and this phenomenon was obtained under very good conditions of control. We can perhaps explain this by posing the question: how would a four-dimensional entity appear to our senses if it were to be slowly intruded into 3-space? We must remember that the millennia of evolution have shaped and adapted our eyes and brains to deal with ordinary three-dimensional existence. When the brain is confronted with something totally unfamiliar, it automatically attempts to interpret it in terms of its previous experiences. It is just possible, therefore, that some of the vague shapes observed by the witnesses may have been genuine intrusions from the world of hyperspace, misinterpreted by the sensory systems of the observers.

Although the theory of hyperspace can certainly explain what is observed during the occurrence of a PK event, it does not solve all our problems. We still have to answer a number of important questions concerning these events. For example, if all objects have extension in the fourth dimension, why are they not constantly moving into and out of that dimension, changing shape, appearing and disappearing, all the while? In short, *why are PK phenomena so uncommon?* In chapter 13 I suggested that PK effects may indeed be more common than we generally suppose, but that our minds refuse to recognise them as such. Even if this viewpoint is accepted, however, the fact remains that most of the objects in our world remain remarkably stable for most of the time. Tables and chairs do *not* undergo weird distortions of shape, jump around the room, appear or disappear in a haphazard manner. Fortunately for our sanity, the objects around us seem to be quite determined to obey the laws of Newtonian physics, at least as long as there are no poltergeist agents in the vicinity. If we accept the existence of a hyperspace in order to explain PK phenomena, we then have to explain why most objects are so rigidly locked into that particular three-dimensional section which we regard as the real world. In terms of our Flatland analogy, this is equivalent to asking: what keeps the Flatlanders and their objects confined to the surface?

Clearly, at this point we need to make a further assumption, and I suggest that 3-space, as we know it, is filled with a force-field which keeps objects from moving out of it into other dimensions. No doubt this force-field could itself be interpreted as a curvature in still higher dimensions, but there is nothing to be gained by taking such a step here. For the moment, let us assume that all physical objects will remain orientated at a constant angle to the higher dimensions unless a force is applied to alter that orientation. This means that the shapes and sizes of objects will, in general, remain constant. Applied to the time dimensions, it means that objects will continue to move in a straight line at a constant speed unless acted upon by a force, which is Newton's first law of motion. Just as a magnetic field can hold a piece of metal firmly suspended in 3-space, so the force-field filling the visible universe prevents objects from rotating or moving into other dimensions. In order to overcome this force-field and bring about a PK event, a considerable quantity of energy may have to be expended, at least at the macroscopic level. This expenditure of energy should have certain predictable consequences which would appear in the experimental records.

Whenever a force is applied to cause an object to move against a field (whether gravitational, electrostatic or magnetic), *heat* is invariably generated. In cases of apportation or teleportation, therefore, where objects are moved right out of 3-space, we would expect to find that they have become hot as a result of the movement. This is in good accord with the available evidence. Of the 500 poltergeist cases analysed by Gauld and Cornell, 53 involved incendiary effects of one sort or another, and in 18 cases objects which had been transported by the 'geist' were found to be hot.[58]

Although this is not a very high percentage of the whole sample, it must be remembered that in most cases observers would be unlikely to pick up an object immediately after it had been thrown, so there would be no knowledge of whether it was hot or not. The average person's reaction to a paranormal occurrence is to back away from it, rather than put out one's hand to touch it! If the reader will turn back to chapter 8 and re-read the account of Zöllner's experiments, he will find further examples of the heating effect.

Not only is heat generated when an object moves against the constraining effect of a force-field, but there is also some distortion of the field itself. Thus, pulling a piece of iron away from a magnet distorts the lines of force in the space round about. If PK events involve the wrenching of objects out of their normal spacetime alignments, we might expect distortions of the spacetime metric to occur in the vicinity. Thus, we conclude that a powerful PK event should have an influence on other objects which may be some distance away. Once again, when we examine the voluminous literature on physical mediumship, we find plenty of evidence to support this expectation. During séances with Slade objects some distance away also began to move, and a heavy screen was shattered by an unexplained force. It is interesting to note that the 'spirits' apologised for this event, which was apparently unintentional (p.101); it seems that the effort needed to displace an object into 4-space is liable to spread to other objects in the vicinity, whether the operator wishes it or not. This spreading effect is particularly noticeable in some of the D. D. Home séances. For example, in 1858 he gave a séance to a group of Dutch intellectuals known as the *Dageraad,* men described by George Zorab as 'typical die-hard rationalists'. The following description is taken from their report:

'Hardly had we seated ourselves – within ten seconds – than we heard soft rappings that soon changed into loud knocks. These raps were heard to come from all sides of the large room. They were accompanied by a complete rocking movement of the ceiling which became so violent that, together with the chairs on which we were seated, we felt ourselves going up and down as if on a rocking-horse. We experienced the same sensation and movement as when sitting in a carriage on springs while driving along the highroad.

'The table behaved more or less in the same manner observed in the former two sittings, i.e. rising high and then descending smoothly to the floor without any abrupt movements.'[193]

This 'earthquake effect', reported frequently with D. D. Home and occasionally with other mediums, remains one of the most puzzling features of nineteenth century mediumship. It is evident that, if the whole building was *really* rocking violently in the manner suggested, enormous cracks would have appeared in the brick and plaster-work! However, if the effects were distortions of the spacetime metric rather similar to the Fitzgerald contraction in Relativity, no such physical collapse would be expected. The apparent rocking of the ceiling might have been due to the observers themselves being rotated into 4-space and back again, the changing angles from which they viewed the room producing something akin to vertigo.

The purpose of this chapter has been to demonstrate how very useful the concept of a higher-dimensional space can be in parapsychology. Zöllner was quite correct in his belief that most of the physical phenomena of mediumship can be interpreted in terms of a fourth spatial dimension; in fact, it is difficult to see how such phenomena as apportation and teleportation could be explained in any other way. Unfortunately, Zöllner lived in the days before Einstein had made geometrical theories of the universe fashionable, and in any case, the mathematical techniques needed to develop such theories were not then available. Einstein was able to use the tensor calculus to give mathematical expression to his theory of a curved spacetime continuum, but this calculus was not developed until 1887, five years after the death of the much-maligned Zöllner. Of course, the notions presented in this chapter do not constitute a *theory* of PK; they are no more than suggestions upon which a theory may one day be built. If a scientific theory is to be of any practical use, it must be worked out in detail so that specific predictions can be drawn from it: I have suggested that macroscopic PK phenomena can be understood in terms of rotational and translational movements of objects in hyperspace; however, a great deal of mathematical work needs to be done before the implications of such a suggestion become clear. Only then will we be in a position to know whether the theory fits the facts accumulated by more than a century of psychical research.

Even if this geometrical theory of PK turns out to be correct, it still leaves one important question unanswered. Assuming that PK effects are indeed distortions of spacetime, or intrusions into it from other dimensions, who – or what – is the agency producing such effects? Clearly, both in poltergeist cases and in séance-room phenomena, some kind of intelligence is at work. If this intelligence is able to manipulate objects from a higher-dimensional space, it must itself exist in that space. I would suggest that what we call 'mind' is actually a material structure existing in hyperspace, and that our visible bodies are merely three-dimensional sections of that structure. This is not exactly a novel idea; in fact, something rather like it was suggested by Professor Smythies in 1967,[165] but it seems to have attracted only minimal attention at the time. It has the advantage of providing a rather neat solution to the so-called 'mind-body' problem. According to this view, mind and matter are simply different aspects of a single multidimensional entity, the three-dimensional section of which we happen to be conscious at any particular time being referred to as 'matter', and the rest as 'mind'.

No doubt some people will see this suggestion as merely a more sophisticated version of the old discredited materialism. However, it should be remembered that when we pass from a world of two dimensions (Flatland) into a world of three dimensions, the whole nature of reality is enlarged, for the entities of that higher world have new and unexpected properties. As a trivial example, it is possible to tie a vast number of interesting knots and hitches in 3-space, whereas the very concept of a knot is meaningless in 2-space. Consider what would happen if the inhabitants of Flatland tried to build a computer; since all the connecting wires must lie in a plane (no wire can pass *over* or *under* another) the complexity of the device would be very severely limited. Indeed, it is doubtful whether the Flatlanders could build anything remotely resembling a computer as we know it. However, once a third dimension becomes available, components can be linked in a great variety of different ways, making it possible to construct calculating machines with enormous mathematical potential.

By analogy, therefore, we can see that the addition of just one extra dimension – from 3-space to 4-space – would lead to a vast enlargement of possibilities. Attempts to account for the properties of mind in purely physical terms (that is, in terms of 3-space concepts) have been singularly unsuccessful. However, those very properties which now seem so inexplicable may become much more understandable when viewed from the perspective of hyperspace. The study of memory, for example, has always been divided between those who hope to explain it in purely physical terms ('memory molecules', neuronal circuitry, etc), and those who postulate a 'nonphysical memory matrix'*. According to the hyperspace theory, both views are partially correct. Whenever we experience an event, whether in the 'physical' (3-space) or 'mental' (hyperspace) realms of our being, some part of us is thereby altered. These alterations are our memories, and some will persist in the 3-space part of our being, some in the hyperspace part, and some in both. It is likely that those memories which are considered to be of the greatest importance are permanently stored in various hyperstructures. It is possible that when that section of our being which lies in 3-space wears out, we merely shed it as a snake sheds its skin, our centre of consciousness then withdrawing into another part of our multidimensional being. Thus, the theory outlined here does not exclude the possibility of 'survival after death'.

It is important to emphasise that the hyperspace world in which, according to this theory, our minds and personalities exist, is not *less* real than the world of three dimensions. On the contrary, it is very much *more* real, in the same way that a cube is more real than a square. What we regard as 'reality' – the everyday world with its three spatial dimensions and linear time-flow – is no more than an abstraction from a much more complex universe. We are indeed like the men in Plato's allegory who, seeing the shadows of a higher reality on the walls of their cave, mistake those shadows for reality itself.

---

*Cf. Lester Smith (Ed): *Intelligence Came First*. Theosophical Publishing House, 1975.

16 Beyond the Quantum

> 'No development of modern science has had a more profound
> impact on human thinking than the advent of quantum mechanics.
> Wrenched out of centuries-old thought patterns, physicists of a gen-
> eration ago found themselves compelled to embrace a new
> metaphysics. The distress which this reorientation caused continues
> to the present day. Basically physicists have suffered a severe loss:
> their hold on reality.'
>
> Bryce S. DeWitt, 1971 (quoted by Schmidt[161])

Many people, including many scientists, still find it difficult
to come to terms with the extraordinary revolution in physics
which took place during the first thirty years of the present
century. The Quantum Theory and the Theory of Relativitiy
are now taught as a routine part of all advanced physics
courses, and their formulae find standard applications in
many laboratories. Nevertheless, there is still a considerable
amount of disagreement among experts as to the exact interpretations which should be placed upon the concepts
which underlie these great theories. This is particularly true
of the Quantum Theory, whose implications seem so bizarre
and so remote from the 'commonsense' view of reality that
we prefer, whenever possible, not to think too deeply about
them. Even the most dedicated quantum theorist thinks in
Newtonian terms when he is going about the business of
everyday life!

The quantum revolution was initiated by the Berlin physicist Max Planck, in a paper which he delivered to the German
Physical Society on December 14th, 1900. In that paper he
suggested that radiant energy is emitted from hot bodies in
the form of discrete units which he called *quanta*. The energy
of each quantum is given by the formula $E = h\nu$, where ν is
the frequency of the radiation and h is a constant, now known
as Planck's constant. This simple assumption proved to be
very effective in solving many of the problems which had
been causing great perplexity among physicists. A few years
later Einstein used it to explain the photoelectric effect, which
is the emission of electrons from a metallic surface when it is
exposed to light. Then in 1913 the great Danish physicist

Niels Bohr applied the quantum principle to account for the internal structure of atoms. On the assumption that energy can only be emitted in discrete units (quanta) he was able to show that the electrons circulating round the nucleus must be confined to certain definite orbits. If an electron jumps from one orbit to another, a quantum of radiation is emitted. When developed mathematically, Bohr's theory provided a beautifully neat solution to the problem of calculating the spectrum lines of the various chemical elements; it also helped to explain the chemical properties of many elements, and their relationship to one another.

So far, everything seemed to be going well. Although physicists had been rather surprised to find that energy only appears in packets, there was nothing particularly bizarre about the concept, and it did seem to account for a lot of otherwise inexplicable phenomena. Then in 1924 came a further suggestion, which shattered their complacency once and for all. It came from Prince Louis de Broglie, a French nobleman who had turned from the study of mediaeval history to devote himself to physics. De Broglie suggested that the quantum principle should be extended to include matter as well as energy. Just as light was now known to possess particle-like properties as well as wave-like ones, so the particles of matter – electrons, protons, atoms, etc., – should, in some experiments, appear like waves. He proposed that a particle of mass m moving with a velocity v should have associated with it a wave of wavelength λ, where $\lambda = h/mv$.

In olden times an actor would don the mask of tragedy or comedy, depending on the part he had to play. So the fundamental components of the physical world appear to us sometimes as waves and sometimes as particles, depending on the experiment we decide to perform. Our natural human curiosity makes us want to ask: what are they *really* like, these building-bricks of the universe? Unfortunately the question seems to be a meaningless one, for we can know nothing whatever about the world except in so far as it impinges upon our senses. Whenever we try to make observations upon an electron we find it wearing one or other of its two masks; there seems to be no way of getting behind the mask and finding out what the real actor is like – if, indeed, there *is* a real actor.

It is hardly surprising that the physicists of the 1920s found De Broglie's idea difficult to digest, and some were rather scornful of it. George Gamow tells us that it was referred to as 'la Comédie Française'![54] Comedy or not, the idea was taken up by Erwin Schrödinger, who developed it into a theoretical system known as *wave mechanics*. In Schrödinger's hands De Broglie's waves proved to be highly successful in accounting for many atomic and molecular phenomena which could not be explained in terms of the old Bohr theory. Almost at the same time another physicist, Werner Heisenberg, developed a rather more abstract mathematical approach to the structure of the atom which became known as *matrix mechanics*. Later, Schrödinger succeeded in proving that wave mechanics and matrix mechanics are mathematically identical, and always lead to the same conclusions; either approach may be used to solve a particular problem, depending on one's personal preference. The fact that De Broglie's waves are real and are not merely mathematical fictions was proved in 1927, when Davisson and Germer passed a beam of electrons through a crystal, and found that the beam was diffracted in the same manner as a beam of light. Today, the wave-like nature of electron beams is utilised in the electron microscope, which is one of the most useful tools of twentieth century science.

There have been many attempts to account for the wave-particle duality in terms which can be grasped by the human mind. One of the earliest was due to Heisenberg himself, who in 1927 put forward the famous Heisenberg Uncertainty Principle, sometimes known as the Principle of Indeterminacy. He argued that in order to observe an electron or any other particle, we must reflect some kind of radiation from it. As the radiation bounces off the electron it will inevitably alter the particle's velocity. Thus, in the very act of observing the particle we disturb it, making its future path uncertain. Since the smallest amount of energy which we can use for an observation is a single quantum, it follows that we can never obtain absolutely accurate information about the position and velocity of a particle at any particular moment. In fact, the uncertainty in the particle's position multiplied by the uncertainty in its velocity can never be less than h/m, where h is Planck's constant and m is the mass of the particle. Since we can never be quite sure where the particle is or how fast it is moving, all our calculations must be concerned with probabilities rather than certainties. Max Born developed this idea, and showed that the square of the Schrödinger wave function (ψ^2) at any point in space can be interpreted as representing the probability of finding the particle there. This has since been adopted as the official interpretation of the Quantum Theory; it is sometimes known as the 'Copenhagen Interpretation', since much of the work on it was done at Niels Bohr's Institute for Theoretical Physics in Copenhagen.

The reader who has followed the story so far may wonder why I referred to the concepts behind the Quantum Theory as 'bizarre and remote'. There is surely nothing very surprising in the fact that we cannot obtain absolute accuracy in our measurements, and must therefore resort to probability calculations. Can we not simply assume that the De Broglie waves arise as a result of the limitations which nature imposes on our observations? Perhaps behind the waves, like the actor behind his mask, lies a real particle behaving in the traditional Newtonian manner, as all good particles should. Unfortunately for common sense, it can be shown that this interpretation is incompatible with the basic principles of the Quantum Theory. There is no 'real' particle at all, and the uncertainty is not merely a consequence of our inability to make accurate observations; it is an inherent property of the natural world. In the words of Dr Paul Davies: 'It is not just that we cannot know what an electron is up to, it is that the electron simply does not possess a definite position and momentum simultaneously. It is an intrinsically uncertain entity.'[31]

In present-day Quantum Theory the state of a physical system before an observation is made upon it is represented by a mathematical device called a *state vector*, which is equivalent to the wave-function of the earlier Schrödinger formulation. The state vector is represented as existing in a multidimensional Hilbert space; in effect, it contains within itself representations of all the possible states which the system might assume when an observation is eventually made. As soon as the observer makes his observation (for example, by interposing a fluorescent screen to detect the position of an electron) the state vector 'collapses', and the system is found to be in one of the possible observational states. This collapse of the state vector (or 'collapse of the wave-packet' as some writers call it) has caused a great deal of heart-searching among quantum theoreticians. It seems to imply that nature is indeterminate until a conscious observer forces it to behave in a particular manner. Indeed, we are almost driven to wonder, as some philosophers have done, whether the world exists at all when no one is looking at it. All that seems to exist in the absence of the observer is a mathematical abstraction, an assortment of probabilities known as the state vector.

The strange nature of the Quantum Theory is highlighted by the famous Einstein–Podolsky–Rosen (EPR) paradox, first put forward in 1935 and still discussed today. Suppose we have a pair of protons which are brought together in the configuration known as the singlet state, and then allowed to separate. Each proton possesses a property known as its *spin*, a component of which can be measured along any arbitrarily chosen axis in three dimensional space. It is known that, if we measure the spin components of the two protons along the same axis (for example, in an east-to-west direction) we shall always find that one is clockwise and the other anticlockwise. Now suppose we allow the two protons to separate until they are thousands of miles apart, and we then measure the spin component of proton A along a particular axis. As soon as we make the measurement the state vector collapses, and the spin component of proton A, which up to now has been an indeterminate quantity, takes on a definite value. The curious feature is this: at the very same instant that we determine the spin component of proton A *the spin component of proton B also becomes fixed*, since the two spins must be equal and opposite. Thus, an observation made in a laboratory here on earth can cause the instantaneous collapse of the state vector for a particle which may be thousands or even millions of miles away, perhaps across the other side of the universe! Furthermore, we can *choose* which component of proton A's spin momentum to measure, and our choice will automatically affect the corresponding component of the spin momentum of the distant partner. Weird as this instantaneous action-at-a-distance may seem to be, it is nevertheless supported by some good experimental evidence.[34] No wonder that Arthur Koestler felt that 'the seemingly fantastic propositions of parapsychology appear less preposterous in the light of the truly fantastic concepts of modern physics.'[97]

Quantum physics, therefore, confronts us with a world whose basic constituents are little more than insubstantial ghosts, occupying no definite localities in either space or time. In so far as we are able to represent these strange entities at all, we have to do so in terms of probability distributions, state vectors, or similar mathematical devices. However, the ghosts have the property of materialising instantaneously whenever we try to observe them; thus, the conscious observer interacts with the shadow world to bring about the crystallisation into reality. The observer can no longer be regarded as separate from the thing he observes, for both are inextricably interwoven in the process of creating the phenomena which we regard as the components of the real world.

In view of the extraordinary nature of these ideas, it is hardly surprising that some modern thinkers have refused to accept the Copenhagen interpretation, and have sought to explain the obvious practical successes of the Quantum Theory in other ways. In 1952 David Bohm published the first of several papers in which he tried to interpret the formulae of quantum mechanics in terms of a *hidden variable* theory. According to Bohm, the movements of electrons and other small particles are actually governed by factors which, by their very nature, lie outside our field of observation. Because we cannot measure these factors we are unable to give a precise description of the trajectory of the particle, and have to rely upon the probabilistic equations of the Quantum Theory. However, if we *were* able to measure these hidden variables, we should find that the particle was behaving in a predictable manner. Bohm's efforts were encouraged by Einstein who, to the end of his life, refused to believe 'that God plays dice with the world'.

In 1957 an even more radical re-interpretation was proposed by Hugh Everett. The paradoxical aspect of quantum mechanics arises from the fact that the state vector apparently 'collapses' when an observation is made, thereby fixing the system in one of its possible forms. Everett cut the Gordian knot by suggesting that the state vector does not collapse at all. Instead, the world divides into a number of parallel worlds, in each of which one of the possible states of the system is realised. As a simple example, we may take the well-known experiment in which an electron is fired at a screen with two slits in it. Through which slit will the electron pass? According to Everett's 'many worlds' theory, at the instant of decision the universe divides into two universes, lying parallel to one another in hyperspace; in one of these universes the electron passes through the left-hand slit and in the other it passes through the right-hand slit. The conscious observer also divides, amoeba-fashion, one of his two selves going into universe A and the other into universe B. Thus, in this theory we are presented with a fantastic endless proliferation of universes, cosmos piled upon cosmos in an unimaginable multidimensional space, for every single quantum event splits the entire world. It can be shown mathematically that Everett's theory is perfectly consistent with the principles of quantum mechanics, and it certainly provides a neat solution to some of the quantum paradoxes. However, many scientists reject it on the grounds that it cannot be tested or falsified by observation, and is therefore not a scientific theory in the strict sense of the term. Everett's own arguments show that there is no way in which the hypothetical splitting of the world could be observed, either directly or indirectly; it therefore remains nothing more than an interesting speculation.

To attempt to explain psi phenomena in terms of the Quantum Theory may seem to some people to be a case of the blind attempting to lead the blind! Nevertheless, several such attempts have been made. One of the most impressive is by Evan Harris Walker, formerly of the NASA Electronics Research Centre in Cambridge, Massachusetts.[184] Walker accepts the existence of consciousness as a real, although non-physical entity, and regards it as the source of the hidden variables which bring about the collapse of the state vector. The term 'non-physical' as used in this context has no supernatural overtones; it simply means 'not accessible to physical measurement'. Pursuing this line of thought, Walker has developed a very sophisticated model of mind-brain interaction in which the hidden variables of consciousness are coupled to the moving electrons in the brain by means of the quantum mechanical wave function. As far as I am aware, this is the first coherent attempt by any scientist to solve the age-old philosophical problem of the relationship between mind and matter, and it is certainly an impressive theory. Having developed this 'Quantum Mechanical Theory of Consciousness', Walker went on to apply it to elucidate the nature of psi phenomena.[120] He has shown that the theory encompasses the existence of ESP and PK, and indicates that they should be independent of space and time. He has also made certain predictions, based on the theory, about the effect of PK upon different kinds of objects, and these predictions seem to be consistent with the results of dice-throwing experiments performed by Cox, Forwald, and others. Many parapsychologists shy away from Walker's theory, possibly because they find it conceptually and mathematically difficult. This is a pity, for the theory is undoubtedly one of the most promising which has so far been developed. The creation of a theory which leads to definite, experimentally-testable predictions is a rare event in psychical research, and it is to be hoped that others will pursue and develop the lines of thought opened up by Walker.

Another modern thinker who has explored the possibility of establishing a link between parapsychology and quantum physics is Dr D. F. Lawden, Professor of Mathematics at the University of Aston, Birmingham. He points out that the Quantum Theory, 'the most fundamental of all physical theories governing the behaviour of matter and radiation', strongly suggests the existence of an interaction between mind and inanimate objects, and this interaction is precisely what we need in order to explain PK and poltergeist effects. Lawden postulates that the observer's mind interacts psychokinetically with the physical world, suppressing certain terms in the state vector which would otherwise lead to rather bizarre consequences:

'For example, according to the principles of quantum theory, it is possible for a body to be in two different places at the same time, so that a meter can be registering two different readings simultaneously. Experience, however, shows that this type of state is never consciously observed and, in line with our ideas, this implies that the structure of the psyche is such that it coerces these systems into an admissible state via the psychokinetic interaction. This raises the possibility that certain basic modes of our experience (e.g. that two bodies cannot occupy the same space at the same time) may be revealed as consequences of our psychic structure, instead of being accepted axiomatically as irreducible properties of physical objects and space.'[101]

In our everyday life we seem to look out through the windows of the senses at a world which is independent of ourselves, an external reality which we can only influence to a limited extent by using the muscles of our body. Modern physics has completely shattered this tidy, commonsense view of a world 'out there'. Reality, it seems, is a much more subtle thing than we imagined, and the observer is somehow involved in creating the very thing which he observes. If Dr Lawden is correct, so-called paranormal events (such as the disappearance of an object from one place and its reappearance elsewhere) are only prevented from happening through the interaction of our own minds with the cosmos. The stable external world in which we live is partly our own creation; we create it by suppressing those possibilities which are permitted by the quantum equations, but which, if allowed to occur, would generate a world in which it would be impossible to live. On this view, paranormal events are rare occurrences which take place when, for some reason or other, this normal mind-control is temporarily relaxed or disturbed.

It is almost certain that we have not yet heard the last of the Quantum Theory in connection with the phenomena of psychical research. The ideas put forward in this chapter are, of course, highly controversial; nevertheless, they represent an encouraging step in the right direction. One of the greatest drawbacks in the past has been the lack of testable theories, for without these no branch of science can make much progress. Now, it seems the theorists are producing something which the experimentalists can put to the test. This may be a sign that parapsychology is about to move into a period of more systematic development in which the cooperation between physicists and parapsychologists will begin to yield fruit.

Epilogue

Our survey of PK phenomena is now at an end. We have seen how, throughout all recorded periods of human history and in all the countries of the world, some individuals have reported the occurrence of events which seem to run contrary to our everyday experience of physical reality. We have also examined the efforts of a relatively small company of scientists and scholars who, in the teeth of much opposition from their confreres and ridicule from society as a whole, sought to establish the truth about those events by impartial investigation and experimentation. As a result of their work, we now have a very strong body of evidence in favour of the occurrence of the PK effect. Finally we have made a tentative attempt to classify the various forms of PK, and we have considered some of the approaches towards a theoretical understanding of the phenomena which can be made through the concepts of modern physics.

Where, then, should we go from here? In the past psychical research has been handicapped by various preconceived ideas and attitudes which have had the effect of restricting certain lines of enquiry. In this concluding section I want to draw attention to some of the mistaken attitudes which, in my opinion, have had the effect of retarding the research effort, and suggest ways in which they can be avoided in the future.

Firstly, some psychical researchers have been far too strongly obsessed with the possible existence of fraud, leading at times to an almost paranoid attitude towards anyone who reports significant results. Of course, every possible attempt should be made to guard against fraud, and I am not for one moment advocating the introduction of lax experimental conditions. However, when a responsible scientist reports that he obtained PK effects in an experiment which appears to have been competently conducted and accurately recorded, his results should not be discarded merely because some sceptically-minded person suggests that a deception *might* have occurred. The fear of being deceived is a natural one, but it must not be allowed to exercise a stultifying effect upon research policy. As we saw earlier, the attitude of Sidgwick and some other leaders of the SPR almost led to the Society missing its opportunity to do a valuable piece of research with Eusapia Palladino (see chapter 9), and there have been other instances where the fear of being deceived has deterred researchers from following up a useful line of investigation. To refuse to investigate a phenomenon because it occurs among people who may be dishonest is rather like a bacteriologist refusing to work with the organism *Escherichia coli* because it normally lives in human faeces! We must face up to the unpleasant aspects of our task, not seek to avoid them.

Secondly, there has been a strong tendency for psychical researchers of each new generation to discount the work of the preceding one, thus making 'null and void' what has already been achieved.[45] The same phenomena, therefore, have to be 'discovered' over and over again, while a great deal of valuable research material is relegated to the archives. One way in which psychical research could make better progress would be by disinterring this mass of material and subjecting it to detailed analysis. As far as I know, no one has ever attempted to compare and collate the voluminous reports of nineteenth and early twentieth century physical mediumship. I am quite certain that, if such a task were attempted (perhaps with the help of computers) some useful new lines of investigation would appear. Throughout the course of this book I have drawn attention to certain features of PK which seem to crop up again and again as accidental side-effects, but which have never been systematically studied. The production of heat during teleportation or apportation is one such example. If the records were to be systematically compared and their common features extracted, the underlying patterns would become much clearer. Gauld and Cornell have already done this for the poltergeist;[58] There is no reason why it should not also be done for the phenomena of the séance-room.

Thirdly, I would suggest that psychical researchers need to form much stronger links with the practitioners of the physical sciences. In the past, psychical research has been severely handicapped by the lack of an adequate conceptual background. As I have tried to show in the last two chapters, the problems of modern physics are in many ways startlingly similar to the problems of parapsychology. In recent years a number of physicists, both experimental and theoretical, have begun to take an interest in parapsychological phenomena. Schmidt, Walker, Hasted, Taylor and Lawden are just a few who spring to mind in this connection. We need the co-operation of physicists such as these in order to work towards a proper theoretical framework for psi phenomena. The 'Einstein of Parapsychology' has not yet appeared, but we have the task of preparing the ground for him.

There are many people whose interest in psychical research springs from the belief that it points toward a non-physical or spiritual reality, and thus acts as a form of defence against the depressing doctrines of materialism. These people may, perhaps, be disturbed by my suggestion that we should seek for a *physical* theory of psi. However, I would remind them that in modern physics matter is no longer the hard, irrefragable thing it once appeared to be. Quantum theory has taught us that *mind* participates in the very nature of matter in some mysterious way; the two seem to be inextricably entwined. Thus the old materialism – and the old idealism – are superseded by our new understanding of reality. There may well be a sense in which the mind is a physical or material structure, but it is not a structure limited to the three dimensions of space and one of time in which our conscious awareness seems to be confined. We need not be afraid to formulate 'materialistic' theories of psi, for they will inevitably involve a totally new concept of matter which passes far beyond our naive sensory experience of it. Long before the Quantum Theory and the Theory of Relativity were conceived, Thomas Henry Huxley sensed prophetically that matter was not everything it was made out to be. Accused of preaching materialistic doctrines, that great nineteenth century genius replied:

'For what, after all, do we know of this terrible 'matter' except as a name for the unknown and hypothetical cause of states of our own consciousness? And what do we know of that 'spirit' over whose threatened extinction by matter a great lamentation is arising, like that which was heard at the death of Pan, except that it is also a name for an unknown and hypothetical cause, or condition, of states of consciousness?'[26]

Postscript

After the main text of this book was written several new developments in the study of macroscopic PK came to my notice. Perhaps the most important of these is the use of the 'minilab', a technique which was pioneered in the United States by John G. Neihardt, formerly Professor of English Literature in the University of Illinois at Columbia. During the early 1960s Neihardt founded a research group known as SORRAT (Society for Research into Rapport and Telekinesis) which, over a period of years claimed to have obtained striking evidence for the reality of large-scale PK. In many ways the work of this group resembles that done by Batcheldor, Brookes-Smith, and the Toronto group led by Dr Owen (see page 165), but for some reason the SORRAT work went almost unnoticed in the parapsychological literature. If the accounts are to be believed, the SORRAT experimenters were successful in obtaining most of the classical phenomena of physical mediumship, including raps, falls in temperature, levitation of physical objects (including, on one occasion, a table weighing 82 lbs), lights, apports, and teleportations. Detailed records of the group's researches were kept by Dr. J. T. Richards, who acted as their archivist and photographer.

As the SORRAT group's phenomena developed they came to the notice of Dr. J. B. Rhine, who in turn brought them to the attention of veteran PK researcher W. E. Cox. Neihardt had already experimented with the notion of trying to obtain PK effects inside a closed glass container, but the results had not been particularly striking. Cox adapted the technique and produced a number of shallow wooden boxes with dried coffee grounds sprinkled inside. Small objects were placed inside the boxes, which were then sealed in such a way that they could not be opened without revealing the fact that they had been tampered with. It was hoped that the objects inside the box would move under the influence of PK, leaving trails in the coffee grounds which could be photographed when the box was opened. If anyone attempted to move the objects by tilting the box the trails would all lie in the same direction; however, genuinely spontaneous movements should leave trails which would be incompatible with this interpretation. Using members of the SORRAT group as 'mediums', Cox obtained a number of apparently successful results with this technique.

Neihardt died in 1973, but some members of the group continued to experience PK effects. In 1977 Cox moved to Rolla, Missouri, with the specific intention of making a careful study of the phenomena occurring in the home of Dr. Richards. It was here that the first really successful minilab experiments were performed. A typical Cox minilab consists of a glass aquarium tank turned upside down on a heavy wooden board. A steel strip passes tightly round the tank and through two slits in the baseboard. The ends of the strip are fastened together with a high-quality padlock, which is further sealed with tape and superglue. The narrow slit between the tank and the baseboard is sealed with a rubber gasket. Cox went to the trouble of getting an independent expert witness (a Rolla locksmith) to examine the sealing of the tank both before and after the phenomena, and to certify that the seals had not been tampered with. He also set up an 8 mm. movie camera in order to obtain a permanent record of any paranormal events which might occur inside the tank.

An astounding variety of PK events are said to have occurred inside the Cox minilabs, and many were recorded on film. Thus, in one sequence a pen can be seen levitating inside the tank, and performing 'direct writing' on a notepad. On another occasion a white envelope is seen to move from inside a yellow envelope in which it had been sealed, the outer envelope remaining closed. The linking together of two leather rings has been filmed on several occasions, although the rings never remain linked. (The reader will recall that this was one of the classic experiments of the Zöllner era). There is also a rather striking film sequence in which the hands of a clock are seen to move *backwards* while the PK phenomena are occurring. The clock had been placed on the table just outside the minilab in order to have a record of the exact time at which various events occurred. It is interesting to speculate on whether or not a real distortion of time occurred in this instance. As I suggested in Chapter 15, it is certainly possible that some of the more violent kinds of PK phenomena involve a distortion of the spacetime metric.

There are very few full-time parapsychologists in Britain, but one such is Mr Julian Isaacs, who has been conducting research into PK phenomena for several years under the auspices of the Department of Applied Psychology at Aston University, Birmingham. Isaacs believes that PK effects may be much more frequent than we imagine, most of them being trivial incidents which go unnoticed unless they happen to coincide with some remarkable event (such as a death), or unless they occur repeatedly, as in poltergeist outbreaks. This is also the view proposed in Chapter 13 of this book. Isaacs has used mass screening techniques to identify potential PK agents in various parts of the country, and he claims to have located more than 50 people with possible PK ability.* In 1980 he began minilab experiments with some of these subjects, modifying Cox's experimental designs in various ways to make the results more informative. So far these British experiments have had only a modest success, but Isaacs has obtained some evidence of metal-bending occurring inside a minilab, and a few cases of object-movements.

What, then, can we make of the minilab research? Obviously with a development as recent as this it would be unwise to commit oneself to too many firm conclusions. Nevertheless, it is clear that the only alternative to a paranormal explanation of the Cox work is the hypothesis of deliberate fraud on the part of Cox, Richards, or both. Such fraud would have to be very carefully planned and executed, and it would involve the use of a film laboratory in order to produce animated sequences of objects moving inside the minilab. As Isaacs has pointed out, there is nothing whatever in Cox's background to suggest that he would be party to such a deception: 'in 30 years in J. B. Rhine's laboratory there was never any occasion to doubt his honesty and integrity'. Of course, those who believe that PK events are physical impossibilities will inevitably prefer the fraud hypothesis; the rest of us must keep an open mind, and await further developments.

*See *Psychoenergetics* 1981, 4, pp. 125–158.

In conclusion, it is worth remarking that the phenomena reported by Cox are in no way unique. They are merely a recurrence, in the second half of the twentieth century, of phenomena which have been reported for well over a hundred years. The only novelty lies in the methods used to study them, and we may reasonably hope that the use of minilabs, suitably equipped with micro-switches and video or film cameras, may eventually give us a much deeper insight into the nature of the phenomena than was possible in the days of Zöllner, Crookes, and Lodge.

Glossary of Technical Terms

(In the following glossary, qualifying adjectives such as 'alleged', 'claimed', etc., have been omitted for brevity. This should not be taken to imply that the phenomena described do, or do not, exist.)

ANTHROPOLOGY: The study of ancient and primitive human societies.

APPORT: An object which appears inside a closed room during a Spiritualist séance. From the French word *apporter,* to bring.

ASCENSIONS: In ancient texts, the rising of the human body into the air. See also *levitation.*

ASCETICISM: Self-denial, as in the practices of certain mystics who go without food and subject their bodies to various physical discomforts in order to attain spiritual benefits.

CLAIRVOYANCE: Awareness of the state of some object or event without the use of any of the bodily senses, as when someone successfully identifies a card sealed in an envelope and unknown to anyone else. A form of extrasensory perception (q.v.)

DERMO-OPTIC VISION: The ability to 'read' colours, etc, when blindfold, using the tips of the fingers.

DIRECT VOICE: A phenomenon of physical mediumship in which spirits speak directly to the sitter, 'out of the air', rather than through the lips of the medium.

DISAPPEARANCE-REAPPEARANCE EVENTS: Term used by Prof. Hasted and others to describe occurrences in which an object vanishes, for no apparent reason, and reappears in a different location at a later time. See also *apport.*

ECTOPLASM: Term invented by Richet to describe the whitish material which exudes from the bodies of certain physical mediums. The word has a different meaning in orthodox biology.

ESP: See Extrasensory perception.

ESP CARDS: A set of cards used in laboratory tests for extrasensory perception, each card bearing on its face one of five symbols: a cross, a star, a square, a circle, or some wavy lines.

EXORCISM: A religious rite designed to expel evil spirits from a person or a place.

EXTRASENSORY PERCEPTION: Awareness of some external state or condition without the use of the bodily senses. The term includes clairvoyance, telepathy, and precognition.

FLAGELLATION: The practice of some religious ascetics of flogging themselves in order to attain a state of spiritual awareness; it may also be a form of deviant sexual behaviour.

FLIGHTS: In ancient texts, the movement of the human body through the air; see also *ascensions* and *levitation*.

GELLER EFFECT: The bending or breaking of physical objects, usually pieces of metal, without the application of sufficiently large physical forces. Also known as *paranormal metal-bending*.

HYPERSPACE: A space of more than three dimensions.

HYPNOSIS, HYPNOTISM: The inducing of a state of increased suggestibility, by the deliberate application of certain psychological techniques. The term was invented by Braid to replace the older term *mesmerism* (q.v.)

HYSTERIA: In general parlance, the word is used to describe any display of uncontrolled emotion, such as extravagant weeping, screaming or laughing. In psychiatry it is used in a more specific manner to describe a form of neurosis which is characterised by severe anxiety, and which may produce bodily symptoms with no obvious physical causes ('conversion hysteria')

LEVITATION: The rising of the human body, or some other physical object, into the air, without the use of any known physical force.

MATERIALISATION: This word is used by Spiritualists in two different contexts: (i) to describe the appearance of an apport (q.v.), or (ii) to describe the gradual shaping of faces, hands, or complete human forms out of ectoplasm (q.v.)

MEDIUM: A person who acts as a channel of communication between this world and the world of departed spirits.

MESMERISM: The techniques of trance induction developed by Franz Anton Mesmer (1733–1815), and the theories associated with them.

METAL-BENDING: see GELLER EFFECT.

METAPSYCHICS: Term invented by Richet and used in France as equivalent to psychical research. Not to be confused with *metaphysics,* which is a branch of philosophy.

MINI-GELLERS: Children who possess similar metal-bending abilities to those of Uri Geller (see Geller Effect).

OCCULT: Literally 'hidden'; occultism is the idea that there are certain forms of knowledge which are hidden from the majority of mankind, but may be revealed to a few chosen adepts. The 'occult sciences' include such practices as alchemy, astrology, and necromancy.

OCCULTATION PHENOMENON: During a séance, the interruption of a beam of electromagnetic radiation (usually infra-red) when no visible object is present in the beam.

PARANORMAL: Incapable of explanation in terms of known physical forms of energy.

PARAPSYCHOLOGY: The application of scientific methods to the study of allegedly paranormal events; a more modern term for Psychical Research.

PK: See psychokinesis.

PLACEMENT EXPERIMENT: A PK experiment in which the subject tries to influence the fall of small objects so that they drop into a designated area.

POLTERGEIST: Literally 'racketing spirit'. A recurrent phenomenon in which noises occur and objects are thrown around, for no apparent reason and without the use of any known form of energy.

POSTCOGNITION: Alternative term for retrocognition (q.v.)

PRECOGNITION: Extrasensory awareness of a future event; knowledge of a future state of affairs which cannot be logically inferred from the current situation.

PSI: The first letter of the Greek word for mind or spirit, 'psyche'. The term 'psi' is used to designate any occurrence which involves the operation of ESP or PK. It is often used in compound expressions, such as 'psi-effect' or 'psi-phenomenon'.

PSYCHICAL RESEARCH: Term originally used in Britain and America to denote the scientific study of paranormal phenomena.

PSYCHOKINESIS: The direct action of the mind upon a physical system, without the mediation of the muscular system of the body.

PSYCHOSOMATIC MEDICINE: The study and treatment of bodily ailments which are caused by underlying psychological factors such as stress.

RANDOM EVENT GENERATOR: An electronic device which generates electrical pulses on two or more outputs, the pulses being randomly distributed between the outputs. It may be used to drive various pieces of equipment used in parapsychological laboratories.

RANDOM NUMBER GENERATOR: Alternative term for *random event generator* (q.v.)

RECURRENT SPONTANEOUS PSYCHOKINESIS (RSPK): Modern term for a poltergeist outbreak (q.v.)

RETROCOGNITION: Extrasensory awareness of a past event or events.

RSPK: See *Recurrent Spontaneous Psychokinesis.*

SAMADHI: State of blissful union with the Divine achieved through the practice of Yoga.

SEANCE: A sitting held for the purpose of contacting departed spirits.

SIDDHIS: Paranormal faculties acquired through the practice of Yoga.

SOMNAMBULISM: Sleep-walking, or walking in a trance.

SPIRITISM: Alternative term for Spiritualism, usually applied to the French variety developed by Kardec.

SPIRIT PHOTOGRAPHY: The appearance of faces or figures of departed persons on photographs of the living.

SPIRITUALISM: The name given to the movement which began in the U.S.A. during the nineteenth century, and which claims to afford communication with the dead and the healing of certain diseases.

SPONTANEOUS HUMAN COMBUSTION (SHC): The bursting into flame of a human being, for no apparent reason.

SUPERNORMAL: Alternative word for paranormal.

TABLE-RAPPING: In Spiritualism, the occurrence of rapping noises on table-tops or other surfaces, said to convey messages from the spirits.

TABLE-TURNING: The movements of tables during séances, such movements being attributed to the activity of spirits.

TELEKINESIS: Paranormal movement of a physical object.

TELEPATHY: Extrasensory awareness of another person's thoughts or emotions.

THEURGY: The doctrines and practices of a neo-platonic sect which flourished during the third and fourth centuries A.D.

THOUGHTOGRAPHY: Term used by Fukurai to describe the paranormal impression of thought imagery upon film.

TRANSCENDENTAL MEDITATION: A form of mind control based upon Yoga, and brought to the western world by the Maharishi Mahesh Yogi and his followers.

TRANSFIGURATION: The apparent change of form of a medium's face or body during a séance, so that she takes on the characteristics of a deceased person.

TRANSVECTION: Term used to denote the levitation and flight of witches.

YOGA: Ancient Indian system of mind and body training, the object of which is to attain union with the Divine.

ZENER CARDS: Old-fashioned term for ESP cards.

References

(1) ABBOTT, E. A.: Flatland: A Romance of Many Dimensions. Basil Blackwell, Oxford, 1978 (reprint of 1884 edition).

(2) BARBANELL, M.: This is Spiritualism. Spiritualist Press, London, 1959, specifically p. 181.

(3) BARCLAY, G.: Mind Over Matter. Arthur Barker, London 1973.

(4) BASTIN, E. W. (Ed): Quantum Theory and Beyond. Cambridge University Press, 1971.

(5) BASTIN, E. W. & PADFIELD, S.: Comment: Uri Geller and the Conjurers. *Theoria to Theory* 1975, *9,* pp 229–231.

(6) BATCHELDOR, K. J.: Report on a Case of Table Levitation and Associated Phenomena. *J. Soc. Psych. Res.* 1966, *43,* pp. 339–356.

(7) BATCHELDOR, K. J.: PK in sitter groups. *Psychoenergetic Systems,* 1979, *3,* pp. 77–93.

(8) BAYLESS, R.: Letter in *J. Soc. Psych. Res.* 1976, *48,* p. 322.

(9) BELL, E. T.: Mathematics, Queen and Servant of Science. G. Bell & Sons, London, 1952, specifically p. 138.

(10) BELL, M.: Francis Bacon: Pioneer in Parapsychology. *Int. J. Parapsychol.* 1964, *6,* pp. 199–208.

(11) BELOFF, J.: Parapsychology and its Neighbours. *J. Parapsychol.* 1970, *34* pp. 129–142.

(12) BELOFF, J. (Ed): New Directions in Parapsychology. Elek Science, London 1974, specifically p. 133.

(13) BENDER, H. & VANDREY, R.: Psychokinetische Experimente mit dem Berner Graphiker Silvio. *Zeit. für Parapsychol. und Grenzgebiete der Psychol.* 1976, *18,* pp. 217–241.

(14) BENDER, H., HAMPEL, R., KURY, H., & WENDLANDT,

S.: Der 'Geller-Effekt' – eine Interview und Frageboge-nuntersuchung. *Zeit. für Parapsychol. und Grenzgebiete der Psychol.* 1975, *17,* pp. 219–240 (Part I); 1976, *18,* pp. 1–20 (Part II); 1976 *18,* pp. 105–116 (Part III).

(15) BRIER, R. M. & TYMINSKI, W. V.: Psi Application: Part I. A Preliminary Attempt. *J. Parapsychol.* 1970, *34,* pp. 1–25.

(16) BRIER, R. M. & TYMINSKI, W. V.: Psi Application: Part II. The Majority-Vote Technique – Analyses and Observations. *J. Parapsychol.* 1970, *34,* pp 26–36.

(17) BROAD, C. D.: Lectures on Psychical Research. Routledge, London, 1962.

(18) BROOKES-SMITH, C.: Review of *The World of Ted Serios. J. Soc. Psych. Res.* 1968, *44,* pp. 260–265.

(19) BROOKES-SMITH, C.: Data-Tape Recorded Experimental PK Phenomena. *J. Soc. Psych. Res.* 1973, *47,* pp. 69–89.

(20) BUEHLER, W. J. & CROSS, W. B.: 55-Nitinol; Unique Wire Alloy with a Memory. *Wire Journal,* June, 1969.

(21) BURTON, J.: Heyday of a Wizard. George Harrap & Co., London, 1948.

(22) BUTTON, W. H.: The Margery Mediumship. *J. Amer. Soc. Psych. Res.* 1932, *26,* pp. 298–323.

(23) CARRINGTON, H.: The American Séances with Eusapia Palladino. Garrett Publications, New York, 1954, specifically p. 249.

(24) CASSIRER, M.: Letter in *J. Soc. Psych. Res.* 1977, *49,* p. 474.

(25) CHARI, C. T. K.: Letter in *J. Amer. Soc. Psych. Res.* 1978, *72,* pp. 66–69.

(26) CLARK, R. W.: The Huxleys. Heinemann, London, 1968, specifically p. 72.

(27) CLARKE, A.: Memoirs of the Wesley Family, Vol. I. London, 1836.

(28) COX, W. E.: Note on Some Experiments with Uri Geller. *J. Parapsychol.* 1974, *38,* pp. 408–411.

(29) CRUSSARD, C.: Rapport sur les essais psychocinetiques effectues par J. P. Girard. Privately circulated report, 1976.

(30) DAVID-NEEL, A.: Magic and Mystery in Tibet. Souvenir Press, London, 1967, specifically p. 156.

(31)   DAVIES, P.: Other Worlds. J. M. Dent & Sons, London, 1980, specifically p. 62.

(32)   de GASPARIN, Count Agénor: Des Tables Tournantes, du Surnaturel en Général, et des Esprits. Dentu, Paris 1854.

(33)   de MARTINO, E.: Magic Primitive and Modern. Tom Stacey, London, 1972, specifically pp. 41–3.

(34)   d'ESPAGNAT, B.: The Quantum Theory and Reality. *Scientific American* 1979, *241,* pp. 128–140.

(35)   DINGWALL, E. J.: Some Human Oddities. Home & Van Thal Ltd, London, 1947, specifically p. 17.

(36)   DINGWALL, E. J.: Psychological Problems Arising from a Report of Telekinesis. *Brit. J. Psychol.* 1953, *44,* pp. 61–66.

(37)   DINGWALL, E. J.: Abnormal Hypnotic Phenomena (4 vols); London, 1967.

(38)   DODDS, E. R.: Supernormal Phenomena in Classical Antiquity. *Proc. Soc. Psych. Res.* 1971, *55,* pp. 189–237.

(39)   DOYLE, C.: The History of Spiritualism (2 vols). Cassell, London, 1926, specifically Vol. I, p. 301.

(40)   DUNNE, J. W.: An Experiment with Time. Faber & Faber, London, 1934.

(41)   DUNRAVEN, Earl of: Experiences in Spiritualism with D. D. Home. Robert Maclehose & Co. Ltd., Glasgow, 1924, specifically pp. 64 and 209, 133–4.

(42)   EBON, M. (Ed): The Amazing Uri Geller. New American Library, 1975.

(43)   EDMUNDS, S.: 'Spirit' Photography. Society for Psychical Research, London, 1965.

(44)   EISENBUD, J.: The World of Ted Serios. William Morrow, New York 1967.

(45)   EISENBUD, J.: How to Make Things Null and Void. *J. Parapsychol.* 1979, *43,* pp. 140–152.

(46)   ELIADE, M.: Shamanism: Archaic Techniques of Ecstasy (trans. by W. Trask) Routledge & Kegan Paul, London, 1970, specifically pp. 304, 243–4, 474, 411, 46

(47)   FARMER, J. S.: Twixt Two Worlds: a Narrative of the Life and Work of William Eglinton. The Psychological Press, London, 1886.

(48)   FEILDING, E.: Sittings with Eusapia Palladino and Other Studies. University Books, New York, 1963,

specifically pp. 17, 81, 105.

(49) FISK, G. W. & MITCHELL, A. M. J.: The Application of Differential Scoring Methods to PK Tests. *J. Soc. Psych. Res.* 1953, *37,* pp. 45–61.

(50) FISK, G. W. & WEST, D. J.: Dice-Casting Experiments with a Single Subject. *J. Soc. Psych. Res.* 1958, *39,* pp. 277–287.

(51) FODOR, N.: A Letter from England. *J. Amer. Soc. Psych. Res.* 1936, *30* pp. 225–232.

(52) FUKURAI, T.: Clairvoyance and Thoughtography. Rider, London, 1931.

(53) FUNDERBURK, J.: Science Studies Yoga. Himalayan International Institute of Yoga Science & Philosophy, U.S.A., 1977.

(54) GAMOW, G.: Thirty Years that Shook Physics. Heinemann, London, 1972, specifically p. 81.

(55) GARDNER, M.: The Ambidextrous Universe. Allen Lane, London, 1967, specifically p. 171.

(56) GAULD, A.: The Founders of Psychical Research. Routledge & Kegan Paul, London, 1968, specifically pp. 7, 164, 230, 338.

(57) GAULD, A.: Review of *Anatomy of a Fraud. J. Soc. Psych. Res.* 1978, *49,* pp. 828–835.

(58) GAULD, A. & CORNELL, A. D.: Poltergeists. Routledge & Kegan Paul, London, 1979, specifically p. 227.

(59) GELLER, U.: My Story. Robson Books, London, 1975.

(60) GLANVILL, J.: Sadducismus Triumphatus. London, 1689.

(61) GRAD, B., CADORET, R. J., & PAUL, G. I.: An Unorthodox Method of Treatment in Wound Healing in Mice. *Int. J. Parapsychol.* 1961, *3,* pp. 5–24.

(62) GREEN, C.: The Decline and Fall of Science. Hamish Hamilton, London, 1976, specifically pp. 137–8.

(63) GREGORY, A. K.: The Medium Rudi Schneider and his Investigators. Unpublished manuscript, available in the SPR library, London.

(64) GREGORY, A. K.: Anatomy of a Fraud: Harry Price and the Medium Rudi Schneider. *Annals of Science* 1977, *34* pp. 449–549.

(65) GREGORY, R. L.: Eye and Brain. World University Library, London, 1966.

(66) GREGORY the GREAT: Life of St. Benedict (Second Book of the Dialogues) translated by Dom Justin McCann. St. Benet's Hall, Oxford, 1941, specifically Ch. III pp. 15–16, 27–8.

(67) HALL, T. H.: The Spiritualists: The Story of Florence Cook and William Crookes. Duckworth, London, 1962.

(68) HALL, T. H.: Search for Harry Price. Duckworth, London, 1978.

(69) HANLON, J.: Uri Geller and Science. *New Scientist* 1974, *64*, pp. 170–185.

(70) HANLON, J.: Spoon-bending Science. *New Scientist* 1977, *67*, pp. 80–82.

(71) HANSEL, C. E. M.: ESP: A Scientific Evaluation. Charles Scribner's Sons, New York, 1966.

(72) HANSEN, C.: Witchcraft at Salem. Hutchinson, London, 1969, specifically pp. 183–4.

(73) HARALDSSON, E. & OSIS, K.: The Appearance and Disappearance of Objects in the Presence of Sri Sathya Sai Baba. *J. Amer. Soc. Psych. Res.* 1977, *71*. pp. 33–43.

(74) HARE, R.: Experimental Investigation of the Spirit Manifestations. Partridge & Brittan, New York, 1855.

(75) HARRISON, M.: Fire From Heaven. Sidgwick & Jackson, London, 1976, specifically pp. 193–4.

(76) HART, H.: The Psychic Fifth Dimension. *J. Amer. Soc. Psych. Res.* 1953, 47 pp. 3–32 & 47–79.

(77) HASTED, J. B.: Letter in *New Scientist*, 1974, *64* p. 356.

(78) HASTED, J. B.: An Experimental Study of the Validity of Metal-Bending Phenomena. *J. Soc. Psych. Res.* 1976, *48,* pp. 365–383.

(79) HASTED, J. B.: Physical Aspects of Paranormal Metal Bending. *J. Soc. Psych. Res.* 1977, *49,* pp. 583–607.

(80) HASTED, J. B.: The Metal-Benders. Routledge & Kegan Paul, London, 1981, specifically p. 175.

(81) HASTED, J. B. & ROBERTSON, D.: Paranormal Action on Metal and its Surroundings. *J. Soc. Psych. Res.* 1980, *50*, pp. 379–398.

(82) HAYNES, RENÉE: Philosopher King: The Humanist Pope Benedict XIV. Weidenfeld & Nicolson, London, 1970.

(83) HERODOTUS: The Histories. Trans. by Aubrey de Sélin-

court. Penguin Books, Middlesex, 1954, specifically pp. 30–31.

(84) HINTON, C. H.: The Fourth Dimension. George Allen & Unwin, London, 1904, specifically p. 57.

(85) HOLMS, A. C.: The Facts of Psychic Science and Philosophy, Kegan Paul, Trench, Trubner & Co., London, 1925, specifically pp. 316–7, 317, 318, 157.

(86) HONORTON, C.: Apparent Psychokinesis on Static Objects by a 'Gifted' Subject. In *Research in Parapsychology, 1973* edited by W. G. Roll, R. L. Morris & J. D. Morris. Scarecrow Press, Metuchen, New Jersey 1974.

(87) HUNT, D.: Exploring the Occult. Pan Books, London, 1964, specifically p. 81.

(88) HUXLEY, A.: The Devils of Loudun. Chatto & Windus, London, 1952.

(89) HYDE, D. H.: A Report on some English PK Trials. *Proc. Soc. Psych. Res.* 1945, *48,* pp. 293–296.

(90) IAMBLICHUS: On the Mysteries of the Egyptians, Chaldeans and Assyrians. Translated by T. Taylor. Bertram Dobell, Reeves & Turner, London, 1895, specifically pp. 125, 123–4.

(91) INGLIS, B.: Natural and Supernatural. Hodder & Stoughton, London, 1977, specifically pp. 70, 280, 365, 414.

(92) JEANS, J.: The Growth of Physical Science. Cambridge University Press, 1950, specifically pp. 4–5.

(93) JOSEPHUS, F.: Jewish Antiquities. Trans. H. St. J. Thackeray & R. Marcus. Loeb Classical Library, specifically Ch. 8 pp. 46–48.

(94) JUNG, C. G.: Memories, Dreams, Reflections. Fontana, London, 1967, specifically pp. 125–7.

(95) KEIL, H. H. J., HERBERT, B. ULLMAN, M., & PRATT, J. G.: Directly Observable Voluntary PK Effects. *Proc. Soc. Psych. Res.* 1976, *56,* pp. 197–235.

(96) KNOWLES, E. A. G.: Report on an Experiment Concerning the Influence of Mind Over Matter. *J. Parapsychol.* 1949, *13,* pp. 186–196

(97) KOESTLER, A.: The Roots of Coincidence. Hutchinson, London, 1972, specifically p. 78.

(98) KRIPPNER, S. (Ed): Advances in Parapsychological Research, Vol. 1: Psychokinesis. Plenum Press, New

York & London, 1977.

(99) LANG, A.: Cock Lane and Common-Sense. Longmans, London, 1896, specifically pp. 48, 50, 173–6.

(100) LAMBERT, H. C.: Notes on Current Periodicals. *J. Amer. Soc. Psych. Res.* 1925, *19,* pp. 173–175.

(101) LAWDEN, D. F.: Possible Psychokinetic Interactions in Quantum Theory. *J. Soc. Psych. Res.* 1980, *50,* pp. 399–407.

(102) LAWMAN, P. D.: Article on 'Spiritualism' in the privately-circulated Journal of the Society for Psychical Research at University College, Leicester, October, 1955.

(103) LEROY, O.: Levitation: an Examination of the Evidence and Explanations. Burns Oates & Washbourne Ltd, London, 1928.

(104) MANNING, M.: The Link. Colin Smythe, London, 1974.

(105) MARKWICK, B.: The Soal-Goldney Experiments with Basil Shackleton; New Evidence of Data Manipulation. *Proc. Soc. Psych. Res.* 1978, 56, pp. 250–281.

(106) MEDHURST, R. G.: Crookes and the Spirit World. Souvenir Press, London, 1972, specifically p. 35, 57, 2.

(107) MEDHURST, R. G. & GOLDNEY, K. M.: William Crookes and the Physical Phenomena of Mediumship. *Proc. Soc. Psych. Res.* 1964, 54, pp. 25–156.

(108) METTA, L.: Psychokinesis on Lepidopterous Larvae. *J. Parapsychol* 1972, *36,* pp. 213–221.

(109) MILLAR, B.: Thermistor PK. In *Research in Parapsychology 1975,* Edited by J. D. Morris, W. G. Roll & R. L. Morris. Scarecrow Press, Metuchen, New Jersey.

(110) MONROE, R. A.: Journeys out of the Body. Souvenir Press, London, 1972.

(111) MOODY, R. A.: Life After Life. Bantam Books, U.S.A., 1976.

(112) MOSS, T.: The Probability of the Impossible. Routledge & Kegan Paul, London, 1976.

(113) MYERS, F. W. H.: The Experiences of W. Stainton Moses. *Proc. Soc. Psych. Res.* 1894, *9,* pp. 259–260.

(114) NEEDHAM, J.: Science and Civilisation in China, Vol.

5, Part. 2. Cambridge University Press 1974, specifically p. 106, 105.

(115) NICOL, J. F.: The Founders of the SPR. *Proc. Soc. Psych. Res.* 1972, *55,* pp. 341–367.

(116) NICOL, J. F. & CARINGTON, W. W.: Some Experiments in Willed Die-Throwing. *Proc. Soc. Psych. Res.* 1946–9, *48,* pp. 164–175.

(117) ORNSTEIN, R.: The Psychology of Consciousness. Penguin Books, 1975.

(118) OSIS, K. & McCORMICK, D.: Kinetic Effects at the Ostensible Location of an Out-of-Body Projection During Perceptual Testing. *J. Amer. Soc. Psych. Res.* 1980 *74,* pp. 319–329.

(119) OSTRANDER, S. & SCHROEDER, L.: Psi: Psychic Discoveries Behind the Iron Curtain. Sphere Books Ltd, London, 1970.

(120) OTERI, L. (Ed): Quantum Physics and Parapsychology. Parapsychology Foundation, New York, 1975, specifically p. 130.

(121) OWEN, A. R. G.: Can We Explain the Poltergeist? Taplinger, New York, 1964.

(122) OWEN, A. R. G: Psychic Mysteries of the North. Harper & Row, New York, 1975, specifically p. 15.

(123) OWEN, A. R. G. & SPARROW, M.: Conjuring up Philip: An Adventure in Psychokinesis. Fitzhenry & Whiteside, Ontario, 1976, specifically pp. 11, 12.

(124) PANATI, C.: The Geller Papers. Houghton Mifflin Co., Boston, U.S.A., 1976, specifically pp. 157–167.

(125) PARSONS, D.: Experiments on PK with Inclined Plane and Rotating Cage. *Proc. Soc. Psych. Res.* 1945, *48,* pp. 296–300.

(126) PEARSALL, R.: The Table-Rappers. Michael Joseph, London, 1972, specifically pp. 23, 36, 223–4.

(127) PHILOSTRATUS, F.: Life of Apollonius of Tyana (2 vols). Translated by F. C. Conybeare, Loeb Classical Library, specifically Vol. I pp. 257, 391–3.

(128) PLAYFAIR, G. L.: This House is Haunted. Souvenir Press, London, 1980.

(129) PODMORE, F: Modern Spiritualism: A History and a Criticism. Methuen, London, 1902 (2 vols), specifically Vol. I.

(130) PRICE, H.: Stella C.; An Account of Some Original Experiments in Psychical Research. Hurst & Blackett, London, 1925.

(131) PRICE, H.: Rudi Schneider; A Scientific Examination of his Mediumship. Methuen, London, 1930.

(132) PRICE, H.: Fifty Years of Psychical Research: A Critical Survey. Longman, Green & Co, London, 1939, specifically pp. 203, 102.

(133) PRICE, H.: Search for Truth: My Life for Psychical Research. Collins, London, 1942, specifically pp. 208–210, 84.

(134) RANDALL, J. L.: An Attempt to Detect Psi Effects with Protozoa. *J. Soc. Psych. Res.* 1970, *45,* pp. 294–296.

(135) RANDALL, J. L.: Experiments to Detect a Psi Effect with Small Animals. *J. Soc. Psych. Res.* 1971, *46,* pp. 31–39.

(137) RANDALL, J. L.: Two Psi Experiments with Gerbils. *J. Soc. Psych. Res.* 1972, *46,* pp. 22–30.

(138) RANDALL, J. L.: Parapsychology and the Nature of Life. Souvenir Press, London, 1975, specifically pp. 23, 155.

(139) RANDALL, J. L.: Tests for Extrasensory Perception & Psychokinesis. Society for Psychical Research, London, 1980.

(140) RANDI, J.: The Magic of Uri Geller. Ballantine Books, New York, 1975, specifically pp. 264–280.

(141) RANKY, Illusionniste: Compte Rendu d'expertise cas Jean-Pierre Girard. Privately circulated report, 1976, specifically p. 6.

(142) RHINE, J. B.: Extra-Sensory Perception. Faber & Faber, London, 1935.

(143) RHINE, J. B.: The Reach of the Mind. Faber & Faber, London, 1948, specifically p. 89.

(144) RHINE, J. B.: Comments: A New Case of Experimenter Unreliability. *J. Parapsychol.* 1974, *38,* pp. 215–225.

(145) RHINE, L. E.: Spontaneous Physical Effects and the Psi Process. *J. Parapsychol.* 1963, *27,* pp. 84–122.

(146) RHINE, L. E.: Mind Over Matter. The Macmillan Company, New York, 1970, specifically p. 67, 338–9.

(147) RICHMOND, N.: Two series of PK Tests on Paramecia. *J. Soc. Psych. Res.* 1952, *36*, pp. 577–588.

(148) ROLL, W. G.: The Poltergeist. Wyndham Publications, London, 1976.

(149) RUSHTON, W. A. H.: Serios-Photos: If Contrary to Natural Law, Which Law? *J. Soc. Psych. Res.* 1968, *44*, pp. 289–293.

(150) ST. FRANCIS, The Little Flowers of: Trans. by L. Sherley-Price, Penguin Books, 1959, specifically pp. 102, 53.

(151) ST. TERESA, the Life of: Trans. by J. M. Cohen, Penguin Books, 1957, specifically pp. 137–8.

(152) SALTER, W. H.: The Society for Psychical Research: An Outline of its History. Society for Psychical Research, London, 1970.

(153) SCHETKY, L. M.: Shape-Memory Alloys. *Scientific American* 1979, *241*, pp. 68–76.

(154) SCHMEIDLER, G. R.: PK Effects Upon Continuously Recorded Temperature. *J. Amer. Soc. Psych. Res.* 1973, *67*, pp. 325–340.

(155) SCHMEIDLER, G. R., MITCHELL, J. & SONDOW, N.: Further Investigation of PK with Temperature Records. In *Research in Parapsychology 1974*, Edited by J. D. Morris, W. G. Roll, & R. L. Morris. Scarecrow Press, Metuchen, New Jersey, U.S.A.

(156) SCHMEIDLER, G. R. (Ed): Parapsychology: Its Relation to Physics, Biology, Psychology, and Psychiatry. Scarecrow Press, Metuchen, New Jersey, U.S.A. 1976, specifically p. 156, pp. 76–89.

(157) SCHMIDT, H.: Precognition of a Quantum Process. *J. Parapsychol.* 1969, *33*, pp. 99–108.

(158) SCHMIDT, H.: A PK Test with Electronic Equipment. *J. Parapsychol.* 1970, *34*, pp. 175–181.

(159) SCHMIDT, H.: PK Experiments with Animals as Subjects. *J. Parapsychol.* 1970, *34*, pp. 255–261.

(160) SCHMIDT, H.: The Comparison of PK Action on Two Different Random Number Generators. *J. Parapsychol.* 1974, *38*, pp. 47–55.

(161) SCHMIDT, H.: PK Effect on Pre-Recorded Targets. *J. Amer. Soc. Psych. Res.* 1976, *70*, pp. 267–291.

(162) SCHMIDT, H. & PANTAS, L.: Psi Tests with Internally

Different Machines. *J. Parapsychol.* 1972, *36*, pp. 222–232.

(163)   SMITH, N. C.: Replication Studies: A Neglected Aspect of Psychological Research. *American Psychologist* 1970, *25*, pp. 970–975.

(164)   SMYTHIES, E. A.: A Case of Levitation in Nepal. *J. Soc. Psych. Res.* 1951, *36*, pp. 415–426.

(165)   SMYTHIES, J. R. (Ed): Science and ESP. Routledge & Kegan Paul, London, 1967.

(166)   SOMERLOTT, R.: Modern Occultism. Robert Hale & Co., London, 1971.

(167)   STAFF OF ROUGE ET NOIR: Winning at Casino Gaming. Rouge et Noir Inc., New York, 1966.

(168)   STEVENSON, I. & PRATT, J. G.: Exploratory Investigations of the Psychic Photography of Ted Serios. *J. Amer. Soc. Psych. Res.* 1968, *62*, pp. 103–129.

(169)   STEVENSON, I. & PRATT, J. G.: Further Investigations of the Psychic Photography of Ted Serios. *J. Amer. Soc. Psych. Res.* 1969, *63*, pp. 352–364.

(170)   SUETONIUS: The Twelve Caesars. Trans. by Robert Graves, Penguin Books 1957.

(171)   SWANN, I.: To Kiss Earth Goodbye. Hawthorn, New York, 1975.

(172)   TABORI, P.: Pioneers of the Unseen. Souvenir Press, London, 1972, specifically p. 134.

(173)   TARG, R. & PUTHOFF, H.: Information Transfer under Conditions of Sensory Shielding. *Nature,* 1974, *252*, pp. 602–607.

(174)   TARG, R. & PUTHOFF, H.: Mind-Reach. Jonathan Cape, London, 1977, specifically pp. 20, 21.

(175)   TAYLOR, J.: Superminds. Macmillan, London, 1975.

(176)   THOULESS, R. H.: Some experiments on PK Effects in Coin Spinning. *Proc. Soc. Psych. Res.* 1945, *48*, pp. 277–281.

(177)   THOULESS, R. H.: A Report on an Experiment in Psychokinesis with Dice, and a Discussion on Psychological Factors Favouring Success. *Proc. Soc. Psych. Res.* 1951, *49*, pp. 107–130.

(178)   THURY, M.: Les Tables Tournantes. Geneva, 1855.

(179)   TIETZE, T. R.: Margery. Harper & Row, New York, 1973.

(180) TONDRIAU, J.: Occultism: Secrets of a Hidden World. Tom Stacey, London 1972, specifically pp. 18, 52.

(181) TROCHU, F.: The Curé D'Ars. Trans. Dom Ernest Graf. Burns Oates & Washbourne Ltd, London 1927, specifically pp. 120, 203, 204, 237.

(182) TYRRELL, G. N. M.: Homo Faber: A Study of Man's Mental Evolution. Methuen, London, 1951.

(183) VASSE, P. & VASSE C.: Influence de la Pensée sur la Croissance des Plantes. *Revue Metapsychique,* Nouvelle Serie 1948, *2,* pp. 87–94.

(184) WALKER, E. H.: The Nature of Consciousness. *Mathematical Biosciences* 1970, 7, pp. 131–178.

(185) WEST, D. J.: A Critical Survey of the American PK Research. *Proc. Soc. Psych. Res.* 1945, 48, pp. 281–290.

(186) WEST, D. J.: Psychical Research Today. Duckworth, London, 1954.

(187) WILSON, C.: The Geller Phenomenon. Aldus Books, London, 1976, specifically p. 118.

(188) WOLMAN, B. B. (Ed): Handbook of Parapsychology. Van Nostrand Reinhold, 1977, specifically p. 676, 803–879.

(189) WOOD, E.: Yoga. Penguin Books, 1959, specifically pp. 258, 104.

(190) YOGANANDA, PARAMHANSA: Autobiography of a Yogi. Rider, London, 1969.

(191) ZÖLLNER, J. C. F.: Transcendental Physics. W. H. Harrison, London, 1880, specifically pp. 126, 17.

(192) ZORAB, G.: Were D. D. Home's 'Spirit Hands' Ever Fraudulently Produced? *J. Soc. Psych. Res.* 1971, *46,* pp. 228–235.

(193) ZORAB, G.: Test Sittings with D. D. Home at Amsterdam. *J. Parapsychol.* 1970, *34,* pp. 47–63.

Index

Abbott, E. A. : 202–203.
Adare, Lord: 83, 162.
Aksakoff, A. N. : 92, 113, 118.
American Association for the
  Advancement of Science: 84.
American Society for Psychical
  Research: 74, 114, 124, 131–133,
  142, 151–152.
Amiens, phenomena at: 64.
Apollonius of Tyana: 43.
Apports: 17, 28, 75, 130, 181–184,
  194, 209–211, 225, 227.
Aquinas, St. Thomas: 79.
Aristotle: 41.
Arnaud, Pére: 18.
d'Ars, Curé: see Vianney.
Ascensions: 24.
Aubrey, John: 80.
Aüfklarung: 60.

Bacon, Francis: 80–81.
Baggally, W. W. : 124–126, 190.
Barbanell, M. : 132.
Barclay, G. : 35, 179.
Barrett, W. : 114.
Bastin, E. W. : 166, 183.
Batcheldor, K. J. : 165, 185.
Bayless, R. : 180.
Bell, E. T. : 111, 129.
Bellachini, S. : 98–99, 109, 191.
Beloff, J. : 159.
Benedict of Nursia, St. : 12–13, 46,
  50, 194.
Benedict XIV, Pope: 79–80.
Bender, H. : 174–176, 182.
Benson, E. W. : 84.
Béraud, Marthe: 129–130.

Bild newspaper: 173.
Blavatsky, H. P. : 36, 121.
Blundun, J. : 148.
Bohm, D. : 183, 222.
Bohr, N. : 218–220.
Bolyai, J. : 200–201.
Borley Rectory: 136.
Born, M. : 220.
Boston Society for Psychic
  Research: 133.
Boutleroff, A. von: 92, 99, 113.
Braid, J. : 66.
Briscoe, M. : 171.
Broad, C. D. : 207.
Brookes-Smith, C. : 158, 165.
Buehler, W. J. : 170
Button, W. H. : 131, 132, 181, 185,
  194.
Byrd, E. : 170, 173.

Card-guessing: 80, 81, 143, 152.
Carington, W. W. : 147.
Carpenter, W. B. : 85, 91.
Carrington, H. : 124–126, 141, 190.
Carroll, L. : 188.
Cassirer, M. : 160, 180.
Challis, Prof. : 94.
Children, as psychics: 44, 70, 74,
  75, 84, 134, 150, 171, 176.
Clare, St. : 47, 50.
Cock Lane Ghost: 64.
Cold, paranormal production of:
  102, 139–140, 195.
Cold, abnormal resistance to: 36.
Collyer, R. : 97–98, 109.
Contraction of the body: 42, 73, 74,
  208.

Cook, Florence: 88, 91, 92.
Coolican, D. : 172.
Copernicus, N. : 59, 193.
Cornell, A. D. : 18, 51, 212, 227.
Cox, E. W. : 76, 85, 89, 98, 100, 109, 113.
Cox, W. E. : 149, 172–173, 224.
Crandon, Mina ("Margery"): 130–134, 142, 143, 155, 194, 209.
Cranshaw, Stella: 138–140.
Croesus of Lydia: 41, 79.
Crookes, W. : 72, 82, 87–94, 95, 97, 99, 113, 116, 149, 141, 165.
Crussard, C. : 174–175.
Curie, Pierre & Marie: 123.

Darwin, C. : 67, 93, 129.
Davenport brothers: 19, 74.
Davenport, R. B. : 71.
David-Neel, A. : 35, 36.
Davies, David: 175.
Davies, Paul: 220.
Davis, Peter: 171.
De Broglie, L. : 218–220.
Defoe, D. : 80.
Deism: 59.
De Martino, E. : 20.
Democritus: 41.
Dempster, H. : 172.
DeWitt, B. : 217.
Dialectical Society of London: 74, 85, 86.
Dice-throwing experiments: 80, 81, 143–149, 152, 155–156, 179, 189.
Dickson, A. : 191.
Dingwall, E. J. : 65, 130, 132–134, 139.
Dodds, E. R. : 41.
Duke University: 142–149, 181.
Duncan, Helen: 53, 155.
Dunne, J. W. : 207–208.

Earthquake effect: 73, 214.

Ecstasy: 16.
Ectoplasm: 42, 83, 129–130, 140, 195, 211.
Eddington, A. S. : 199.
Edmunds, S. : 158.
Eglinton, W. : 93, 191.
Einstein, A. : 96, 205–206, 214, 217, 222.
Eisenbud, J. : 141, 157.
Eliade, M. : 16–19.
Elisha: 39.
Elongation of the body: 28, 42–44, 73, 74, 208.
EPR Paradox: 221.
Epworth, phenomena at: 64.
ESP: 17, 28, 41, 55, 63, 79, 80, 143, 145, 146, 148, 152, 164, 191, 197, 203, 208, 224.
d'Espérance, Madame: 93.
Euclid: 199 et seq.
"Eva C.": 129–130.
Evans, C. : 175.
Everett, H. : 222–223.
Extrasensory Perception: see ESP.
Eysenck, H. : 190.

Fahler, J. : 161
Faraday, M. : 81–82, 87–88, 92, 129.
Fay, Eva: 88, 92.
Fechner, G. : 100, 101, 110.
Feilding, E. : 124–6, 130, 139, 141, 185, 190.
Fisk, G. W. : 147, 148.
Flammarion, C. : 142.
Flatland (Abbott): 202–203.
Flights: 19, 25, 26.
Fodor, N. : 180.
Forwald, H. : 149, 224.
Fourth dimension: 96–97, 202, 204, 210, 211, 214.
Fox sisters: 67–71, 88.
Franklin, R. L. : 29.
Francis of Assisi, St. : 47, 50.
Freud, S. : 115.

Fukurai, T. : 158.
Fullerton, G. S. : 110.
Fyall, A. : 172.

Galileo: 59, 67, 90, 193.
Gamow, G. : 219.
Gardner, M. : 95, 107, 111.
Garrett, E. : 139, 140.
de Gasparin, A. : 82, 92, 113.
Gauld, A. : 18, 51, 76, 114, 127, 138, 212.
Gauss, K. F. : 200.
Geley, G. : 114, 130, 142.
Geller, Uri: 13, 22, 28, 70, 156, 166–173, 180, 182–183, 191, 227.
Geller effect: see metal-bending.
Girard, J. P. : 174–175.
Glanvill, J. : 80.
Glass-breaking effects: 12, 13, 194.
Goldney, M. : 88, 113.
Grad, B. : 81, 150.
Grandier, Urbain: 53–55.
Grassmann, H. : 202.
Gregory, A. : 135, 137, 138, 165.
Gregory the Great, Pope: 11.
Green, C. : 179.
Gurney, E. : 114, 127.

Hall, T. : 91.
Hallucinogens: 26, 28.
Hanlon, J. : 169.
Hansen, C. : 56, 57, 58.
Haraldsson, E. : 33, 34.
Hare, R. : 83, 84, 92, 113.
Harrison, M. : 18, 161, 178, 179.
Hasted, J. : 167, 169, 176–177, 182–183, 194, 196, 197, 228.
Heat, abnormal resistance to: 17–18.
Heat, paranormal production of: 17, 52, 105–107, 161, 163, 212–213.
Hebard, A. : 164.
Heisenberg, W. : 219.

Herbert, B. : 161.
Herder, J. G. : 60.
Herodotus: 41.
Hidden variables: 222–223.
Hinton, H. : 201.
Hobbes, T. : 60.
Hodgson, R. : 116, 121, 122.
Home, D. D. : 17, 28, 70–74, 82–85, 88–90, 92, 93, 101, 102, 116, 118, 133, 140, 155, 156, 162–165, 194, 213, 214.
Honorton, C. : 162, 168.
Hope, Lord Charles: 137, 138.
Hume, D. : 61.
Hunt, D. : 52.
Humphrey, Betty: 145.
Huxley, Aldous: 54, 55.
Huxley, T. H. : 85, 228–229.
Hyde, D. : 147.
Hydesville, phenomena at: 67–70, 81.
Hyperspace: 96, 97, 102, 210, 214–216, 220.
Hypnotism: 64.

Infra-red occultation phenomenon: 136–138.
Inglis, B. : 41, 111, 116, 124.
Institut Métapsychique: 114, 136–137.
Isaac, John: 183.

James, W. : 114, 115, 122.
Jeans, J. : 24, 59.
Joseph of Copertino, St. : 48–50, 58.
Josephus Flavius: 40.
Jung, C. G. : 13, 113, 115, 194.

Kardec, A. : 72–73.
Keil, J. : 160.
Kellar, H. : 109, 126, 191.
Kelson, Prof. : 172.
King, Katie: 91, 92.

Knowles, E. A. G. : 147, 148.
Koestler, A. : 221.
Krippner, S. : 168.
Kulagina, N. : 22, 156, 159–162, 164, 194.
Kuleshova, R. : 160.

Lambertini, Prospero: 79–80.
Lang, A. : 18, 44, 64.
Lankester, R. : 99
Lawden, D. F. : 224–225, 228.
Lawman, P. D. : 42.
Leroy, O. : 31.
Leslie, Leo: 191
Lessing, G. E. : 60.
Levitation: 19, 20, 25, 26, 28–34, 44, 47–49, 52, 55–58, 63, 74, 75, 81, 82–84, 124–125, 126–127, 165, 194.
Levy, W. J. : 191.
Lewis, C. S. : 178.
Living systems, P. K. upon: 80, 81, 150, 151.
Lobatschewsky, N. I. : 200–201.
Lodge, O. : 93, 120, 121, 131, 132, 139.
Lombroso, C. : 117–119, 141.
Loudun, phenomena at: 53–56.

Maimonides Dream Laboratory: 162.
Malleus Maleficarum: 53.
Mann, T. : 134.
Manning, M. : 156, 174.
Many worlds theory: 222–223.
"Margery": see Crandon.
Maskelyne, J. N. : 74.
Mayer, S. : 175–176.
Mayr, R. : 176, 191.
McCabe, J. : 100.
McDougall, W. : 115, 132, 133, 142, 143.
Medhurst, R. G. : 88, 113.
Mediumship, physical: 13, 19, 28, 67–78, 81–94, 97–110, 116–127, 129–141, 155, 189–190, 227.
Memory: 216.
Mesmerism: 65–66.
Metal bending: 13, 166–177, 179–180, 189, 194.
Metal breaking: 13, 180.
Metta, L. : 151.
de la Mettrie, J. : 60.
Millar, B. : 163.
Mind: 215.
Minkowski, H. : 204, 205, 207.
Mitchell, A. M. J. : 147.
Mitchell, E. : 166.
Morselli, E. : 119, 120.
Moses, S. : 75–76, 88, 114, 133.
Myers, F. W. H.: 114, 120, 121, 127, 190.

National Laboratory of Psychical Research: 135, 137.
Nature: 139, 168–169, 175.
Naumov, E. : 161.
Needham, J. : 25, 26.
New Horizons Institute: 18, 174.
New Scientist magazine: 168.
Newton, I. : 59, 67, 196, 212.
Newtonian physics: 59, 61, 62, 212, 220.
Nicola, N. : 183.
Nicol, J. F. : 147.
Nijinsky, V. : 178.
Nitinol: 170–172.
Non-Euclidian Geometry: 200–201, 205, 206–207.

Ochorowicz, J. : 118, 121.
O'Regan, B. : 183.
Osis, K. : 33, 34.
Osty, E. : 136, 138, 141.
Out-of-the-body-experiences: 17, 28.
Ovid: 43.
Owen, A. R. G. : 18, 174.

Owen, Iris: 165.

Palladino, E. : 78, 93, 102, 117–128, 133, 140, 155, 185, 189–190, 227.
Panati, C. : 169.
Paranormal defined: 14.
Parise, F. : 156, 162–164, 194.
Parsons, D. : 146–147.
Patanjali: 20, 27.
Pearce, H. : 149.
Pearsall, R. : 66, 189–190.
Perot, R. : 147.
Peter, St. : 39, 40.
"Philip": 165.
Philostratus: 43.
Photography, paranormal: 22, 33, 157–159.
Placement experiments: 149.
Planck, M. : 217.
Plato: 216.
Podmore, F. : 77, 114, 116.
Poltergeists: 18, 22, 41, 42, 51–54, 64, 68, 84, 166, 174, 176, 180, 184, 186, 196, 212, 215, 224.
Possession: 16.
Powell, F. : 98, 191.
Pratt, J. G. : 146, 162.
Precognition: 152–153, 207–208.
Price, Harry: 77, 108, 134, 135–140, 142, 155.
Price, Pat: 168.
Prince, W. F. : 133.
Psi; meaning of term: 148.
Psychokinesis; defined: 13, 232.
Puharich, A. : 166.
Puthoff, H. : 163–164, 166, 168, 173, 189.

Quantum Theory: 154, 217–225, 228.

Ramp function: 174.
Randall, J. L., experiments by: 150–151, 171.

Randi, J. : 99, 167–169, 175, 189.
Random number generators: 151–153, 189.
"Ranky": 175, 191.
Rasmussen, A. : 163.
Rasmussen, K. : 16.
Reimarus, H. S. : 60.
Relativity, Theory of: 96, 203–207, 210, 214, 217, 228.
Rhine, J. B.: 66, 132, 133, 142–147, 179, 181.
Rhine, L. E. : 133, 142, 149, 181.
Richet, C. : 81, 83, 115, 118, 120, 123, 129, 130, 141, 142, 211.
Richmond, N. : 150.
Riemann, G. F. B. : 200–201, 206.
Rule, Margaret: 56–58.
Rush, J. : 169.
Rushton, W. A. H. : 159.
Russia, parapsychology in: 161.
Rutherford, Lord: 192.

Sai Baba, S. : 33–34, 182.
Salem, witchcraft at: 56–58.
Scheibner, W. : 100, 101, 110.
Schiaparelli, G. : 118.
Schmeidler, G. : 163.
Schneider, Rudi: 134–138, 140, 142, 155, 165, 211.
Schneider, Willi, 134–135.
Schrenck-Notzing, Baron von: 118, 130, 134–136, 141, 142.
Schmidt, H. : 151–154, 228.
Schroedinger, E. : 219–220.
Sergeyev, G. I. : 160.
Serios, Ted: 157–159, 164, 195.
Seybert Commission: 109–110, 126.
Shackleton, B. : 149.
Shamanism: 15–20.
Shakers: 19.
Showers, Rosina: 88, 92.
Siddhis: 27.
Sidgwick, E. : 121, 123.

Sidgwick, H. : 78, 113–115, 121–123, 127, 190, 227.

Slade, H. : 93, 97–110, 131, 194, 195, 213.

Smith, Lester: 216 (footnote)

Smith, N. : 188.

Smythies, E. A. : 30, 31.

Smythies, J. R. : 215.

Soal, S. G. : 191.

Society for Psychical Research: see SPR.

Spiritualism: 28, 36, 44, 67, 70–72, 76, 81, 85, 114, 117, 142, 157.

Spontaneous Human Combustion: 18, 161.

SPR: 31, 69, 78, 79, 93, 111, 113–128, 132, 138, 140, 142, 147, 155.

Stanford Research Institute: 163, 166, 168.

St. Clair: 23.

"Stella C.": see Cranshaw, Stella.

St. Maur, phenomena at: 64.

St. Médard, phenomena at: 63.

Suetonius: 11, 55.

Swann, Ingo: 156, 162–164.

Table movements: 35–36, 68, 73, 75–76, 81–82, 86, 101, 103, 123–127, 140.

Tabori, P. : 138.

Targ, R. : 163, 166, 168, 173, 189.

Taylor, John: 13, 166–168, 185, 197, 228.

Telekinesis, definition of: 93, 233.

Teleportation: 40.

Tent-shaking: 15, 18.

Teresa of Avila, St. : 47–52, 58.

Thermal effects: see Cold and Heat.

Theurgists: 43–44.

Thouless, R. H. : 147, 148.

Thurston, H. : 126–127, 191.

Thury, M. : 83, 92.

Tillyard, R. J. : 139.

Time, nature of: 153, 203–205, 207–208.

Tondriau, J. : 16.

Toronto Society for Psychical Research: 18, 165.

Transcendental Meditation: 29.

Transfiguration: 42.

Trilles, R. G. : 20.

Tscherepanoff, M. : 35.

Tyrrell, G. N. M. 185.

Ullman, M. : 162.

Uncertainty Principle: 219.

Van de Castle, R. : 22.

Vandrey, R. : 175.

Vasiliev, L. : 160.

Vasse, Paul & Marie: 81, 150.

Vianney, J. B.: 50, 51.

Victoria, Queen: 71, 129.

Vinogradova, A. : 156.

Virgil: 42.

Walker, E. H. : 223–224, 228.

Wallace, A. R. : 67, 72, 85, 99, 100.

Watkins, Graham & Anita: 162.

Watson, Lyall: 166.

Weber, W. : 100, 110.

Wesley family: 64–65.

West, D. J. : 147, 148, 156.

Whitton, J. L. : 174.

Wiesner, B. P. : 148.

Wilson, C. : 167, 179.

Witchcraft: 52–58, 155.

Wood, E. : 27–29.

Wooley, V. W. : 139.

Yoga: 20, 26–37.

Yogananda, P. : 32, 182.

Zöllner, J. C. F. : 94–112, 113, 131, 140, 141, 181, 189, 194, 203, 213, 214.

Zorab, G. : 165, 213.

Zorka, A. : 191.